from
The Japan Foundation

LIVE MACHINES

LIVE MACHINES

HIRED FOREIGNERS AND MEIJI JAPAN

H. J. Jones

UNIVERSITY OF BRITISH COLUMBIA PRESS
VANCOUVER

LIVE MACHINES

Hired Foreigners and Meiji Japan

©The University of British Columbia 1980

This book has been published with the assistance of a grant from the Canadian Federation for the Humanities, using funds provided by the Social Sciences and Humanities Research Council of Canada.

Canadian Cataloguing in Publication Data

Jones, Hazel J., 1927–
   Live machines

   Bibliography: p.
   Includes index.
   ISBN 0 7748–0115–8

   1. Aliens – Japan. 2. Technical assistance in Japan.
   3. Japan – History – Meiji period, 1868 – 1912. I. Title.
   DS882.5.J65   952.03′1   C79–091161–2

International Standard Book Number 0–7748–0115–8

Printed in Canada

For Mickey and Tom Murata

Contents

Tables

Meiji Government Foreign Employees

1. Areas of Service by Nationality (1868 – 1900)
2. Periods of Service: Man Years by Area of Government (1868 – 1900)
3. Periods of Service: Man Years by Nationality (1868 – 1900)
4. Ministry of Public Works: Areas of Service (Man Years by Nationality)
5. Ministry of Public Works: Periods of Service (Man Years by Nationality)
6. Monthly Salaries of Foreign Employees in the Meiji Government (1868 – 1900)
7. Ministry Expenditures for Overseas Students (1876 – 86)

Appendices

1. Instructions for Hiring Foreigners (Gaikokujin yatoiirekata kokoroe jōjō), March 1870 (Meiji 3/2). Foreign Ministry Records Bureau, Tokyo.
2. Regulations for the Employment of Foreign Teachers and Others and Their Expenses while in Japan (Gaikoku kyōshi nado yatoiirekata oyobi zairyūchū shohi kisokusho), September 28, 1873, including Table for Expenditures for Foreign Employees. Foreign Ministry Records Bureau, Tokyo.
3. Yatoi Licence for William Elliot Griffis. Foreign Ministry Records Bureau, Tokyo.

Acknowledgements

Over the years, research for this study has been generously funded by the Fulbright-Hays Area Fellowship, the University of Michigan, the Canada Council, and the University of Alberta. This aid is gratefully acknowledged. As with all continuing research, assistance from colleagues has been invaluable. Particular debts of gratitude are owed to Roger F. Hackett (Michigan) and Umetani Noboru (Osaka) and to Ardath Burks (Rutgers), William Holland (British Columbia), Konishi Shirō (Tokyo University), Ogata Hiroyasu (Waseda), Ōyama Azusa (formerly of the Foreign Ministry Diplomatic Documents Research Unit), Sakata Yoshio (Kyoto), E. Patricia Tsurumi (Victoria), and numerous others.

Responsibility for errors in fact or interpretation is solely the author's.

HJJ

Abbreviations

FS	Fuken shiryō
GHS	Gaimushō hikitsugi shorui
GK	Gaimushō kiroku
HBT	*Hōki bunrui taizen*
JKK	*Jōyaku kaisei kankei Nihon gaikō bunsho*
KS	Kaigunshō shiryō
MZKS	*Meiji zenki zaisei keizai shiryō shūsei*
NB	Naikaku bunko shiryō
NGB	*Nihon gaikō bunsho*
ŌM	Ōkuma monjo (manuscript items only)
SY	*Nihon teikoku tōkei nenkan*
TJK	*Tsūshō jōyaku kankei Nihon gaikō bunsho*

Introduction

A striking aspect of the history of Japan in the nineteenth century is the government's employment of thousands of foreigners to aid its modern development. The use of foreign personnel by developing nations has become commonplace in the process of modernization in the second half of the twentieth century, but Japan was the first of the late modernizers to use such aid on a large scale. As may be expected, attitudes and activities of foreign employees in Japan show many similarities with those in other modernizing countries today. The sharp dissimilarities in the Japanese case are, however, more significant. While Japan's leadership drew heavily on the resources of other nations as many developing nations do today, at the same time they marshalled indigenous resources, selected from among the successful nineteenth-century Western models of modern development, adhered firmly to a policy of Japanese control and management, assumed total responsibility for the cost of modernizing, and carried out their decision to replace foreigners with trained Japanese as rapidly as possible. These were specific aims of the Japanese in hiring foreigners, and in these respects Japan's experience has few, if any, parallels. A New Japan emerged.

In the historical continuum there have been many New Japans. One may surely apply this comment to other nations as well. However, Japan's location on the periphery of world civilizations has caused the role of geography in Japanese development to be accentuated in Japanese history studies. The locus of this slender arc on the Pacific ring of fire separate from the mainland of Asia has had unquestioned influence as the last relay station for expanding civilizations. As sociologist Tsurumi Kazuko has so well illustrated in *Curiosity and the Japanese*, an innate and persistent curiosity is manifested in the historical phenomena of Japanese proclivity for cultural borrowing. Also, whereas curiosity appears to decrease in the degree to which nations experience the modernizing process, it has not abated among the Japanese because they continue to feel themselves country yokels (*inakamono* is Yanagita Kunio's phrase). The traditional distinction between capital and countryside is extended to the world. Perhaps stemming from this special penchant for curiosity, from whatever age the Japanese can be designated Japanese, they have found their value system in the human nexus, as Nakamura Hajime asserts. It is perhaps from this presentist viewpoint that an achievement orientation has developed.

Thus, the role of geography and the historically observable psychology of the Japanese people have produced the concept of New Japans in history studies. One of these schema for viewing Japanese history is that of alternate cycles, reception of more advanced cultures followed by adaptation, Japanization, to use Nitobe Inazo's term. In the alternation between opening the country and seclusion, *kaikoku* (open country) is posited as a watershed of change and *sakoku* (closed country) as native adaptation. If each kaikoku experience created a New Japan, it was after the peak of intake subsided that a New Japan emerged. But there were New Japans not preceded by alien stimuli. A major watershed was the confrontation of rival Imperial cadet military houses, perhaps best dated from the Hōgen Insurrection in 1156 and its resolution by the Minamoto with the establishment in 1185 of the Kamakura military government.[1] The refinement of feudal machinery fashioned an emerging warrior (*bushi*) class. There were such New Japans in the primitive era, and one could argue that there were within the Tokugawa or early modern era as well. Numerous historical periods of sufficiently dramatic and enduring socio-political change seem worthy of the appellation "new." What they share in common is a priori native sculpting.

As one reviews the alternate cycle schema, the nature of the kaikoku-sakoku phenomenon is therefore significant. The terms are relative; the country was never totally opened or totally closed. Yet in some interpretations the view is latent that the first decade of the Meiji period (1868 - 78) was open to the world and unlimited in its reception of foreign culture. The politico-legal policy was clearly one of limited kaikoku. Notwithstanding the Imperial Charter Oath of 1868, with its injunctions against class and old usages and its call for knowledge to be sought abroad, and despite broad exposure to that knowledge, ideological borrowing was limited. The ideological switch, more apparent than real, from expulsion of foreigners (*sonnō-jōi*) to revering the emperor by opening the country (*sonnō-kaikoku*) became effective political sloganism. The experience was confined for all practical purposes to a select segment of society, and modernization "strain" provoked varied but indigenous reactions. Germane to the present exploration of the modernization theme in Japan is the quality of its reception.

In the Meiji period, the scope for borrowing was undoubtedly broader than in any previous era. There was a literal inundation of materials and ideas, and the fact that the experience was confined to an élite meant that the new intelligentsia in and out of government bore the brunt of its effects. Those effects are being examined by scholars with a variety of approaches.

As understanding of the totality of the Japanese experience grows, the Japan of a century ago will be better understood. The need to understand it is more than academic because the present age is tangibly an offspring of the Meiji experience. None perceive this better than those Japanese scholars who feel their history.

Between 1868 and 1870, the machinery for political, economic, and social change in Japan was recast; by 1873 reformers had moved into positions of leadership; by 1875 these reformers had arrested Western expansion; and by the end of the decade they had begun to reverse it. In 1878, the new government quelled the last armed challenge to central authority, the Satsuma insurrection (Seinan *sensō*), thus completing the first phase of the Meiji Restoration. Two more decades revealed its full mechanism. One aspect of the Meiji experiment in modernizing was the government's use of foreign assistants. This study is an introduction, nothing more, to that experience. Items extant in original records are scattered and fragmentary, but from them one can determine what government policy was concerning hired foreigners (*yatoi*). An examination of that policy reveals that the Meiji leadership acquired expertise through experiment. This study supports the idea of "pragmatic instrumentalism in leadership" in Japan, as well as the premise that there was political motivation in modernizing, and, contrary to some interpretations, suggests that the "people's response" and that of lower echelon civil servants differed qualitatively from the leadership's.[2]

The use of foreign instructors and the sending of Japanese students abroad were two important modernization factors in Meiji Japan's experience. However, in the early Meiji period the hiring of foreign assistants took precedence over the despatch of students. In the period as a whole (1868 – 1912), the number of foreign employees was well over three thousand in all areas of government. The five or six thousand suggested by yatoi William Elliot Griffis (1870 – 74)[3] is too large if applied to foreign employees in government and perhaps too small if private foreign employees are included. Officially, private foreigners in Japan were not called "yatoi." The formal term in Foreign Ministry records includes an honorific and the word for foreigner (hence *oyatoi gaikokujin*). The phrase was shortened to yatoi by Japanese officials, and in English "yatoi" became a neologism for "government foreign employee."[4] Because the literal meaning of yatoi is "hired menial," a psychological tone was immediately set. Yatoi is a Meiji term. Ogata Hiroyasu suggests that *okakae*, meaning tutor, was a more usual reference to government-hired foreigners in the *bakumatsu* era (1853 – 67.)

Anesaki Masaharu has commented on the need for study of Meiji Japan's foreign assistants: "Their lives and services should be compiled out of the documents of the time, but unfortunately many of those documents stored in government offices were destroyed by fire after the earthquake of 1923.

The sources are therefore to be sought in the native countries and families of those foreign workers."[5] It would be valuable to have this suggestion implemented through co-operative international research.

This book is limited to a study of foreigners employed by the Meiji government. Initially it was thought a good choice because of the massive government involvement in this employment of foreigners. However, it has become evident that research on foreigners in private employment in the Meiji era is also essential for a better picture of industrial and social development. As yet there are few studies of individual foreign employees. Also, an overall study of their social backgrounds, relations with individual government officials and private entrepreneurs, specific contributions and drawbacks, actual levels of competence, activities after resignation, and the like could be pursued profitably.[6] There are three areas in which continuing research could focus: on the precise work of *komon* (advisers), especially legal advisers, to discern the specific modus operandi, in particular the division of labour with Japanese counterparts in order to enhance understanding of Meiji leadership; on the collective influence of minor yatoi on social change; and on the influence of yatoi on contemporary opinion-makers after return to their home countries.

1

Yatoi in the Meiji Experiment

Meiji Japan set out posthaste in pursuit of modernization. Live machines and living reference books were used. The aim was to replace those rented machines and books rapidly with trained Japanese. The motivations, the self-imposed limitations, the scale and scope, the lack of concerted programme design, and essentially the urgency of that pursuit prompt use of the term "experiment." Nation-building in Meiji Japan was not limited to the employment of foreign instructors. Yet, elusive as the statistics are, even a conservative assessment of utilization of such instructors reveals that this was a salient feature in building the New Japan of a century ago.

HIRED FOREIGNERS IN LATE TOKUGAWA JAPAN

The hiring of foreign assistants by the Meiji government had its antecedents in the preceding era, although the scale was slight in comparison. From the seventeenth century, contrary to a policy excluding foreigners from the main islands, Westerners were found in semi-official and semi-private employment. But, from 1854 to April 1868, at least two hundred foreign technological and language instructors were hired, most by the central government (*bakufu*) and some by regional domains (*han*). Of these more than eighty were French, more than sixty were Dutch, about thirty were British, and Americans and Germans constituted the remainder.[1]

From 1840, with China's entanglement with Britain, bakufu and han became increasingly involved in military preparation for national defence, but the arrival of the "Black Ships" (dark and tall; two were steam frigates) under the command of Commodore Matthew C. Perry, who was seeking to open Japan to obtain refuelling stations and trade with the United States and who promised to return a year hence, spurred anew concrete proposals and actions.

Officials at that time, as in the early Meiji period, were reluctant to hire foreigners, and initially missions were thrust upon them by the Dutch as a condition for receiving ships and machines. Two Dutch naval missions from 1854 to 1858 (the second included doctors and engineers), and the Dutch employees who continued after the Dutch initiated abolition of group missions, made significant contributions to Japanese technology. They were largely responsible for naval training in Nagasaki (the names of many future Meiji leaders were on the rolls of graduates); for building docks and factories, a naval school in Kobe, the Nagasaki vaccination clinic, a hospital and medical school (the base for Nagasaki University); and for providing language services.

In the mid-1860's, the French dockyard and workshop projects at Yokosuka and Yokohama had as a major aim the training of Japanese in ship construction and repair. A language school and military training mission were also part of the French contribution. Some French engineers did exploratory work for han, especially in Kyushu, and for the bakufu as far north as Karafuto.

From the mid-1860's, British technicians were han employees; the largest group was from Platt Brothers of Manchester at the Satsuma spinning plant. Erasmus H. M. Gower was hired by the bakufu to explore mining possibilities in Hokkaido. In 1866, in retaliation for the coup of the French minister in Japan, Léon Roches, in arranging a military mission, British minister Harry S. Parkes felt compelled to remind the bakufu of an 1864 request, hitherto ignored, for British military instructors. Parkes insisted that "Instructors in Naval Matters" be substituted for the original request.[2] However, this mission, accepted under duress and arriving on the eve of civil war, achieved little.

Some Germans and Americans were also hired in this period, but other than a German veterinarian and two American mining engineers who went to Hokkaido in the early 1860's, most became teachers in government language schools in the open ports. Some of the latter tutored future Meiji leaders and became yatoi in the Meiji era.

The records suggest that these two hundred or so bakumatsu foreign employees were well-qualified instructors. All were hired for the training of the Japanese, as well as for construction projects. More than half continued in Meiji employ. A pattern emerged in employment procedure and contract stipulations; this pattern and a few departures conditioned the hiring of foreigners in the Meiji era.

In the bakumatsu era, all engagements were made upon recommendation by foreign government representatives or foreign business entrepreneurs residing in the open ports, and the latter all had close ties with their governments. This meant that foreign employees from the outset were under the aegis of their respective nations and, knowingly or not, their employment became a means by which pressure was exerted by those nations. This arrangement also led to nepotism. Erasmus Gower's brother was British consul in Kanagawa and later Nagasaki, and the much-respected bakufu employee Dr. Anthonius F. Bauduin had relatives in business. Many such examples exist in both the bakumatsu and Meiji eras. This phenomenon appears to be related to the view of foreign governments that their nationals in Japan's employ were quasi-commercial agents, a persistent view which cast a shadow on Japanese relations with employees. Also, at the behest of foreign representatives, contract terms for bakumatsu employees providing handsome salaries, transportation, housing, foreign medical services, and naming the employee's government representative as arbiter of all disputes placed the employee firmly under his government's protection, since under the treaties foreigners were not subject to Japanese law.

Although U.S. minister Townsend Harris was instrumental in arranging the appointments of engineers Rafael Pumpelly and William Phipps Blake through Charles Wolcott Brooks, Japan's commercial agent in San Francisco, their 1862 contracts are notable exceptions.[3] They are among the first entered into by the bakufu to bring foreigners into the interior. While they include what by that time had become usual stipulations for transportation, housing, and salary, and implicit approval of the appointments by the United States representative, they reflect several significant departures from earlier contracts.[4]

They include no provision for the employee's recourse to his government representative. The contracts for each man, who would be working in the interior beyond treaty port jurisdiction, state "that full protection of life shall be afforded him by the Government of Japan, while in its service, whether at mines, traveling or in any of the cities or towns, he acting in conformity to the laws and regulations of said [Japanese] government" (Article 4).[5] This clause, drawn up by Brooks and accepted by Harris, whose name heads the contracts, conforms literally to the treaty arrangements. Foreigners could reside and work only in the defined port area, and there they were subject only to their own consular jurisdiction. The logical implication of these treaties, then, was that foreigners travelling beyond the defined area not only required Japanese permission to do so, but came under Japanese protection and were required to conform to Japanese laws.

These contracts are unique in their observance of the legal implications of early treaties. Even in the bakumatsu period, there were numerous exceptions to restriction of foreign residence to the treaty port areas; the French at

Yokosuka were the largest exception. Foreign representatives insisted that, even when their work took them into the interior, foreign employees were still under consular jurisdiction, in effect flouting Japanese sovereignty and the treaties as well. This stance had hardened by the early years of the Meiji period, and Japanese officials were then obliged to address themselves to this challenge.

In a lighter vein, another stipulation, rarely explicit in contracts although carefully adhered to, stated that the employee would "have a social position and rank in Japan relatively equal to that of scientific men in similar positions in other countries."[6] Japanese officials tried to base status treatment on the employee's position in his home country. Bakumatsu Dutch, French, and most British employees had military, naval, or government rank, so assessment was not difficult. Non-military citizens of a republic presented a puzzle no less to the employees themselves than to Japanese officials. In Blake's self-description, he listed his bachelor of philosophy degree, his work experience—solid but not exceptional—and numerous learned society affiliations as addenda to a letter in which he wrote;

> In reply to the inquiries by Your Excellency of my rank and position in the United States, I would state that in America, Scientific men take position according to merit and public services or experience and as Engineers, they rank with officers of Engineers of the Army, from whom the most able Generals and Commanders are selected. When distinguished by ability, accomplishments, and public service, they are received with great honor and attention by the highest officers of the country, by Governors and Ministers of State and their society is courted.[7]

This concern for status reached ludicrous proportions in the Meiji era, and Meiji officials were to have even more difficulty over status than did the governor of Hakodate regarding Blake and Pumpelly.

Yet it was the bakumatsu experience with foreign assistants which prepared the way for their employment in the Meiji era. In this sense, Umetani Noboru's comment is especially significant:

> Although the bakufu fell when it was engulfed by the stream of world history, amidst political and economic difficulties, it eagerly sought to assimilate material aspects of the West, and in foreshadowing the building of Meiji Japan, these experimental preparations should be given proper weight.[8]

Bakumatsu foreign employees were the forerunners of Meiji yatoi. From its launching, the new Meiji ship of state was caught up in the same stream of world history which engulfed the bakufu. Like their predecessors, Meiji leaders had reservations about the wisdom of using foreign assistants; yet their ship had to be rendered seaworthy and the Japanese crew required training. In commenting on Japan's response to the West at that time, Umetani has suggested that first there was an attempt simply to adjust, to find a modus vivendi, but that soon a more positive decision was taken to use all phases of Western development—in a sense an adjustment to external pressure by use of that pressure.[9] Soon a large-scale experiment in foreign borrowing was undertaken, the immediate motivation for which was the acquisition of competitive economic strength leading to political independence.

HIRED FOREIGNERS IN MEIJI JAPAN

Throughout history there are examples of nations using foreign tutors. In the nineteenth century, the Middle East, Russia, China, and South America all used foreign assistants. However, the Meiji Japan experience is without analogy in numbers, varieties of persons selected and the many areas in which they were employed, the fact that total financing was borne by the Meiji government, and in the policy devised for their control.

In any given year in the Meiji era, the number of foreigners in Japan for all purposes was a fairly constant eight thousand, although it was considerably less in war years. Usually half were Chinese.[10] It is not possible to arrive at a firm picture of the numbers of either private or government foreign employees from official published sources. It was not until 1882 that the government began to publish official statistics: in that year a Cabinet Statistics Bureau began editing the *Imperial Japan Statistical Yearbook* (SY).[11] In the early volumes, some statistical reports for yatoi go back to 1872. For the years 1876 through 1898 there are two annual tables on numbers and salaries of foreign employees. However, individual names are not supplied in context and, where these tables can be compared, the numbers of foreign employees and monthly salaries do not agree for half the years cited.

In a number of Japanese publications, lists have been compiled which represent patient digging. The two most extensive and reliable are those by Ogata Hiroyasu and by Saigusa Hiroto and his colleagues.[12] Shigehisa Tokutarō made a pioneering contribution, and there are detailed lists for particular projects and missions published in various articles and monographs and in some government histories.[13] Excluding the inevitable overlapping, there are published sources for more than two thousand government and private employees.

Figures in this book have been drawn from manuscript sources, principally from Foreign Ministry records, Navy files, the Ōkuma Papers, prefecture documents, the Cabinet Collection, and other library holdings. These have been checked against published names including those in some foreign directories. The number of employees listed in SY to 1887 are markedly lower than employees clearly identifiable by name. However, from 1887 through 1898, SY figures for each year indicate from twenty to one hundred employees more than those this study has been able to find names for. These discrepancies point to the inherent difficulties in this undertaking. Several limitations are imposed by extant materials. Foreign Ministry records provide a rich source of information, but the Foreign Ministry by the 1880's had relinquished its direct administrative role in the employment of foreigners in favour of Cabinet supervision and the latter records are sparse. By the 1890's the term oyatoi gaikokujin disappeared from the records, although foreigners continued to be employed after the turn of the century.

Records have been lost, and Anesaki Masaharu declares that "the memory of these foreign advisers has been much obliterated, partly wilfully, due to the conservative reaction of the nineties."[14] Although the Foreign Ministry co-ordinated the administration of foreign employees, its efforts to maintain complete records were foiled by activists. With little interest in mundane record-keeping, government officials consistently flouted operating procedures even when they became standardized. Despite the fact that in early years there was constant inter-ministry change, particularly in the top three ministry positions, ministerial insularity was pronounced. Incumbents guarded their domains jealously in the face of urgent calls for financial retrenchment, and the employment of foreigners was invariably the focus of criticism. General records or "no records" were most easily manipulated.

Even in keeping records, the inveterate use of the Japanese syllabary (*kana*) for foreign names and the omission of given names despite directives stipulating full romanization often makes it impossible to determine spellings or full names except for long-term and better-known employees. Simultaneous multiple employment by several bureaus or by more than one ministry presents further complications, especially for similar-sounding names. But, by cross-checking sources, it is possible to determine that on occasion many more persons were employed than official administrative reports indicate.

Despite the fragmentation of existing records and the futility of transliterating kana, more than 3,000 foreign employees in government service have been counted. Because of similarities between names, duplicates have been discarded, though some *may* have been different persons. It is also difficult to deal with the numerous temporary and part-time workers in the lower echelon. Unevenness in data has reduced the sample to 2,050 individuals. The tables on pages 145 – 54 are not viewed here as hard data, but rather as imprecise indications of the variety and magnitude of the Meiji undertaking.

The origins and activities of these foreign employees are diverse. More than twenty-five national groups are represented (Table 1, p. 145); countries providing the largest numbers were Britain, France, the United States, and Germany. The British account for half of all nationals and two-thirds of those who were employed by the Public Works Ministry (Tables 4–5, pp. 150–51), which sponsored major technological projects and model industries.[15] The total of 2,400 (Table 1) includes 350 cases of multiple, inter-ministry employment.

In the sample, man years of service by area of government (Table 2, pp. 146 – 47) total more than 9,500 years. Man years by nationality (Table 3, pp. 148 – 49) indicate that the British contributed more than 4,300 years, the French more than 1,500, and the Germans and Americans more than 1,200 years to building the New Japan.

The New Japan required refurbishing of administrative organs. Major reorganization in 1868 was followed in August 1869 by the establishment of the Council of State (*Dajōkan*) system (which had an executive council and six executive sections: imperial household, civil affairs, military affairs, finance, justice, and foreign affairs), on a model dating from the eighth century. Subsequent internal alterations and divisions transformed these executive offices into modern ministries. From 1869, civil enterprises dealing with the development of industry and technology were directed by Civil Affairs and from 1870 to 1873 they were divided among the new Finance, Public Works, Education, and Home ministries. Military-related activities were directed by Military Affairs and separated in 1872 into the Navy and Army ministries. With the abolition of Public Works in 1885, Agriculture-Commerce and, later, the Communications ministries were set up. By the second decade, the Council of State was replaced by a Western-style cabinet system in preparation for modern constitutional government. With each reorganization, yatoi activities and projects were subject to transfer to other offices.

The Council of State figures for yatoi are abnormally high in the early years because in 1868 British lighthouse technicians and civil engineers and French engineers and workers, principally in the Yokohama foundry and Yokosuka dockyards, were placed under the foreign affairs section. Technically these yatoi were administered by the Kanagawa local government. The number of regular employees in the Council of State was always slight, but the noticeable increase in 1874 was owing to the employment of foreigners by a special office (*Banchi jimukyoku*) set up to handle affairs relating to the Taiwan punitive expedition. Some foreigners continued to be employed after the office was abolished in 1875. For its own office work the Council of State used French, American, and Austrian translators, two of whom, Albert Charles Du Bousquet, 1867 – 82, and Guido F. Verbeck, 1864 – 78, were also general advisers prior to 1882. In the 1880's, German advisers in finance and law helped prepare for the new cabinet system.

In December 1885, the Cabinet replaced the Council of State. The Public Works Ministry was also abolished and railway employees were transferred to Cabinet administration between 1885 and 1890; hence, figures for British employees in 1885 include seventeen railway employees, a number which was gradually reduced through 1890. Cabinet advisers included British architect Josiah Condor, 1877 – 87, and constitutional adviser, Francis Piggott, 1887 – 91; a French legal adviser, Emile Boissonade, who served the Cabinet while employed by the Justice Ministry from 1873 to 1895; an American translator; and German legal advisers for local government, constitution preparation, the court system, and civil law from 1883 to 1894. German legal advisers were conspicuous from the early 1880's, but the basis of their employment was laid in the Foreign Ministry in the 1870's.

The national origins of employees in the Foreign Ministry were particularly diverse. That some of the earliest employees were American and German reflected Japanese hopes of altering British dominance in treaty revision negotiations. Between 1871 and 1914 there was always an American adviser on international law. Japan's awakening interest in its own boundaries, in its neighbouring territory, and in the position of the United States in the Pacific was reflected in the continued employment of Americans (Henry Willard Denison, 1880 – 1914; Charles LeGendre on Taiwan, 1872 – 75; Durham H. Stevens on Korea, 1884 – 1907). In the early 1870's, German interpreters and language teachers were numerous; German legal translators and legal advisers were employed through the 1880's. A Russian, an Italian, and a Swiss are included among the translators and language teachers, and a British adviser on treaty revision was stationed in London, while an English secretary/public relations man was employed in Japan.

The Imperial Household Ministry employed several foreign language teachers and physicians, including a part-time music teacher. However, the only high-ranking foreign employee was a German adviser on court etiquette named Ottmar von Mohl, 1887 – 89.

Although the preponderance of German advisers involved in later institutional and legal revision has often been noted, almost all law instructors in the Justice Ministry during the last quarter of the century were French. There were also French legal translators and court advisers. The large number of French specialists was related to the employment of Boissonade, who was in charge of revision of legal codes. While a German translator and legal adviser were used in the mid-1870's, it was not until after 1890 that two German specialists edited some of the French work. British legal translators and advisers were employed from 1879 to 1901. Apart from being employed to undertake legal revision, British, French, Americans, and Chinese were used as court interpreter/translators under the requirements of the treaty system.

As Table 2 indicates (pp. 146 – 47), employment of foreigners by the Finance Ministry was heaviest through 1881, the peak years being 1871 – 76. Early figures refer to persons hired by the finance section of the Council of State or directly for the Civil Affairs Ministry before its establishment. There were customs and mint employees, all but one of whom were British. For the peak years numbers were bolstered by Mint Bureau employees (twenty-six of a total of thirty-two were British) and French workers in the Tomioka model spinning plant. It is difficult to define other areas by particular nationals. Both British and Americans were prominent in banking development and tariff matters; customs, with a few British and French exceptions, came to be handled by Americans. General legal and financial advisers as well as translators were British, American, German, and Russian. In the Printing Bureau, two Americans (a chemist to develop an ink process and a teacher of printing), a British bookbinder, three German teachers, an Italian engraver, and an Austrian photographer were employed.

The activities of the Home Ministry, however, can be more clearly classified by reference to particular nationals. British were used in the 1870's in agriculture (a few Americans were also employed), in surveying (transferred from the Public Works Ministry in 1874), in commercial shipping offices of the 1870's, and in the railways, which from 1890 to 1892 were administered by the Home Ministry. The employees hired for postal revision, some thirty persons, were almost entirely American. In the 1870's most of the hydraulic and construction engineers engaged in harbour development and most of the pharmacologists for new municipal sanitation offices were Dutch. From the mid-1880's through the 1890's, police advisers, as well as architects and engineers employed to design state buildings were German. The Senjū Woollen Mill was staffed from the mid-1870's through 1890 by Germans. Home Minister Yamagata Aritomo's preference for German systems, seen in his restructuring of the army, was also reflected in his organization of police, the woollen mill, which was the major supplier of uniforms, blankets, and so on, and in his choice of Cabinet employee Albert Mosse as adviser on local government. Other nationals were also used in small numbers in these various areas.

Foreign employee activities in the Public Works Ministry are illustrated by Tables 4 and 5 (pp. 150 – 51). From 1870 to 1885 this ministry hired 60 per cent of all foreign employees. Only 15 per cent of these were office personnel; all others were engineers, technicians, and field workers.[16] Fifty per cent of those in the field were day labourers. British were without question predominant in all bureaus, although French and Germans had strong representation in the Mines Bureau. Employees listed from Manila, in the Philippines, were seamen and lighthouse tenders, and Chinese were seamen and cooks. Italians were teachers of fine arts, and Danes were hired in communications, especially telegraph communication.

With the abolition of the ministry in 1885, employees were transferred to the new Communications or Agriculture-Commerce ministries. Others were temporarily in other offices. Most employees in the Communications Ministry from the 1880's to 1900 were British, and in the same period in Agriculture-Commerce, most were German. From about 1880, German employees superseded both British and Americans in the field of agricultural development. The British, however, were retained in the government shipping branches of both ministries, just as they had been dominant in various government shipping offices in the 1870's.

Throughout its decade of operation, the Commission for Hokkaido Development (Kaitakushi) was served largely by Americans in a broad programme of surveying, mining, railway construction, soil improvement, dairy and stock farming, fruit and grain experimentation, canning and other refineries, leather tanning, and small-ship transportation. However, the Commission also employed Chinese and German leather tanners, Chinese farmers and German beer brewers, Russian carpenters, Dutch and British civil engineers, and an Austrian photographer. After 1881, the agricultural school continued to be staffed principally by Americans, but in the early years Dutch and English women were employed to teach girls. Americans continued as science teachers, but other nationals were engaged as language teachers.

In the Navy Ministry all training was done by British employees. Yokosuka dockyards and part of the Yokohama foundry came under Navy administration in 1872, with almost fifty French workers. A handful of other nationals were employed: Germans (including one woman) in teaching music and in gunpowder manufacture; Dutch as physicians and English-language teachers; Swiss and Americans as language teachers. An American navy paymaster was hired to revise payroll accounts, a Portuguese hired as an interpreter, a Chinese hired as a metal worker, and in later years a prominent French ship architect and designer was hired.

In the Army Ministry, French instructors were used throughout the 1880's to conduct cavalry, artillery, and infantry training and also to teach calisthenics and music. Germans appear in the 1880's as language teachers, strategy instructors, and advisers on general staff reorganization. Italians were employed as cannon-makers, Belgians as gunsmiths, and British as English teachers.

The Education Ministry employed many nationals throughout the Meiji period, but the fields given consistent and major attention were medicine, the natural sciences, and language. On all levels of education, Germans accounted for 37.2 per cent of foreign employees, British for 22.5 per cent, Americans for 20.1 per cent, French for 13 per cent, Swiss for 1.8 per cent, Austrians for 1.2 per cent, and others for less than 1 per cent each. These figures were compiled (by name) by Ogata Hiroyasu, largely from Cabinet Collection records.[17] Although based on fewer names, Ogata's percentages correspond closely to those in this study.

The costs of employing so many foreign assistants placed a formidable burden on the Meiji government, which assumed direct, total financial responsibility. From the outset, the medium of payment generated argument. Even in the bakumatsu era, foreign employees had begun to insist on payment in Mexican silver dollars (*yōgin*), the most common currency for foreign exchange in the treaty ports. In the 1860's Dutch contracts stipulated Mexican silver dollars, and contracts of other nationals demanded their own currency or equivalent. Following serious arguments over the rate of exchange, the bakufu was obliged to make reimbursements and to accept adjustments made by foreign representatives in Japan.[18]

Meiji officials inherited these financial problems, and even when the new silver yen reached full production in 1872, foreign employees insisted on yōgin. The payment-medium crisis reached a peak in the Navy Ministry in 1874 – 75 after the British mission arrived. Since the problem was government-wide, in 1876 senior councillor Iwakura Tomomi directed each office to use whatever medium was convenient.[19] Meiji officials fought hard for the foreign diplomatic and trade community's acceptance of the new monetary system, but throughout the first decade they faced an adverse exchange ratio.[20] Silver thus became the standard officially authorized for foreign employees and was a dollar equivalent whether listed as yōgin, gen (indicating coin), or yen.[21]

Salaries were the major expense recorded (See Table 6, p. 152).[22] In salaries alone, foreign employees were without doubt an alien élite. Based on yatoi remarks in newspapers and memoirs, salaries were often double the U.S. average and more than double the European average in many categories. The upper 7 per cent in this study received salaries equivalent to or exceeding those of Japanese officials who were full generals and admirals (*taishō*), chief officials (*chōkan*), department ministers (*-kyō*), inner council chairmen (*gichō*), or councillors (*sangi*), all of whom in the early 1870's had salaries of 500 yen a month; ministers of the legislative and administrative chambers (*Sa-U daijin*) at 600 yen, or the Council of State prime minister (*Dajō daijin*) at 800 yen.[23] At least two yatoi received salaries more than double that of the prime minister.[24] Almost all foreign employees, even the lowest unskilled persons, except Chinese hired for Hokkaido Development and foreign police, received salaries in excess of rank eleven of the third civil service category (*hannin*). In fact, three-quarters of all yatoi received salaries equivalent to those of the upper two levels of Japanese civil service (*sōnin* and *chokunin*).[25]

The disparity between emoluments of foreign employees and Japanese officials is even more significant in the light of comments by Shibusawa Keizō. In 1871 the government began paying officials a certain amount each month, partly in rice. By 1875 scales were quite firmly established. But, "in fact, the government did not pay the salaries listed, and there is evidence that at times it was unable to pay officials anything."[26] Monthly salaries were a financial strain and in subsequent years were revised downward. Disparities between salaries for foreign employees and lower level Japanese officials were particularly wide. Although foreign engineers and technicians were paid between $400 and $800 a month, the highest paid first class Japanese engineer received 250 yen.[27] It was common for one foreign teacher's salary to exceed the total of all student tuition in a given school, and, naturally, it exceeded that of the Japanese principal.[28] Foreign unskilled labourers received 80 to 90 yen a month compared with 12 to 13 yen for Japanese section officials.[29] If Japanese officials were under stress, the ordinary Japanese labourer was never able to stretch his meagre income to cover basic necessities.[30]

Expenditures for foreign employees are more overwhelming when one considers additional emoluments. By the fall of 1873 salary scales were established. The preparation allowance (a lump sum compensation for moving), class of transportation, per diem for baggage, food, and lodging en route, class of housing and allowances in lieu of housing, and per diem for official travel within Japan were determined on the basis of salary (see Appendix 2, pp. 159 – 65). However, additional stipends and additional part-time employment payments were often not formally accounted for.

Published sources on the funding of yatoi are limited to sporadic records given in SY and to compilations of government documents made later.[31] These fragmentary samples are out of context and do not reflect the practice revealed in directives and government correspondence. For example, according to MZKS, from December 1867 to December 1868, when government expenditures were declared at 30.5 million yen, expenditures for yatoi were listed at almost 71,000 yen. The amount is scarcely enough to cover even the salaries for Yokosuka French employees. The 1870 Civil Affairs-Finance Ministry report, in a review of the early years, estimated salaries for an average of forty-five French yatoi a year (even in 1868 closer to fifty-five, according to Yokosuka records of actual employees by name) at $80,820.[32] (This figure may or may not include the salary increase received in 1870.) In comparison, forty-three Japanese officials received one-third of that amount.

But the Japanese government after April 1868 was also responsible for the military, and perhaps the naval mission through July, high-priced foreign engineers, a whole crew of foreign lighthouse technicians, and others for a total of at least ninety-two, excluding the military. By extension, the figures reported through September 1871 can hardly cover yatoi salaries, let alone other emoluments. The same deficiencies apply to official reports found for 1876 – 77 and 1880 – 81.

For 1872, Osatake Takeki has found a document listing 214, actually 213, individuals with their monthly salaries, nationalities, and offices of employment.[33] Neither the numbers (SY reports 369 yatoi and government files reveal 674 yatoi for that year) nor the salaries (534,492 yen) in that document reflect the actual situation. In 1874, the peak year of employment, with 858 yatoi (SY reports 524), the count of actual salaries alone exceeds $1.8 million. Other commitments would raise that figure considerably.

For 1876 – 77, government-published expenditures for yatoi (MZKS and HBT) were almost 1.4 million yen. When, by 1881, the number of yatoi had been reduced to a third of the peak employment, HBT figures for July 1880–June 1881 record expenditure of more than 800,000 yen. Yet, in the cry for retrenchment, the Army Ministry received in 1881 an allotment of 2.5 million yen for ten years in order to build fortifications and hire foreigners.[34]

For another key year, 1886, when the Cabinet was reorganized, SY reports 169 yatoi with aggregate monthly salaries of 44,731 yen. Estimated on a twelve-month basis, although employment dates are not given, the amount would exceed one-half million yen. But salaries alone computed from government files amounted to more than $650,000 for 204 known employees.

Because the country was under financial stress, all officials were obliged to give assurance of economy and retrenchment. Foreign employees were expensive and their alien presence conspicuous. It was perhaps natural that calls for economy focussed on their overpayment. Funding from outside the regular budget was a common practice for all government purposes and expenditures for yatoi were deliberately played down by offices employing them. For many years, half of the Education Ministry budget was spent for foreign employees, but this cannot be ascertained from published annual reports.[35] However, those reports do show that from the mid-1870's the Education Ministry allotted an average of 70 million yen annually to local education; much of that was paid to foreign teachers. The Education Minister admitted that in 1877 – 78 one-third of the Tokyo University budget (98,279 out of 282,035 yen) constituted salaries for the foreign faculty exclusive of travel allowance, housing and repairs, surely a low estimate.[36] In 1879, after major attrition, the Public Works Ministry expended 66 per cent of its budget for foreign employees; expenditures were never less than one-fourth to one-third of the budget.[37]

These data indicate that while the cost of the use of foreign assistants in Meiji Japan's nation-building eludes computation in this study, it was a tremendous amount for those times and conditions. Yet the most important single statement that can be made about Japanese government expenditures for foreign employees is that its officials remained willing to make those expenditures under the internal economic and political stress of the times. In hiring American experts for Hokkaido Development in 1871, Kido Takayoshi (Kōin) told Itō Hirobumi that, however great, the expense was justified.[38] He was expressing the opinion of a core of Meiji leaders intent on a policy of economic growth.

THE MEIJI EXPERIMENT

Bakumatsu foreign employees had prepared the ground for the Meiji yatoi experience. Not only did they help lay a concrete project base but through the encouragement and good offices of these employees, Japanese students were sent abroad for study. Their intangible contributions were perhaps even greater, as they helped create a climate favourable to international educational exchange. The precedent was there for enterprising Meiji leaders to build on. At the same time, contractual obligations incurred by the Japanese and the fact that foreign employees were under the legal protection of their countries put Japan at a disadvantage with respect to treaty port politics, in which it was to negotiate acquisition of modern technology.

Of necessity, political independence was the immediate motivation for the employment of foreign assistants. However, Japanese officials and intellectuals were soon swept up in the challenge and magic of the "new enlightenment." One recalls how Ōkuma Shigenobu persuaded Shibusawa Eiichi to enter the new Finance Ministry. The latter demurred on the grounds that he had no experience. Ōkuma likened restoration times to when the ancient gods (*kamiyo jidai*) after consulting among themselves, brought their world into being. The new government was gathering knowledge to create a new political world. Experience was not a criterion for office; the gods had had no previous experience for their grand enterprise. Dedicated effort was the prime criterion for building a new nation.[39]

Evidence of dedicated effort abounds. But the pressure, self-imposed limitations, scale and scope of change, and the whole phenomenon of cultural symbiosis took their toll. Was it not as Shibusawa remarked about Ōkuma? He was a man of great capacity and spirit who thought nothing was impossible, but sometimes he spread his *furoshiki* (scarf for carrying things) a little too wide, did not tie the ends, or did not notice holes and leaks. Ōkuma had both virtues and shortcomings.[40] So it was with the Meiji experiment. The scale of the experiment was so large that it is difficult to distinguish between what was expedience and what was soundly considered, what was veneer and what was core change. Georges Bousquet (1872 – 76), the first lawyer hired by the Justice Ministry, wrote: "I have seen unfolded before my eyes a civilization very, very old, refined and no less mature than our own."[41] But in cataloguing the changes observed, he noted they were more revolutionary than evolutionary. Motivation for the feverish activity he assessed as vanity, an attempt to show Europe a décor of Western civilization. The Japanese were so able that their progress would be no less useful if accomplished on a more moderate footing. As it was, Bousquet felt their efforts too grand, too ostentatious, not in keeping with indigenous qualities.[42] This assessment represents a fair consensus of opinion among yatoi, but it ignores the domestic and foreign pressure experienced during the Meiji experiment.

However, Japan's nation-building did in fact require experience as well as dedicated effort. The first decade was characterized by a frenzy of activity, indicated by the numbers of foreigners hired and the multiple uses to which they were put. In one sample of a little more than 2,000 yatoi, 350 cases of simultaneous or multiple inter-ministry employment were counted. Intraministry employment by more than one bureau is more than double that count. Memoranda and correspondence show that yatoi were often hired and paid additional sums for work over and above their contracts. The uses of foreign employees were extended to every conceivable limit.

Despite the numbers engaged, a shortage of foreign workers and the time consumed by recruitment processes encouraged officials to lure employees from one office to another.[43] Yatoi took advantage of demands for their services and engaged in moonlighting. By 1875, the situation was so bad that the Council of State insisted that, in cases of employment by more than one ministry, the original employer's permission had to be obtained.[44] Yatoi moved from one office to another by a natural momentum, so that even those discharged for negligence could take advantage of the situation. As a preventive measure, ministries were ordered in 1876 to investigate new employees with previous service in Japan.[45]

Haste and uneven emphasis is seen in all government efforts. In the constant crises and reshuffling of government affairs in the 1870's, officials were also subject to frequent change. The existence of shifting intra-government coalitions and a pervasive concept that an official could and should function in any area meant not only that transfers often occurred but also that officials were assigned multiple responsibilities. Projects suffered as a result. The displacement of the samurai class was at the centre of domestic problems.

Ways were sought of assimilating the former civil-warrior class into the new social and economic framework which involved dissolution of the han and establishment of the prefectural system for co-ordinated local administration. Government payment of samurai stipends took 23 per cent of government funds from 1868 to 1886, a sum equal to the total expenditure for the Public Works Ministry.[46] By 1876 the drain on finances was so great that pensions were commuted to reduced lump sum payments and government bonds. The further hardships of this displaced group precipitated the Satsuma Rebellion in 1877, which required almost 42 million yen for its suppression.[47]

This period of internal crises, accompanied by retrenchment in the Public Works Ministry, has been described by a yatoi as follows:

This autumn was remarkable for a great "jishin": or earthquake—in the official world, that is to say. The Japanese give this name to an administrative crisis that arrives periodically,—it is difficult to say whence or why,—and involves a re-construction of the ministry (always, however, composed of nearly the same persons, but with a different distribution of duties); a general dismissal of all officials in the government service, immediate re-appointment of three-fourths of them temporarily, that is to say, until the next "jishin"; and a strenuous effort to get rid, or get credit for getting rid of foreign assistance by all the departments.[48]

Factional strife and political rivalries, even more than financial difficulties, contributed to the controversy over the use of yatoi. Thus, often there was duplication of effort, inconsistent support of projects, and premature cancellation of programmes. For example, when the development of the Kitakami valley was undertaken by the Home Minister, the Vice-Minister of Public Works disassociated himself from the project.[49] Schools were opened only to be closed; training programmes were often begun only to be suspended, reorganized, and started again, as yatoi complaints attest. Sometimes interest was lost in a particular project by one office, and it changed hands until a hospitable office or official decided to shelter it. This was the case with the Senjū Woollen Mill, which was eventually revived by the Home Ministry. The Tomioka model spinning factory, the training base for the important textile industry, was operated first by Finance and then by the Home Ministry.

The Hokkaido Development programme provides a clear example of a project which was prematurely cancelled. Despite bakufu efforts, the northern island was not until the Meiji era "felt" to be part of Japan proper. A fascinating social aspect of the programme to subsidize colonization was the effort by the government to inculcate in the Japanese positive attitudes towards that then inhospitable northern land.[50] The Commission for Hokkaido Development had envisioned a twenty-year programme in two ten-year stages. In the first decade the exploration and development of natural resources, the introduction of new techniques and tools, agricultural and livestock experimentation, roads and railway construction, numerous infant industries, and agricultural schools were scheduled.

Commissioner Kuroda Kiyotaka engaged former U.S. Commissioner of Agriculture, General Horace Capron, who, as his background showed, was competent.[51] But Capron's authoritarianism and the jealousies among the foreign staff caused problems. By 1874 most contracts had expired and most of the original party in the north had drifted into government employment near the capital. Later, good teachers and technicians were hired at moderate salaries. William S. Clark, for example, gave new impetus to the training programme and to the Sapporo Agricultural School during his nine-month stay in 1876–77.[52] However, in 1881, after ten years of activity, the programme was cut short because of internal instability, lack of funds, and intra-government rivalries.[53] Some activities were continued by local government.

Thus, projects in the first decade of the Meiji period had an aura of experiment, and crucial areas such as mining, shipping, rail transportation, and heavy industry were slow to develop. Foreigners blamed premature dismissal of yatoi before the end of the first decade for this, but, in critical areas, some foreigners did continue to be employed into the twentieth century.

In critiques submitted to the government, mining engineer Dr. Curt Netto (1873–85) argued that Japan's refusal to allow foreign investment and its dismissal of foreign engineers before the Japanese were fully trained were major reasons for failures in mining development.[54] In the mid-1870's, in order to develop maritime commerce so essential to an island country, the main government shipping office (Kaisō toriatsukaijo, later Kansenkyoku), using largely British assistants, attempted to organize several semi-public companies, but these went bankrupt. Several shipping company histories blame this failure upon high salaries for yatoi, but factionalism and inexperience were also factors. Eventually the Japan Mail Line (N.Y.K.) succeeded, as did shipping companies of several other cartels. But N.Y.K. used foreign employees for many years.[55]

In the first decade rail transportation received major emphasis, but the construction of a basic rail network required more than three decades. The first attempt required heavy foreign tutelage. Even so, a yatoi chief engineer attributed delays in the first decade to understaffing. The reduction of foreign staff and replacement by "unseasoned Japanese" resulted in many accidents.[56] The manufacture of heavy machinery and rails was not possible

until the turn of the century. It was the beginning of the Taishō period (1912 –
26) before domestic production met half the demand. Obstacles of terrain,
the need for tunnels and bridges, made work slow and difficult. Especially in
bridge engineering, foreign assistance was required long after other work was
being performed entirely by the Japanese.

Many yatoi, such as engineer Edmund G. Holtham (1873 – 81) thought that
the government was being hoodwinked by officials claiming economy by
citing discharge of foreigners. The usually judicious yatoi Dr. Erwin von
Baelz (1876 – 1903), personal physician to many Meiji leaders and a university
professor, commented that medical students returning from abroad in the
first decade in Germany would not even be called doctors. Despite dismissals
of yatoi, the Japanese in 1879 were still not sufficiently trained.[57] Japanese
leaders like Itō Hirobumi fully agreed that the Japanese were, at the end of
the first decade, as yet insufficiently trained, especially to replace foreign
engineers.[58]

Yet, in spite of criticism, heavy expenditures for telegraph lines and railways were vindicated because these provided rapid communication and
logistical support for the new conscript army which responded to the Satsuma
Rebellion, the last military challenge to centralization and national unity.[59]
However, by the end of the first decade, there was an alteration in government priorities, as indicated by the reduction in foreign technologists and the
decision to turn over most government enterprises to private interests. It has
been pointed out that,

> ready as political leaders were for sacrifices, the government could not
> indefinitely stand the financial strain of heavily subsidizing the new
> industry for it was simultaneously investing lavishly in related forms
> of modernization—public education, for example—and liquidating the
> old regime at great financial cost.[60]

From the second decade, for political as well as financial reasons, priority
shifted to the development of government machinery and institutional specialization for public control.

Maruyama Masao has commented succinctly on this transition to government specialization, citing the Home Ministry as an example. He observes
that from the time of Ōkubo Toshimichi as Home Minister, the meaning of
home or interior affairs included almost every administrative field in the
nation. As state functions grew complicated though, the various sections
became independent. With a characteristically ironic touch, Maruyama concludes that the meaning of "interior" shrank until the so-called proper

interior affairs work was social traffic regulation, that is, police work.[61]

Meiji leaders sustained this massive programme of foreign assistance with relatively few foreign loans. Traditionally, the heaviest sacrifice was demanded of the agriculturalist. Although new government industries introduced new technological methods and alleviated some regional imbalances, they did not provide capital. In the 1870's and 1880's, land tax accounted for four-fifths of total government revenue and 50 to 60 per cent thereafter. But international financial trust in Japan's foreign trade was not established until the First World War; hence there was heavy reliance on foreign resident traders and foreign financial corporations.[62]

Thomas C. Smith has commented that lack of capital precluded development being left to private initiative. He notes that the government was willing to foster enterprises even at a loss as long as they were deemed useful, and argues that the sale of government industries was the direct result of its inability to sustain the financial burden. Smith has made a cogent case for the positive role of government enterprise from 1868 to 1880. However, W. W. Lockwood's conclusion is still valid: "direct entrepreneurship passed rather quickly . . . . In most industries it never went beyond the pilot venture."[63]

The Meiji experiment with foreign instructors inevitably caused cultural tensions. Contrary to Thomas C. Smith's assertion that "it is easy to overlook the significance of labor in Japanese industrialization because it posed no major problem," a grave problem facing Meiji modernizers was the absence of a modern labour force.[64] The transition to a modern Japan was not made with ease, as is indicated by the nature of the labour force, the labourers' plight, and labour unrest, especially during the first thirty years of the Meiji period.

The absence of a modern labour force was another pertinent reason for the wide use of foreign unskilled labour in major initial projects. Despite the potential for modernization, early Meiji commoners had the same prejudices towards foreign machines and the factory system as they demonstrated towards the foreign-style national conscript army. Initially these changes were viewed as disruptions which offered little promise of enhancing their lives. For the most part, factories were set up in open fields. As there was no local labour supply to draw on, railways were laid through the countryside and coolie labour was brought in. Theoretically, according to modern experience, anyone should be able to swing a pick or shovel and master simple machine operations, but the tools, technique, timetable, administrative concepts, and handling and organization were all modern and quite literally foreign. Paul Akamatsu has written: "Given that the nobles and then the imperial government were skipping various stages in moving from craftsmanship (to a large extent pre-capitalist) to modern industry, the concentration of qualified and suitable manpower could not be rapidly obtained.[65]

The government itself was never a major employer of industrial labour. According to G. C. Allen, even by 1880 the government employed less than one-fifth of the working population (about 37,000 persons). From the 1880's to the First World War, industrial labour in Japan consisted mainly of women workers hired for a few years, women and men moving back and forth between farm and factory (*dekasegi*), and floating labour pools under independent boss contractors (*oyakata*).[66] Thus, the "labour force" was composed largely of short-term or temporary unskilled labour being paid low wages. Allen has noted that only when permanent skilled labour was required in engineering, metal, and chemical industries were high wages necessary, and then in order to overcome resistance to factory work.[67]

Early labour practices smacked of conscription. In textile industries in particular (and textiles were at the centre of the early industrial base), the largely female labour force was actually in bonded servitude, employees being indentured by their families. However, the dire conditions of women in the Meiji factory system—starvation, torture, bondage—developed after the government turn-over of model industries to private hands. For example, in the Tomioka spinning plant under government management, the regulations of the factory adviser, Paul Brunat (eight hours of work in a nine and a half-hour day, no night work, Sunday holiday and New Year holiday from December 29 to January 3, one- to three-year contracts) were implemented for women workers. These conditions promoted efficiency and were not devised just because daughters of samurai and rich agricultural families, such as the niece of Inoue Kaoru and the sister of Tokutomi Sohō, were hired for élan. Ability was the criterion for position, and daughters of outcasts (*burakumin* or *"shinheimin"*) taught daughters of the élite. However, social factions developed as women from Yamaguchi (Chōshū) exerted élitest pressure. Even so, hundreds of leadership models were produced for the nation and some of these women returned to rural areas to set up small local factories, continuing to use enlightened regulations.[68] Some scholars have suggested that it was not until heavy industry developed in the 1930's and the numbers of males in the Japanese labour force for the first time exceeded females that a proletariat was born.[69]

The early pace was too rapid; labour seemed to pass from infancy to adulthood without experiencing a healthy childhood. Akamatsu remarks:

It would not be an exaggeration to say that industrialization in the Japan of the 1870's corresponded neither to economic *need* nor a social reality. Industrialization had been adjudged necessary to Japan's political independence, first by the Bakufu and then by the imperial government . . . . A long time was to pass before a working class took shape.[70]

Perhaps there was no way for leadership to opt for a "balanced economy." Specialization for export had to be chosen. As G. C. Allen remarks, all exports with the exception of copper were produced from small-scale or peasant cottage industries. Early Meiji development coincided with a demand for raw silk in Europe. Besides 1868, 1876 was the only year exports exceeded imports, and nearly half of all exports consisted of raw silk.[71] Some economic scholars assert that industrial take-off occurred in the 1890's, but it is generally conceded that competitive economic strength was not achieved until the First World War, when Japan moved from the status of debtor to creditor nation. However, political independence was achieved at the end of the third decade of the Meiji period as a result of bureaucratic and legal specialization developed in the second decade.

Also in the second decade, the government gave renewed emphasis to the overseas student (*ryūgakusei*) programme. The employment of foreign instructors and the sending of students abroad were two aspects of Japan's modernizing experiment. In theory, Meiji leaders gave them equal emphasis. In practice, the overseas student programme suffered even more than that which regulated the hiring and control of foreign assistants because of financial constraints and intra-government factionalism. And, in practice, for the first decade and a half of the Meiji period the employment of foreign employees took precedence over sending students abroad.

It is to the credit of foreigners in Japan and yatoi in particular that they consistently endorsed this programme. Building on earlier precedents and personal experience, many Meiji modernizers encouraged sending students abroad. In 1869 the Meiji government assumed responsibility for the programme begun in 1862 under bakufu and han auspices.

In the first plan, one hundred students drawn from ministries, bureaus, and han were to be screened on a basis of talent, regardless of social status. In this undated but pre-1871 proposal, the average length of study proposed was five years. Of the one hundred students, twenty-five each were to be sent to England, France, and Prussia. Of the other twenty-five, some were to be sent to Holland and some to the United States.[72]

The despatch of students abroad was recommended in most early project proposals. In 1870, Iwakura Tomomi, Terajima Munenori, and Inoue Kaoru concurred that it would be a pity to prolong the use of foreign instructors. Japanese should not only be trained in the new Mint in Osaka, but also some should be sent abroad for seven or eight years of training.[73] In the

Public Works proposal, the academic group was drawn from the upper classes. Academic representatives were to be skilled in a Western language, but prior language skill was not required of those in technology, who were to be selected from mines, foundries, dockyards, and various construction and manufacturing sections. Returning students would be obliged to work for the government for seven years.[74]

In 1871, the central government assumed control of private han students as well. The Education Ministry supervised and co-ordinated regulations for all students, but problems in funding and in the quality of those selected were noted. Inoue Kaoru and Yoshida Kiyonari, especially concerned because funding was from outside the regular budget, criticized the appointment of upper class students. They wanted assurance that only candidates with a prospect of success would be chosen.[75]

In 1872, the Education Ministry instituted more careful screening before selection and more stringent supervision abroad. Even so, some officials not only maintained that the quality of returning students was so poor that most failed the Education Ministry examinations, but also that students were reluctant to serve in government offices to repay their scholarships. From the letters and reports of some students through the bakumatsu era to the first Meiji decade, it appears that although they were assigned designated areas of technological study, on arrival abroad they often showed more or equal interest in the social sciences and humanities.[76]

In 1873, when 18 per cent of the Education Ministry's budget was being spent on overseas students, the programme was suspended because in the opinion of some officials the 500,000 yen spent between 1868 and 1872 had been fruitless. Officials tried to devise a better system. Putting selected students through a nine-week preparatory course was tried, but did not work. As a result, in 1875 eleven students were chosen from Kaisei school, noted for the élite status of its students. Their quality, and that of ten more despatched in 1876, was very high, but this programme lapsed in 1877–78 because of the disorders caused by the Satsuma Rebellion.[77]

At the end of the first decade, Itō Hirobumi and other officials, especially from the Education Ministry, argued on behalf of sending students abroad. Education Minister Tanaka Fujimarō thought that the results of the programme were just beginning to be assessed. Already, faculty positions were being filled by Japanese. The argument for economy was turned against opponents. Noting that one-third of the university budget was allocated to foreign staff, officials claimed that their replacement by Japanese not only would reduce national expenditures but also was essential for future independence.[78] They were echoing the opinions of yatoi such as François Verny, French director of the Yokosuka dockyards, who had written that rescinding the overseas student programme would save money in the short term but

cause great loss in future.[79] Retrenchment nevertheless impeded the programme.

However, in the critical years 1880–81, the Army budgeted 60,000 yen for
overseas students. Other ministries also supported programmes; records are
available for 1876–86 (See Table 7, pp. 153–54). Thus the financial problems
experienced by the Education and Public Works ministries do not reveal the
whole picture. In 1882, regulations for overseas students were revised thor-
oughly and a strict regimentation programme was instituted by the Education Ministry. Tanaka's arguments were heeded, and thereafter only the
better graduates of Japanese institutions were selected. According to Ishizuki
Minoru, throughout the 1870's students abroad were, by and large, at the
grammar school level; only a few actually entered college level programmes,
and only from the late 1870's did entering students complete a programme
for graduation. A clear distinction is noted from 1882, however, from which
time those selected were graduates of Japanese institutions: overseas students
became overseas scholars. This change was the result of the new government
policy, as government students became the mainstream of those sent overseas.
It does appear that those despatched in the late 1870's and early 1880's
returned with greater academic competence.[80]

Student numbers for the first and second decades are difficult to ascertain.
Ogata Hiroyasu has estimated that some 1,500 students went abroad from the
1860's through the 1890's. Watanabe Minoru, in a count based on Education
Ministry annual reports from 1875 to 1894, totals 623 students. He states
that an average of 34 students between 1894 and 1912 were despatched each
year. From 1880 to 1894 an average of 6 returned each year and from 1895
to 1912 about 27 returned each year.[81] These estimates suggest that maturation of the programme was not achieved until the third decade.

Most students trained abroad and graduates of government funded higher
institutions entered government offices and college and university faculties.
Some, especially many overseas students, later moved into private enterprise. Ishizuki points out that it was the government's intention that overseas
students be leadership models upon their return. Even into the third decade,
private students continued to go to various countries to study liberal arts.
But as the overseas student programme became monopolized by government,
(especially from 1884), government preference for German concepts and
technology became dominant. Returning students replaced yatoi, but their
talents were monopolized by government.[82]

As Meiji officials chose increasingly to channel energies into state-building, the borrowing process was narrowed. Because of the government's
increasing debts, insufficient capital, and its difficulties with monetary and
taxation reforms, bonds were forged between government and financial
families, thereby precluding separation of state and business interests in

banking, transportation, industry, and trade. Thus, social safeguards for ordinary citizens were compromised. The experiment, because of its élitest emphasis, posed obstacles to emerging social democracy and to the adoption of economic and political models such as Western-style capitalism and the the British parliamentary system.

It was, however, with the help of yatoi, students trained by yatoi, and students trained abroad that Tokyo University produced 12,235 graduates between 1876 and 1912, a formidable cadre of leadership models (in law, 4,151; letters, 1,545; medicine, 1,932; natural science, 674; engineering, 2,815 agriculture, 1,118).[83]

Intrinsic to the élitest nature of the Meiji experiment was the presence of plus-minus factors in every undertaking. The initiators were a socio-political élite. Despite the fact that many were proponents of ability as the sole criterion for selection of individuals for higher training, the majority of trainees were drawn from a social élite, though admittedly the social base was broadened in the course of the Meiji era. And leaders within this social élite did succeed in making educational ability the criterion for administrative office. Yet, until the middle of the Meiji period, radical change touched only a limited segment of the population. Thereafter, it slowly filtered to a wider circle, and from the second decade the shift from nation-building to state-building is perceptible, as new constraints were imposed by an emerging nationalist philosophy.

2

Yatoi under the New Management

In machine technology, nineteenth-century Japan was far behind advanced Western nations. Differences had not been so pronounced at the time of Japan's first meeting with European nations in the sixteenth century, but the intervening industrial revolution in the West had reversed the balance, at least vis-à-vis Britain, France, and the United States. However, in terms of its bureaucratic institutions and psychological finesse, Japan easily matched the West. Even before the imperial capital was moved from Kyoto, Meiji officials acted to assert their authority upon foreigners in Japan. They did this in the face of commitments made by the bakufu to Western powers and despite de facto (military) power held by foreigners.

THE NEW MANAGEMENT

The new Meiji leaders set in motion this grand experiment in foreign borrowing; their thinking was integral to the experiment. In the Japan of the 1860's civil war had ostensibly erupted from the debate waged over the unwanted presence of foreign powers and the treaties with those powers which the Tokugawa shogunal government had been forced to accept.[1] Emerging from the conflict as the new government, the anti-Tokugawa leaders were no more able to expel the foreigner and reject the treaties than the previous regime had been. Many views and shades of opinion were held by parties in the opposing camps during the civil war. But some bakufu adherents, for example, had defined expulsion of the alien barbarians (*jōi*) as co-operation with foreigners who came to Japan for friendly purposes and exclusion only of real enemies. They argued that expulsion should be applied strictly only to closed ports, that is, areas outside the open treaty ports.[2] It was this definition, a limited opening of the country, which new leaders propounded in the slogan "Revere the Emperor and Open the Country" (*sonnō-kaikoku*). Within the new leadership, some envisioned a central government gathering to itself talented candidates and transcending regional loyalties.[3] This concept of a New Japan initially created severe factionalism within the new government, caused it to forfeit han support, incurred the disaffection of a broad segment of the samurai class, and gave a new incentive to the need to succeed.[4]

A majority of the emerging élite rejected traditional concepts of status. This probably happened because some 70 per cent of the new leadership encountered Western learning directly through study at home or visits abroad.[5] Major leaders came from outer domains (*tozama*), but many of the professional bureaucrats staffing various government offices, some rising to key positions, were of pro-bakufu origins. Many had Western educational experience, and they held a variety of ideological viewpoints. Significantly, most of the core leadership had been active in pre-restoration reform politics in both bakufu and han. Some of those with bakufu backgrounds, were more favourable to intercourse with the West than han reformers.

An initial aim of the Meiji reformers was to implement national defence and economic development more effectively than their predecessors had done. While the core of the leadership argued for centralization in government, some put heaviest emphasis upon the need for economic and technological strength (*fukoku*) and others upon the need for a strong army (*kyōhei*). Accordingly, two major factions emerged in the early Meiji government. Sakata Yoshio has described one group as a "modern bureaucratic faction" (*kindai kanryō gun*). With Ōkuma Shigenobu at its centre, it included Itō Hirobumi, Inoue Kaoru, Godai Tomoatsu, Yoshida Kiyonari, and others.[6]

The other major grouping Sakata describes as "new knowledge military bureaucrats" (*shinchishiki gunji kanryō*) because they drew knowledge from Europe. Yamagata Aritomo was soon a central figure in this faction.[7] Kyōhei was the pivot of its thinking on all policy. This group initially opposed priority for any technological project or government reorganization which they felt did not directly assist the new military programme. A major instance was the railway project against which Kuroda Kiyotaka led vociferous opposition.[8]

In early Meiji this polarization created problems: Civil Affairs-Finance Ministry (Mimbu-Ōkurashō) adherents of fukoku (kyōhei) would pull government members in one direction and the Military Affairs-Justice Ministry (Hyōbu-Gyōseishō) proponents of kyōhei would tug them another. in With factionalism and friction rampant, five years were required to stabilize the civil reform policy and another five to assure the authority of the central government.

Nevertheless, despite superficial evidence to the contrary, gravitation of power to these two major groupings—the progressive modernizers and the conservative modernizers—enabled a cohesive official response to internal and external crises. Innocuous elements were eased aside and obstreperous elements eliminated. For the most part, compromise and decision by a kind of bureaucratic collegial consent were skilfully practised. With a few exceptions, a common front was erected against foreign pressures. To a degree, ambition was cloaked by self-effacement. The more conservative Council of State (Dajōkan), originally composed of many court nobles (*kuge*) and regional lords (*daimyō*), many of whom were still thinking in terms of an older political order of familiar political patterns such as a "council of lords," controlled the upper five levels of appointments. Progressives held lower positions, but important decision-making—in the early years of the Finance and Public Works ministries, for example—was often done in subordinate offices.[9]

As Sakata Yoshio has pointed out, the new progressives differed from any previous Japanese leaders in determination and character. They were to bring into existence the first modern bureaucracy. The group originally in the finance section was very important. Ōkuma Shigenobu, prior to 1868, unlike most other leaders, had no special history of political endeavour. He had studied with Guido F. Verbeck in the Nagasaki bakufu school, Seibikan. Verbeck had worked closely with him in the dispute with foreign representatives over the forced evacuation of Japanese Christians from the Nagasaki area. Ōkuma's argument was so successful that Parkes, the British minister to Japan, was moved to remark that he had never met such a logical Japanese before.[10] That not only began a friendship between Parkes and Ōkuma, but also gained the latter a reputation for diplomacy.

In late 1868, Ōkuma became a foreign affairs officer, and in the spring of 1869 he moved to the finance section. Diplomacy and finance were inseparably linked: the debased monetary system compounded problems with foreign traders. It was in the finance section that the progressive nucleus grew. Progressive modernizers espoused discarding old usages and instituting completely revised programmes. For the first time, a national consciousness supplanted regional consciousness; drawn into this group were others from the former bakufu and pro-bakufu han.

The slogan "Rich Country-Strong Army" (fukoku-kyōhei) had varied interpretations according to era and person, but progressive modernizers recognized that nations possessing both qualitative and quantitative superiority in arms also had advanced technology and wealth. And they understood that the former was dependent on the latter. The finance group thought positive economic activity was absolutely necessary. Economic, political, and social organization would have to be reformed, they thought, through foreign borrowing. It was on this point that finance bureaucrats departed from other officials.

These progressives—and their circle grew—collided continually with conservatives. The finance section was soon linked with the new organ for civil affairs, and the influence of the progressives was strong in the foreign affairs section. They squared off against officials in the military affairs, justice, and imperial household sections.

The progressives were strident exponents of abolition of the han and of the establishment of the new national prefecture system. Until this major reform was successfully carried through in the summer of 1871, such major leaders as Kido Takayoshi, Ōkubo Toshimichi, Sanjō Sanetomi, and Iwakura Tomomi tried to restrain the young progressives.

Sakata says that Council of State ministers Sanjō and Iwakura read each new proposal with wrinkled brows, fearful of the content. Ōkubo and Godai Tomoatsu often cautioned them against hasty progress and provocation of critics. But, young and active, they belittled those outside their clique. They worked hard and played hard, taking their work with them to teahouses, which simply caused more criticism. They felt that the conservatives in justice and the imperial household did little actual work. Thus, they provoked those officials by reducing their salaries. Serious confrontation also occurred over attempts to extend their authority over regional governors.[11]

In a sense, the 1870 revisions establishing the new Finance and Public Works ministries aimed to provide special areas for progressives in order to keep them from clashing with conservatives. When the prefectural system was established and advocates of unified government had weathered the crisis over Korea in 1873, Ōkubo Toshimichi as head of the new Home Ministry took a lead in his positive encouragement of industry. Previously he had been so dedicated to the goal of national unity that he had not actively supported progressive policies. Kido Takayoshi at times had had to defend the young progressives to Ōkubo. But Ōkubo's participation in the Iwakura Mission (1871 – 73; the largest official observation and study tour despatched to the United States and Europe), particularly his observations in England, transformed his thinking on the importance of a viable industrial base for economic and military growth. In setting forth his policy for encouragement of industry, he stressed that the time had come for practical works, that the time for arguments, speeches, temporary methods, threats, power, or tricks was past.[12]

The young progressives gradually advanced with Iwakura and Ōkubo to ranking ministerial posts. Iwakura, Ōkubo, Sanjō, and Kido had helped bridge the old and the new. However, frictions and conflicts between progressives and conservatives over economic development versus national defence continued throughout the experiment in foreign borrowing. Yet, both groups constituted the new managerial élite, both became new civil and military bureaucrats, both were modernizers, and both had to deal with reactionary elements within the government.

In order to build a modern nation, several ways of obtaining the new technology were available: the use of foreign experts and foreign capital, the importation and translation of foreign educational materials, the despatch of observation teams and Japanese students abroad, and participation in world commercial exhibitions and interchanges. In the bakumatsu era, the Japanese government tried all of these. But the two swiftest methods—employment of foreigners and importation of foreign capital—were the least desirable to Meiji leaders, who sought modern technology without further compromising sovereignty.

Perhaps the Iwakura Mission best illustrates the various predispositions of Meiji leaders. The following is a summary of an 1871 proposal. The new government recognized its responsibility to revise the unequal treaties signed by the defunct bakufu. But, to obtain equitable revision, native institutions and practices would have to comply with international law. In any case, this could not be accomplished rapidly, and there was great fear that if revision were forced on Japan, a further loss of national rights would result. Therefore, it was decided that before further foreign interference materialized, a plenipotentiary mission should be despatched to promote general good will and to convey to foreign powers Japan's intentions and desires regarding treaty revision. At the same time, observation was to be made of institutions and laws abroad, and methods for implementing them in Japan were to be explored.[13]

The new government from the outset posited limitations. National sovereignty was the yardstick (or more properly the *monosashi*) against which action and activity were to be measured. Many of the progressives—Ōkuma, Yoshida, Inoue Kaoru, Itō Hirobumi, and a number of others— remained open and flexible to foreign borrowing, but with time and experience, considerations of national sovereignty determined views. Even Ōkuma did not entirely escape this conditioning.

In 1868, when Japan was faced with strife in the countryside, particularly rebellion in the north, the government had to ensure that immediate concerns took precedence over long-term considerations. Japan's sovereignty was no longer intact, a fact that had to be dealt with. Foreign capital and foreign employees were already in Japan, and international treaties, foreign employee contracts, and a complement of foreign troops argued that the foreign vanguard would remain. Anti-foreignism, financial concern, and the delineation of a restricted kaikoku (open country) policy were issues which led Meiji leaders to remove foreigners from the interior, tentatively dismiss foreign employees, and prohibit the private employment of foreigners. In 1868 bakufu and han foreign employees were placed under the administration of the local government of the open port area in which they worked, and initially the central government declined responsibility for their support.[14] The central government first focussed its attention on the three official missions of bakufu foreign employees.

THE FIRST DECADE: MANAGERIAL CONTROL

In the spring of 1868, the French were advised to withdraw from Yokosuka to the open port of Yokohama. Director François Verny (1865 – 76) refused and added that a French warship in Yokosuka provided protection for French employees.[15] The French minister to Japan, Léon Roches, took the same strong stand on the legal aspect of the bakufu debt. Either the $500,000 owing was to be paid within seven months or the French right to sell the Yokosuka complex would be exercised.[16] Shortly after, Meiji officials acquiesced to these arrangements by bakufu bureaucrats when Roches was informed by them that the financial distress of the new government rendered economy mandatory and that Director Verny must be made to understand this. Administratively, the plants were placed under the Kanagawa court (*saibansho*) and remained closed until Kyoto appointed new officials.[17]

At the same time, other officials protested the illegality of French residence in Yokosuka outside the open port area. Kanagawa court officials took the matter to Iwakura Tomomi, who referred it to the Yokohama court.[18] There the matter rested. The new government was unable to dislodge the French from Yokosuka because their refusal to leave was backed by force.

Parkes, Great Britain's minister to Japan, was agitated by rumours that the French would take over directly, and French personnel were worried about a possible British conspiracy against them. In April 1868 a Yokosuka employee, Dr. P. A. L. Savatier, wrote: "We are now in the midst of revolution in Japan . . . but do not know how the revolution will turn out."[19] Later he wrote:

We have exchanged our badges, and the new government officials have replaced bakufu officials. England plotted to take the place of France . . . England's attitude is bad . . . . Things have settled down now but the new government is the puppet of England . . . . The position of the new French Minister is difficult.[20]

Although Roches was replaced by Maxim Outrey in May 1868, Verny remained as director. Economy was the keynote, and the first confrontation occurred over the government's desire to reduce the number of French employees.[21] Verny held his ground. It was not until the following year that relations entered an amicable phase, when Terajima Munenori assumed responsibility for the Yokosuka-Yokohama projects. Owing to Terajima's intelligence, tact, and his efforts to acquaint himself with the operation, personnel relations proceeded more smoothly.[22] There was some minor friction, but Verny's competence and sense of duty were recognized.[23]

The importance of the Yokosuka plant was fully appreciated by the new management, and in 1870 it was removed from local jurisdiction and placed under the new Finance Ministry. Verny was given a six-month leave, during which he was on half salary while recruiting new employees. On his return, new regulations were drafted with Japanese officials. These were designed to bring the Yokosuka-Yokohama compound under the recently established Public Works Ministry.[24] The revised regulations specified that all work which could be performed by Japanese was to be turned over to them and that the director, subject to the approval of Japanese officials, might extend French employee contracts another year.[25] The administration of the Yokosuka plant (*seitetsujo*), renamed the Yokosuka dockyards (*zōsenjo*) in 1871, was transferred in late 1872 to the newly established Navy Ministry. The importance of this shipbuilding and repair enterprise as well as the growing organization of government may be traced in these administrative moves.

In Verny's last report before he and the dockyards passed under Navy administration, he offered some pointed and thoughtful cirticism. The exasperated manner of his correspondence with the bakufu was replaced by a reserved and quiet tone, and the same restraint permeates private correspondence of Yokosuka employees in this period as well. Verny requested that three points be considered by Japanese officials in full authority: that Japanese be sent abroad for study, that four replacements be found for retiring French employees, and that the matter of timber cutting for Navy warships be reviewed.

Verny was still blunt. He pointed out that since the answers he received varied with each person—Sano, Hiraoka, Nakajima, and Akamatsu—replies from officials in full authority were essential. He wrote that although the work was successful (sixty-two ships, including eight foreign ships, had been repaired in the preceding eighteen months), the government was making changes according to the moment's convenience. He complained of the closing of the factory school and of the revoking of the decision to send students abroad.[26] He asked how the government intended to train engineers and accountants if the overseas student programme were halted. From 1868, he pointed out, section foremen had been training growing numbers of young Japanese workers (450 in 1868 and 1,250 in 1872, and 1,500 if those at Yokohama were included). A new French head was needed to continue this work, and a French engineer was needed to instruct Japanese in better timber cutting methods. Verny closed with the remark that if these suggestions were not adopted as policy, the Japanese would save a little money now but would experience great loss in future.[27]

After the dockyards went under Navy jurisdiction, Verny's recommendations were implemented. The Navy school (*Kaigun heigakkō*) and the Yokohama manual training school utilized foreign employees, for the most part English in the former and French in the latter. By 1872, the transition of the dockyards into a Japanese establishment was well underway. By 1877, the year after Verny's retirement, it was complete.[28] In this last year, Verny had become adviser (*komon*). Jules Thibaudier, his assistant, continued to be employed, but his position was as head of the French workers. Verny's enviable powers in the original agreement (only the director was to deal with management) passed into the hands of the Meiji employers.

Although the Meiji government had been unable in 1868 to sever French relations with Yokosuka, it was successful in cancelling the military and naval missions. Contracts were scheduled to run to 1872, but British minister Parkes did not protest.[29] His overriding interest was British commerce, and he was eager for rapport with Meiji officials. Nor was he unhappy to see the French ousted. However, the new French representative to Japan, Maxim Outrey, protested vociferously and demanded that twelve or thirteen months salary be paid in accordance with Article 5 of the agreement because dismissal was at Japanese convenience. Japanese officials made a serious case against the French because of French assistance to the rebels in the north. Outrey soon regretted his outburst, but he insisted on salary payment for the mission through July and half pay during the return trip. To maintain French interests, he attached the chief of the mission, Captain Jules Chanoine, and Lt. Albert Charles Du Bousquet to the French legation in Tokyo.[30]

Cancellation of the training missions was a minor victory for the new government. It illustrates its intention to act independently when conditions permitted. This is no less true because the decision against using foreign instructors was later reversed. In 1870, the Japanese selected the British model for a new navy and the French model for a new army.[31] The selection of models implied neither the need for official missions nor for the employment of individual foreigners. The programme to employ foreign instructors evolved gradually between 1871 and 1873. In the Army, employment of foreigners was kept to a minimum, but in the Navy the large-scale employment policy advocated by progressive Navy officials met constant opposition.[32]

Initially, the military school bureau (*heigakuryō*) operated under Dutch regulations, but when Japanese students returned from Holland they rejected the Dutch pattern and chose the British model because it was superior.[33] Before the Navy Ministry was established in 1872, instructors were of Dutch, English, and American origins. It was not until 1873 that the British representative in Japan showed positive inclination to assist the Japanese government, and this occurred because Japan finally agreed to invite a "mission navale."

Commander Archibald L. Douglas (1873 – 75) arrived in 1873 to act as head of the British Naval Mission, but, withdrawing early from his contract, he returned to England in July 1875. Navy officials Nakamuta Kuranosuke and Kawamura Sumiyoshi thought that Douglas's involvement should be restricted to revision of regulations and to teaching and so rejected his direction.[34] In 1876, when the first three-year contracts expired, the services of fifty-two employees were terminated in November and their work licences were returned to the Foreign Ministry. Most were rehired under new, individual three-year contracts that had Parkes's approval. These contracts included a stipulation that Japanese officials could punish those guilty of contract infringements.[35] The mission as such dissolved, but British instructors continued to be employed on a large scale through 1878 – 79.

The French model was selected for the Japanese army because an important segment of government opinion actively favoured it. However, the young, eclectic Itō Hirobumi did not. He argued that soldiers in northern han should be incorporated into the imperial guard and be given suitable positions, and then that the good points of all European systems should be utilized to produce an army under direct imperial control which could maintain order within Japan and defend the country against foreign powers.[36]

The military affairs office which was opened in 1868 was reorganized as a Military Affairs Ministry in 1869 and handled both army and navy matters. Ōmura Masujirō became first assistant. He had studied medicine with Dr. Philipp von Siebold in Kyushu and had been encouraged by the latter to concentrate on military studies.[37] It was Ōmura's proposal for national defence which was accepted. He thought that commoners should be conscripted and given Western training and received permission to establish a barracks and a training school in Osaka and a gunpowder factory in Uji.[38] He planned for the military to take over the Yokohama French-language school the bakufu had set up in 1865.[39]

The merger took place before an official decision to use the French model was made. Ōmura's assassination in 1869 by those disgruntled over the inclusion of commoners in the military was incentive enough for his friends to see the plans through.[40] Other Japanese officials, thinking in terms of the British and French models, favoured sending students abroad rather than using foreign instructors. Kuroda Kiyotaka, for example, recommended that Japanese cadets be enrolled in naval and military academies in England and France.[41]

Also prior to an official decision on selection of models, Yamagata Aritomo and the younger Saigō (Tsugumichi) in 1869 went abroad to observe military systems. English, French, and Dutch systems were used in various han, and Yamagata, then third official in military affairs, wanted to organize a uniform training system for han armies. Despite the appeal of the German conscript system, he recognized that there was no foundation yet for German military training in Japan.[42] And, although the Prussian representative in Japan, Maxim von Brandt, favoured close co-operation, the Prussian government, in the throes of unification at home and quarrelling with France abroad, asked that immediate assistance for Japan be postponed.[43] It was at this juncture that Du Bousquet, who as legation interpreter and translator had earned the respect of army officials, provided information on adaptation of the French and other systems.[44] In 1870, although he was still with the French legation, he became an adviser in the Military Affairs Ministry.[45]

Arrangements for French instructors languished from 1870 through 1871. Prussia objected to Japan's hiring French instructors while the Franco-Prussian War was in progress. The Japanese also moved slowly because of French minister Outrey's attempts to use discussions to ease restrictions on Christianity and because they rejected the idea of an official mission with the restraints it implied.[46] In the arrangements finally agreed upon, the mission concept was a mere formality. The first employees, Lieutenant-Colonel Charles Marquerie (1872–75) and Lieutenant-Colonel Munier (1874–80), established immediate rapport with Japanese officials, but senior officers' duties were limited to teaching specific subjects. Later, German instructors and advisers were treated with the same circumspection and professional aloofness.[47]

Although unable to set aside the notion of official missions immediately, the new government brought the activities of these foreign employees within manageable limits. At the same time, Japanese officials rejected bakufu permissiveness towards foreign investment. When one considers the grave monetary crisis of the new government and the suits brought against it, this decisive stance appears the more remarkable. By the end of 1868, paper notes were circulating at a rate between 55 and 60 per cent below their nominal value.[48] In the spring of 1869, Ōkuma Shigenobu brought various problems regarding foreign intercourse to the attention of other officials. He enumerated the debts, indemnities, and loans inherited from the bakufu and han, pointed out the heavy current expenses involving foreign employees in the Nagasaki and Yokosuka foundries, lighthouse construction, mint construction, mine development, and other industries; and pointed out the need to redeem some 30 million ryō (1 ryō = $1.25) of bad money (*akuka*) which was held by foreigners and for which traders were suing through their legations. Accusations of coin debasing and counterfeit operations abounded.[49]

Foreign debts totalled close to 3 million yen. Although at the time of the civil war only one national loan was outstanding (Yokosuka), some thirty-seven regional governments had contracted formal loans totalling 111 cases and involving fifty-seven foreigners.[50] The majority of the latter were private loans, but because they were taken out in the name of han, it was necessary for the Meiji government, if it were to succeed as the responsible centralized authority, to honour these obligations.

In 1869, the government paid the debt incurred with British merchant Thomas B. Glover for the Nagasaki docks. Steps were soon taken to nationalize the mines, despite opposition from regional mine owners and foreign powers.[51] The major suit over the Takashima mine is the outstanding example of this difficult task, involving as it did nepotic ties of foreign government representatives and foreign businessmen. The Dutch firm of Bauduin helped to extricate the Meiji government from its financial difficulties.[52] Government and private mining activities were soon placed under the supervision of the new Public Works Ministry.[53]

Meiji leaders placed heavy emphasis on internal reorganization as a prerequisite to treaty revision. Despite their fear of contracting new debts, the government often found it unavoidable to do so. To repay France and prevent foreclosure of the Yokosuka works, the government borrowed from the British Oriental Bank Corporation (Tōyō ginkō) in Yokohama. To finance the mint construction, in a massive rehaul of the monetary system in an effort to restore fiscal confidence, the government was obliged to borrow from the British firm of Alt and then obliged to borrow from the Dutch firm of Bauduin to repay Alt. The Japanese literally were able to keep afloat by a long series of short-term private loans.[54] They understood that in order to control foreigners they had to control the projects foreigners worked upon. The railway project provides an excellent example of this understanding.

The Meiji government rejected the bakufu arrangement with American engineers largely because by that arrangement the railway system would be collateral. Parkes negotiated a new proposal utilizing British engineers and granting financial assistance which he assured would be on a private basis only. He recommended the agency of his old China crony, Horatio Nelson Lay. Lay, however, floated a public bond issue in England, the outcome of which had serious ramifications within the Japanese government. The astounded Parkes then tried to extricate the Japanese government from its financial problems through the Oriental Bank. In the resulting contract with that bank, the Japanese sustained heavy losses in redeeming the bond issue and in buying up some foreign employee contracts. In the new arrangement there was no question of the railways serving as security or of foreign assistance being prolonged.[55] The Japanese commissioner, Inoue Masaru, rapidly assumed a practical managerial position, supervising construction and the employment of foreign employees.[56]

The project for the imperial Mint also had a stormy beginning. Obviously, British patronage was considered because the British were dominant in the economic scene in Japan. From the outset, the Japanese position was challenged because of ambiguities in the Oriental Bank contract. The rights and privileges of the bank, the rigid control of bullion movement, the engagement of foreign employees, and foreign direction of the Mint were juxtaposed with the financial responsibilities of the Japanese. Japanese officials, however, conceived a certain bifurcation: the foreign director was to have a foreign sphere of interest and the Japanese a Japanese sphere, the Japanese official being in charge of the Mint as co-ordinator. But the bank agreement itself and the independent nature of the contract of the foreign director, Major Thomas W. Kinder, placed the bank and Kinder in a position of authority which conflicted with Japanese intentions.[57] Japanese officials apparently did not understand the contract arrangements.

In the serious contest for managerial power which followed Kinder's arrival from Britain, Japanese officials took decisive action. Inoue Kaoru did not participate in the original agreement, but he did serve in 1869 as chief of the Mint Bureau. A very direct, forthright person, Inoue was dubbed *kaminari-san* ("Mr. Lightning") by his colleagues. During his tenure, the situation was under control. However, his replacement found it difficult to cope with the foreign director. In 1871 Inoue stepped in, disciplined Kinder (who had also earned the name *kaminari-san*—"Mr. Thunder") for irregularities and high-handedness, and revised administrative regulations.[58]

Shortly, however, relations between Kinder and a succession of Japanese officials in the Mint deteriorated further. The official designated to review the situation, Yoshida Kiyonari, initially hoped for an amicable settlement, but he changed his point of view after investigating the problems in the Mint. Where Inoue Kaoru had felt that because of the bank agreement a cooperative policy was necessary, Yoshida offered a strong argument for the mass cancellation of foreign employees' contracts and for the dissolution of the Oriental Bank agreement, "to make the Mint the Japanese government's in name and fact." Council of State officials concurred, and late in 1874 the decision was carried out, despite the financial loss it entailed.[59]

There had been no question among the Japanese that ultimate managerial control would be theirs.

Lighthouse construction and harbour and coastal safety measures posed similar problems. Some problems were residual; the government had obligations under Article 10 of the British treaty. Parkes had initiated an arrangement with the bakufu to employ Chief Engineer Richard Henry Brunton (1868 – 76) and other British technicians. Meiji officials were unable to alter the contract arrangement made by the British secretary of the Board of Trade acting on behalf of the Japanese government.[60] It was left to Sano Tsunetami to assert Japanese control by indirection.

These early struggles for control of foreigners were aided by bureaucratic reorganization. Among the modern ministries giving direction to domestic enterprises was the Public Works Ministry, established in 1870. The policies and activities of this ministry illustrate forcibly the aims in Meiji nation-building of self-direction, managerial control, the temporary use of foreign assistants, and the training of Japanese to replace them. These aims are clear in the 1870 draft proposal prepared by Itō Hirobumi, Yamao Yōzō, and engineer Edmund Morrell, the first Meiji government employee for railway construction. Itō probably submitted the report to the Council of State almost as Morell gave it to him.[61]

In the proposal, it was noted that with the exception of England all governments had a Civil Engineering Bureau under their direction. The work of such a bureau included road construction and the supervision of harbours, coasts, lighthouses, and mines. The establishment of a main office and three sections was proposed—one section for actual work, one for education, and one for accounting. The activities of each section were outlined. All three would employ foreigners.

This proposal provided the first formal statement of the rationale and purpose in hiring foreigners. The proposed ministry was to foster and control industries to advance the state and to lay the foundation for the economic strength needed to compete with foreign countries. Because Japan did not excel in any field of technology, the use of foreign instructors could not be avoided. But borrowing the strength of foreign assistants was a temporary means of competing. The education of talented Japanese was indispensable so that the use of foreign employees and the nuisance which attended their employment could be dispensed with and a lasting foundation for technology laid.[62]

The Yokosuka complex begun by French employees, the Nagasaki area dockyards and factories begun by Dutch employees, the Kagoshima dockyards, and various gold, silver, coal, and other mines (including the Sado, Ikuno, and Miike mines) formed the initial project base for the new government. In 1870 and 1871 regional factories were taken over, as were the spinning mills in Kagoshima, Hiroshima, Sakai, Tomioka, and other places, and a whole series of other projects initiated.[63] The Public Works Ministry became co-ordinator of many of these enterprises. And in 1873, three years after establishment of the ministry, the Engineering School was opened. The first group of instructors were able young men in their twenties, students of M. Rankin of Glasgow University, which was then developing a centre of applied sciences. The principal, Henry Dyer, acting on Itō's eclectic suggestions, selected the best points of Dutch, German, and British systems and used the Zurich Institute as a model. In drafting, design, and fine arts generally, Italian employees were preferred. And Itō specified that he wanted competent instructors in the basics, not specialists.[64]

In education, Meiji officials directed their attention first to standards. This, even more than financial difficulties, may account for the continual opening and closing of schools which marked the early years. With the restoration, foreign instructors were sought by schools throughout Japan. In the first two years the majority of instructors were unqualified and many were opportunistic. As plans were made for reorganization of the liberal arts school (Nankō) and the establishment of the medical school (Tōkō)—both were predecessors of Tokyo University—the best instructors were sought. The Dutch-American missionary Guido F. Verbeck, a friend of Iwakura, Ōkuma, and others, was brought from Nagasaki as head teacher of Nankō. He undertook a general housecleaning, removing at a sweep the butchers, sailors (drunk and sober), the braumeisters, and other frauds from the open ports who had been attracted by the salaries offered.[65] With the help of foreign employees, Japanese officials made concerted efforts to determine standards for selection, employment conditions, and general regulations governing foreign instructors in schools throughout Japan. The nationwide implementation of these regulations in 1873, which was part of the groundwork for thorough revision of the Japanese educational system, made short shrift of incompetents.

By 1878 the Japanese had won the struggle for managerial control of their nation-building. All yatoi were firmly under Japanese administration and Japanese officials administered all projects. Thus, by the end of the first decade of the Meiji period, even titular foreign directorships were abolished. The concept of official groups or teams disintegrated with the alteration of employment contracts between 1875 and 1877—for the French at Yokosuka, for Army and Navy instructors, for Mint employees under the Finance Ministry, and for employees in all the bureaus of the Public Works Ministry. Major contracts such as those for Douglas (Navy) and Kinder (Mint) ended in 1875, for Verny (Navy) and Brunton (Lighthouses) in 1876, and for W. W. Cargill (1872–77), Director of Railways, in 1877.

By 1874, significant change was seen with respect to yatoi in technology.

The Lighthouse Bureau, for example, had largely dispensed with foreign engineers. The Workshop Bureau, which conducted several model factories (ironworks in Yokohama, Nagasaki, and Hyogo, and cement, glass, and other shops especially in the Tokyo area), retained only four engineers and the Communications Bureau only five. These were engineers, not technicians. The largest number of engineers was found in the Railways and Mines Bureaus, but by 1874 the only professionals remaining in the Engineering School were the principal, Henry Dyer, and the electrical engineer, William Ayrton. Thus, by 1874, even though 1874 and 1875 were peak years in the employment of yatoi, there was already a reduction in the number of higher-ranking technologists as Japanese assumed a greater role. The Engineering School became a college in 1877 and later merged with Tokyo Imperial University.

With the end of Cargill's contract (the contract for railway construction was the largest single project), a major reduction in foreign employees occurred in 1877 – 78. Both the peak in yatoi employment in 1874 – 75 and the first pronounced slump in 1877 – 78 were tied closely to the technological projects of the Public Works Ministry and the activities of the Navy, a major employer of yatoi. Although the Public Works Ministry survived until 1885, the phase-out in the use of foreign assistants dates from 1877, years before the financial retrenchment of the early 1880's. Government emphasis on the use of foreign technologists lasted only a decade. A transition of emphasis to institutional building was already underway. Administrative reorganization and the introduction of modern book-keeping, banking, and auditing methods were among early efforts in institutional remodelling.

In the first decade, the majority of yatoi were basic instructors, and in the Public Works Ministry, three-quarters of the employees were literally yatoi (menials or labourers). About a quarter were skilled workers, but 50 per cent were semi-skilled and unskilled labourers. However, in the first decade of the Meiji period most of the yatoi with professional expertise were general experts and were expected to apply themselves as generalists in many areas often outside their training. Towards the end of the decade a change was perceptible.

A vital innovation of the first decade was the employment of foreign lawyers. The Japanese knew that they had to learn to cope with the legalistic character of the Western mentality. They had been forced to become familiar with unpleasant aspects of Western legal processes but were ignorant of the principles upon which they were predicated. Certain general advisers (*komon*), such as Verbeck and Du Bousquet, were also used for the purpose of unravelling Western legal complexities, as may be seen by numerous extant views (*ikensho*) solicited from them and by the books they selected for translation. It may well be that through the use of general advisers, Meiji officials came to the conclusion they required a lawyer, or even a corps of lawyers.

In 1871, J. R. Davidson (1871 – 77), a British subject, was named legal adviser to the main office of the Public Works Ministry (with a salary of $1,000 a month) to safeguard Japanese government rights in technological projects. He was also sent abroad to review the mixed court system in Egypt. The American, Erastus Peshine Smith (1871 – 76), was the first adviser on international law to be employed with the Foreign Ministry for the study of treaty revision (at $10,000 a year). In 1872 British legation legal consultant John F. Lowder (1872 – 88) was employed by the Finance Ministry for land, income, and business tax reform (at $500 a month). Georges Bousquet (1872 – 76), who became the first law instructor employed by the Justice Ministry, had a salary of $500 a month. Also in the first decade the famous Emile Gustave Boissonade de Fontarabie (1873 – 95), vice-rector of the University of Paris, was appointed to act as adviser to each central administrative office and to undertake revision of civil and penal codes. Attached to the Justice Ministry, he received monthly $1,200 in gold and additional stipends for services to the Privy Council and Cabinet. With Boissonade's engagement, institutional change was inaugurated.

Also in the early 1870's, Jouslain, a former Saigon court prosecutor, served as court legal counsellor with the Justice Ministry. And, indicative of future law study diversification, Yale University law professor Henry Taylor Terry (1876 – 1912), an Education Ministry employee, became lecturer in English and American law. He served the institution through its various transitions from the Kaisei school to Tokyo Imperial University (with his initial monthly salary of $320 rising to $500).

Meiji officials made use of general advisers and early legal specialists to initiate study of Western legal practices, to safeguard the Japanese position in the face of foreign economic and diplomatic pressure, and to clarify the legal position of foreign employees themselves. Early contests between Japanese bureaucrats and foreign employees for spheres of authority subsided, and individual employment contract suits in the early years declined. Whereas until 1874 all consular decisions involving foreign employees went against the Japanese government, by the end of the decade Japanese mastery of Western legal techniques reversed the trend.

THE SECOND AND THIRD DECADES: SPECIALIZATION

The Meiji government, entering its second decade, was in serious financial straits. From the outset, officials had overextended resources. In the early 1880's, the massive scale and rapid tempo of activities necessitated a long overdue stringent retrenchment policy. The economy was on the verge of bankruptcy, expenses for yatoi being singled out as a major cause. Innate distaste for foreign tutelage was apparent in the emotional nature of the criticism arising as a result of the heavy expenses. In 1881, Iwakura Tomomi reported that yatoi salaries were a million yen and that each ministry was to terminate their services and pay them off in paper money if termination were impossible.[66] But in 1882 he acknowledged that some foreign employees' salaries had to be paid in coin, even though that greatly reduced national assets.[67]

As the Council of State called for a reduction of foreign employees, each office in requesting budget allowances gave assurance of thrift in cutting back the numbers of foreign employees, but attempts to freeze new engagements were not successful. In 1881, the Home Ministry proposed that foreign employees throughout the government come solely under their employing ministry's jurisdiction.[68] This made it possible for the Home Ministry and others to manipulate funds within each ministry to retain and engage needed yatoi. Even as economy was demonstrated by sizeable cuts in the total number of foreign personnel, this proposal allowed government offices to employ foreign specialists at higher salaries. Throughout 1885, the Council of State continued to exhort offices to be economical and not take on new engagements, but in fact the mid-1880's saw a spate of new engagements, especially of government advisers.[69]

By the second decade, government needs were different. The Army Ministry consistently preferred to send Japanese officers abroad rather than to hire foreigners. By the 1880's it was interested only in hiring advisers for general staff reorganization and for specialized fortification and weaponry techniques and production. The Navy, which had made wide use of yatoi, no longer required instructors in basic skills other than language. And language instructors were screened carefully both for character and ability. Advisers in the specialized areas of ship design and new weaponry techniques account for most of the yatoi employed during the second decade.

By 1874, the Home Ministry was engaged in several major projects utilizing considerable numbers of yatoi: public sanitation, postal revision, weather observation, and construction. For example, from the Osaka chemical laboratory and school (Seimikyoku), which employed Dutch and German scientists, the Home Ministry established the Tokyo and Yokohama, and, later, other municipal health offices. Health problems relating to prostitutes had already been tackled by the Home Ministry's predecessor, Civil Affairs, in conjunction with local government using foreign medical missionaries as paid employees. From these beginnings great strides were made in all areas of public health, water purification, and so on. The Home Ministry also hired engineers, mostly Dutch, to carry out regional projects for waterworks, irrigation, harbour dredging, and the like. Some of these were not only engineering marvels of the day but for many years to come. Some, carefully maintained by local inhabitants, still function today.

From 1880, the Home Ministry began to absorb some of the activities of the Public Works Ministry, slated for abolition in 1885. Separate funds were obtained for the encouragement of enterprises and were largely used for foreign assistants. In 1885 the new Construction Bureau absorbed engineers and technicians from Public Works, and while the railways were placed under Cabinet supervision for four years, the Home Ministry administered them and the foreign engineers from 1890 to 1892. By 1886 all yatoi were professionals: architects, hydraulic engineers, postal and police advisers, and legal advisers for local government reorganization.

By 1886 the Finance Ministry needed few yatoi: two remained in the Mint, one in the Printing Bureau, and one legal adviser in the Tax Office.

In education as well, the trend towards specialization is evident. Part of this trend was indicated in the government's revamping and monopoly of the overseas student programme from the early 1880's. Tokyo University, established in 1877 on a merger of the Kaisei arts school and medical school, was enlarged in 1886 by the addition of the Engineering College from Public Works, the Komaba Agricultural School, and institutions from other ministries. Although Japanese students did not return from abroad in significant numbers until the third decade, institutional growth within Japan was rapid. Students of yatoi trained others, and yatoi in the schools were steadily replaced by Japanese. Yatoi association with Tokyo Imperial University remained strong in the second and third decades. From the second decade, however, there were fewer foreigners in total but more Germans among them, and these foreigners were expected to have established academic reputations *before* coming to Japan. Technologists retained from the 1880's were specialists, and from 1886 many were transferred to the university.

Selectivity, which was in evidence earlier but was not consistently pursued, became more uniform in the second decade. By then, government hiring was limited to specific individuals for specific posts and duties. Foreign Ministry records from 1880 show hundreds of rejections of applications by private foreign persons and distinguished foreign intermediaries.[70] As a sign of bureaucratic maturation within Japanese officialdom, institutional engineering was coached by more than a score of foreign legal specialists replacing the general advisers and miscellaneous informants of the early years. Meiji officials themselves entered an age of specialization. In the transition to the Cabinet era, men of broad learning gave way to professional specialists. As Japanese students who were taught in the first decade completed training, generalists were displaced by the Japanese professional bureaucrats and foreign legal advisers (*komon*) of the second decade.

The prime area of specialization in the second decade was law. A few lawyers had been hired in the first decade, but from 1877 – 78 a corps of foreign legal specialists were employed in the Foreign Ministry, the Justice Ministry, the Cabinet, and the university law school. Contracts show that many were attached to a specific Japanese official. Some combined lecturing with legal work. Some were shared by more than one ministry. But all trained Japanese in the course of their service. Without exception, each was competent, and some were of considerable stature. The Japanese paid well for their services.

Americans were dominant in international law and in teaching theory. Eli Sheppard (1877 – 79) had replaced E. Peshine Smith (1871 – 76) in the Foreign Ministry. In international law, especially that pertaining to the equalization of treaties and the concept of national sovereignty, Japanese policy evolved with the assiduous labour of former United States consular officer, Henry Willard Dension. Legal knowledge for developing Japanese interests in Asia was provided by Durham H. Stevens, who received a monthly salary of $450. His assassination by a Korean dissident was tied to the Korean question. On the law faculty of Tokyo Imperial University, Charles Bigelow Storrs (1886 – 88; paid $370 a month) taught English legal theory, and the distinguished Henry Taylor Terry continued to lecture in English and American law.

The British served in legal finance and other areas as well. J. R. Davidson in the Public Works Ministry was followed by Robert J. Beadon (1877 – 87), legal adviser to the Public Works, Finance, and Home ministries concurrently, each of which paid a third of his services (total: $1,000 a month). In 1881, he became full-time counsel for the Foreign Ministry, receiving in advance each July 1 a retaining fee of $12,950. The architect of tax reform, John F. Lowder, continued in the Finance Ministry Tax Office, and from 1884 to 1888 his services were also shared by the Justice Ministry, which supplied $300 of his $500 monthly stipend. Another member of the British legation was also hired—a crown advocate for the British Embassy, William Montague Hammett Kirkwood (1885 – 1901, with a monthly stipend of $500). Kirkwood's contributions included helping the Justice Ministry with draft negotiations (especially regarding northern boundaries); he drew up a new system of imperial court precedence and rendered into English drafts of laws prepared by German specialists. Prime Minister Itō Hirobumi had assigned to himself Francis Piggott, as special adviser on constitutional law, who was given a monthly salary of $600.

The French pioneered law instruction in Japan. After Georges Bousquet, Boissonade urged continuance of law programmes. Georges Appert (1879 – 89) joined the Tokyo law school faculty and simultaneously acted as legal adviser to the Justice Ministry, with a monthly salary of $300 from the Education Ministry and $200 from Justice. The distinguished Boissonade (1873 – 95) continued revision of legal codes and encouraged the French school of law among Japanese bureaucrats. Auguste Revilliod, a French jurist (1889 – 92), and Michel Revon (1893 – 99), from the University of Geneva, were attached to the Justice Minister personally. Revilliod (at $400 a month) and Revon (at $500 a month) were under special Education Ministry contracts and lectured in their legal specialities at Tokyo Imperial University. An Italian, Alessandro Paternostro (1889 – 93), was also employed by the Justice Ministry for legal research (at $1,000 a month).

Various foreign nationals assisted in the plans of Meiji leaders to establish institutional machinery, peerage, a refurbished Imperial Household Ministry, and an updated cabinet system—the background organs for a new constitution With the inauguration of a Western-style Cabinet system in December 1885, constitutional research proceeded in earnest and varied nationals were involved. But, clearly, German legal specialists worked at the core of this institutional revision.

Initially engaged for commercial law and treaty revision in the Foreign Ministry, Hermann Roesler (1878 – 93) was moved to the new Cabinet as legal and economic adviser to all central offices in order to work closely on constitutional drafts. Hermann Techow (1883 – 91) and Karl Rudolph (1884 – 86), both state councillors in Germany, were legal advisers to the Council of State and the Cabinet (each at $600 a month), and Techow continued as adviser to the Cabinet when it replaced the Council of State. Otto Rudorff (1884 – 87), a magistrate in Prussian lower courts, initially taught Roman and public law in the Tokyo law school, but he was transferred to the Justice Ministry to draft a new courts system. In his last year he also worked for the Foreign Ministry (monthly salary: 1884 – 85 from the Education Ministry $450; 1885 – 87 from the Justice Ministry $550; and in 1886 – 87, from the Foreign Ministry, an additional $200).

Directly assisting the Home Minister in the revision of local government organs was Albert Mosse (1886 – 90), state magistrate in Germany and a Cabinet employee (at $600 a month). In the transition to constitutional government, Heinrich Mosthaf (1891 – 94, at $700 a month), counsellor to the home ministry in Germany, joined other German legal specialists as Cabinet advisers. Among the most distinguished of German specialists was Ludwig S. Loenholm (1890 – 1911), a privy councillor in Germany. Loenholm shared with French specialists Revilliod and Revon the distinction of being attached to the Justice Minister personally and of having a special contract with the Education Ministry for teaching at Tokyo Imperial University.

The variety in specialities of these advisers reflects Japanese syncretism. Ōyama Azusa suggests that Japanese distrust of foreigners dictated the multinational selection. But the different national origins and schools of legal thought were not simply window dressing, although the varied representation undoubtedly enhanced an illusion of a broader institutional selection than occurred. The long service of the French school suggests that dominance of German theory in constitutional preparation did not of itself imply dominance of German theory with regard to legal codes. Even though later revision was assisted by German legalists, the revision of that major French contribution before the codes were ever implemented was part of a conservative reaction to Western theory per se. Law specialists aver that strong French and some English influence is apparent in the New Civil Code (which is the revision of Boissonade's work) and in the Justice Ministry itself; the university law school, while retaining heavy French influence, was also open to considerable English and American influences, as was the Foreign Ministry.

Thus, the diversity of research not only better equipped Meiji officials to pursue different approaches in legal theory but also provided the precedent for diversity in the study of law at a university level. Perhaps most significant of all is the fact that foreign legal experts trained Japanese civil servants throughout their service. Whatever questions may be raised in discussing in-depth selection, the breadth of Japanese selection is a fact. The interests of the core of Meiji modernizers were eclectic. In pursuit of the modern, they grasped that the first essential was security within the world power structure. In their use of foreign assistants they had this goal in mind from the beginning. The importance of the accepted trappings of modernity did not escape them. With high-priced, high-quality foreign legal assistance, the Japanese directed the updating of their institutions. Foreign lawyers helped the Japanese to come of legal age at home and in the world.

By the late 1880's, the Japanese world view had already altered. The fear of inundation by Western culture increased concern for preservation of the Japanese identity and renewed interest in the study of indigenous accomplishments. It also strengthened determination to control foreign advisers. Many yatoi, in fact, spoke and wrote with a sense of trepidation that the Japanese compulsion for modernity would negate and eventually cause them to lose much of their distinct cultural heritage. Also, a growing sense of national consciousness was nurtured not only by the tangible successes of the first twenty years, but also by the realization that everything Western was not superior or even valuable per se. In a quasi-assimilative process, chaff and grain were sifted, thanks in large part to the breadth of selection in the borrowing process. These reactions touched the whole of the bureaucracy and the intelligentsia in and out of government. The Japanese world view was expanding, and the Japanese were demanding equality as well as security in the international community.

The major irritant of treaty revision failure remained. From their foreign legal advisers in the 1870's and 1880's the Japanese received moral support and practical advice. The basic concepts of international law were applied to the treaty system, and Japanese students came to have a clear grasp of how the law was supposed to function. The position of the Japanese was succinctly explained by yatoi adviser Henry W. Denison. As Peshine Smith, Hermann Roesler, and other lawyers had done, Denison informed the Japanese that the opening of the interior and the return of legal jurisdiction were not matters for negotiation. If foreigners had extraterritoriality, they could not have access to the interior. Denison argued further that the most favoured nation clause itself was dependent on give and take.[71] By the second decade the Japanese had gained a clear understanding of their legal rights as a nation. By the crisis of 1887 when reaction to a proposal to use foreign employees as jurists in the new Japanese court system forced the resignation of Inoue Kaoru, the climate of establishment opinion had changed radically. It was natural for the outs of government to be critical, but the nationalistic emphasis of conservative members in the government had begun to infect progressive supporters. This greater national consciousness triggered the reaction which defeated the proposal.[72]

Progressive leaders constantly sought ways to achieve treaty revision and tried to accommodate themselves to existing political realities. Some Japanese officials and foreign legal advisers perceived in the Inoue plan a conflict with the principle of national sovereignty upheld in the proposed constitution. Boissonade's articulation of the problem reflected the position of many Japanese officials:

> Japan in its drive for progress over twenty years has hired many foreigners. In no other country is there precedent for hiring so many. However, in the army, the navy, in administration, in education, foreign employees have been given the name of adviser or instructor only. Never have they been given rights proper to citizens. For the first time [in this treaty revision proposal] foreigners in Japan will engage in official work, that is they will exercise a part of government authority. In every country becoming a government official, exercising government power is a special right of the country's nationals; this is a public right. Judges are the most important government officials in a country and that duty is one of the most important operations of official rights. To entrust this official position to foreigners is improper.[73]

The initial recommendation for use of foreign jurists had been made by British legal adviser J. R. Davidson, using the Egyptian mixed court system as reference. It was his opinion that their use would be the swiftest way of activating Japanese court jurisdiction.[74] After the nationalistic rejection of the Inoue proposal, major Cabinet and Foreign Ministry officials, on the recommendation of German advisers in the Cabinet, then considered the naturalization of foreign jurists as a means of cloaking them with constitutionality. For German advisers the suggestion presented no conflict. As the Italian representative in Japan pointed out, under German law they would remain German, and by naturalization they would in effect enjoy dual citizenship.[75] However, some of the British and French advisers found the suggestion of naturalization repugnant. Thus, when Ōkuma Shigenobu as Foreign Minister included in yet another new plan the proposal that foreign judges be naturalized as Japanese, the whole issue exploded again. By 1889, just two years after the Inoue plan first suggested foreign jurists in the court system, opposition without and within government rejected anything which smacked of compromise in treaty revision. The Ōkuma proposal was squelched almost solely because of opposition to the naturalization of foreign employees.[76]

Although foreign powers failed to recognize it, Japanese bureaucrats quite literally had come into their majority. By the 1880's, pioneering efforts to establish an education merit bureaucracy were underway. It was achieved between 1887 and 1894 with the compulsory higher civil service examination system.[77] Legal reforms had been a sine qua non dictated by Western powers if Japan wished recognition in the world community. Although these reforms had progressed well, Great Britain, the nation with the greatest vested interest in the treaty system and the greatest weight in negotiations, would not recognize the Japanese position. France followed Britain. The United States and various other nations had for ten years conceded willingness to enter equitable treaties. Germany, too, had become co-operative, but British intransigence remained the obstacle. This was naturally resented by the Japanese who, with Western legalists as guides, had mastered Western legal concepts. The Japanese thought it time Western nations honoured their commitments under the laws they espoused.

Yet despite such thinking, some progressives were still openminded about the use of foreign jurists in negotiations in the 1890's. The discussion of such matters in a draft jurisdictional convention dated January 1, 1891, proves that the use of foreign jurists in the Supreme Court and, under certain circumstances, in the Court of Appeals was still entertained.[78] But the majority view held. Treaty revision, an official motivation for the Meiji experiment, was accomplished by the end of the third decade without foreign jurists in the courts.

The government programme of employing foreigners was brought to an end within thirty years. Although the major dismissal of yatoi technicians at the end of the first decade may have been premature, it was evidence not only of financial strain, nationalist sentiment, and xenophobic reaction, but also of Japanese intentions to direct their own nation-building. Yatoi who remained after the second decade of Meiji or who were engaged during the second decade, suffered no identity crisis. They recognized themselves as employees of Japanese employers. In the heyday of Western expansion this was no small achievement.

In a decade and a half, sophisticated bureaucratic management techniques were perfected and the way to a merit bureaucracy was opened. Thus, for three decades yatoi had been used to carve the feet and face of a New Japan. The Japanese themselves filled in the heart and torso. Thereafter, as in other modern countries, foreign consultants were generally restricted to being scholarly and other professional visitors invited by the government. Yet the employment of a few foreign legal advisers over the years through the end of the Second World War attests to Japan's continuing uneasiness in international relations. This was a legacy of the unequal treaties and of Western expansion. But the unequal treaties and Western expansion were both also catalysts for the amazing Meiji experiment in massive foreign borrowing.

3

Regulating the Yatoi

Administrative history is not disposed to excite the imagination. Yet it does in the Japanese case because the Meiji approach to nation-building is revealed in the policy developed to administer foreign employees. It was the Meiji style writ small. In examining how the yatoi were handled, one can trace Meiji growth from enthusiastic amateur fumbling to professional bureaucracy. Regulating the yatoi was a struggle in the hard face of foreign pressure. The obstacles would have intimidated a less determined government.

From 1868 the Council of State required foreign office permission (with full dossier and contract information) for local and national officials to hire foreigners.[1] Compliance was very erratic, but in 1870 a guideline entitled Instructions for Hiring Foreigners (Appendix 1) was issued. This was the base for future regulations which in effect created a civil service for foreigners. Attention was directed to standards, the need to control foreign employees— all of whom were under foreign consular protection—and to the issue of status.

Japanese modernizers recognized "ignorance of employment methods" as a basic cause of the "imprudent selection" of foreigners and of the disputes which inevitably ensued with foreign consuls. Japanese officials were cautioned against accepting at face value the "empty boasts" of some foreigners seeking employment. Emphasis was placed on the grave need for careful prior investigation of candidates' qualifications because "deceitful and frivolous persons [were] not excluded among foreigners who come to oriental countries." Some foreigners were "unsuitable" for the positions they filled. Japanese officials were warned that the statements of Japanese witnesses against foreigners were not considered credible by foreign consuls and so dismissal for due cause was very difficult. Whatever the conditions of a particular dispute, legal-minded foreign representatives argued from the written contract alone. Therefore, candidates were to be selected carefully and their employment was to be precisely defined in Western legal terms.

Foreigners were hired both from the open ports in Japan and from abroad. Many applied directly to Japanese officials. Among them were port tramps and beachcombers seeking their fortunes on Asian coasts. News of the Meiji experiment spread rapidly to Europe and America, and many foreigners made their way to Japan without prior arrangements, confident that chances of lucrative employment, especially for anyone with a little education, were virtually certain. In the early years, despite numerous frauds (*ikasama*), some of these adventurers found their niche in Japan and proved able workers.

A better selection was obtained from those hired abroad. The earliest channels for soliciting employees were through foreign diplomatic representatives or prominent merchants in Japan. These men used their good offices in their home countries to find suitable candidates for specific projects. The same system had been used by bakufu and han from the 1850's. Meiji Japanese also advertised positions in newspapers abroad, and members of various Japanese missions sought candidates. Foreign employees themselves were asked to find other employees.

But the quality of early employees left much to be desired. Even competent employees argued about duties, direction, expenses, treatment, and other matters. Some of these problems had their origin in faulty contracts, but in the background of all problems was the assumption that the foreigner should not be subject to Japanese employers. This attitude surfaced in statements made by foreigners that the success of a particular operation was dependent on an employee's being responsible to his own government representative. This kind of attitude, which is perhaps inevitable in certain personality types, was conditioned by the ambivalent status of yatoi as Japanese government employees and as foreign nationals within the treaty system. Certain temperaments were not amenable to Japanese direction. It was necessary, therefore, for Meiji officials to master Western legal practice to minimize losses, particularly in cases where even an able foreign employee proved refractory. Clarification of the employer role of Japanese officials was essential. The task was made more difficult when group missions were involved, when a foreign government was intermediary, and when a foreign financial agency arranged for contracts.

STANDARDS

Owing to the treaty situation, not only was foreign consular permission required for hiring foreign nationals, but inquiries by foreign representatives about their work, safety, and treatment had to be answered. The Japanese Foreign Ministry, therefore, became co-ordinator of the administration of all foreign employees, private as well as government. The ministry took this responsibility seriously. On March 30, 1870 (Meiji 3/2/29), a Council of State decree (*fukoku*) was issued to all branches of government requiring the seal of the Foreign Ministry for employment of foreigners.[2] A stronger requirement was decreed on June 17, 1870 (Meiji 3/5/19), when a rigid licence system for foreign employee work and travel was inaugurated. This applied to private employees also.[3] However, this action did not solve contract disputes.

On July 16, 1871 (Meiji 4/5/29), for example, the Foreign Ministry complained to the Council of State that government officials were still drawing up makeshift contracts. In reply on August 4, 1871 (Meiji 4/6/18), the legal section of the Council of State issued a notice to all ministries and units of local government requiring that they submit a letter containing consular permission to hire yatoi and requiring that draft contracts be approved by the Foreign Ministry prior to licensing.[4]

At the same time, the Education Ministry undertook to co-ordinate the nationwide employment of foreign teachers. According to an unnumbered notice (*tasshi*) for January 24, 1872 (Meiji 4/12/15), regional as well as national schools were obliged to obtain Education Ministry permission to hire foreign teachers. Officials needed to establish salary scales in accordance with qualifications, delineate work duties and specify supervisers for foreign teachers, set up standard pay scales for travel and emoluments, and determine the medium of payment. Building on information supplied mainly by yatoi,[5] Education officials prepared a set of "Contract Regulations for Hiring Teachers" (Kyōshi yatoiire jōyaku kisokusho).[6] The Education Ministry also prepared model draft contracts for employees hired in Japan and for those hired abroad, as well as drafting model letters to be sent to foreign representatives or teachers who were asked to find suitable applicants. These efforts were made by yatoi and Japanese officials working in close collaboration.

Officials made notes on articles that were to receive special attention. Free housing and repair maintenance were supplied, but more than one family was not to be allowed to occupy a house. Furnishings were not government responsibility. Despite earlier provisions for Western-style houses, there were not enough available. This obliged use of Japanese houses (usually temples), but employees could receive permission to build their own houses. The term of employment was clarified. Because of transportation costs, two or three years were permitted for contracts signed abroad, but contracts entered into in Japan were to be restricted to a six-month trial period followed by a two- or three-year renewal if the candidate proved suitable.[7]

These regulations for foreign educators were approved by the Foreign Ministry and were issued as Education Ministry Notice no. 20 on September

22, 1872 (Meiji 5/8/20). Education officials apparently interpreted approval to mean they had sole administrative responsibility for foreign teachers. The Council of State, at the behest of Foreign Ministry officials, rather sharply informed the Education Ministry on December 15, 1872 (Meiji 5/11/15), that the issuance of work and travel licences was a prerogative of the Foreign Ministry.[8]

The Education Ministry accepted this rebuff, but internally it acted to upgrade further the quality of teacher candidates. In May 1873, officials implemented a system whereby contracts with new teachers hired in Japan were not to be signed until the teachers demonstrated their ability for fifteen days. The Council of State authorized the payment of a single stipend (70 to 100 yen) for the trial period. Even then, under Education Notice no. 88 dated June 14, 1873, only teachers licensed in their home countries were to have their contracts renewed and only teachers of language and very simple subjects could be hired without certification.[9]

Other ministries, as well, had begun regulating the employment of foreigners—especially the Navy and Public Works ministries, which, with Education, engaged the largest number of yatoi. If one thinks roughly in terms of high, mid, and low levels of expenditures among all offices, then the expenditures of these three ministries were consistently high. Navy regulations, drawn up with foreign employee assistance, were issued to all bureaus. In general, provisions of this ministry were the same as those of Education.[10]

Central to the entire question of standards was obviously the need to formulate a pay scale based on employee qualifications. Employee complaints about less qualified or less able persons receiving the same or more salary and employee demands for adjustment also figured in efforts of Japanese officials to apply merit or achievement-oriented standards. The task was formidable. It was a seller's market, and employees, by and large arguing from existing precedents, pressed for what the traffic would bear. To co-ordinate wage practices, Inoue Kaoru in the Finance Ministry gathered the scales suggested by the various ministries and sent reports for study to the central legislative chamber (Seiin).[11]

By September 1873 a firm blueprint emerged. Based on the model prepared by the Education Ministry, salary was to be determined by initial qualifications, and all other emoluments were geared to salary levels (see chart Appendix 2). This approach was codified in "Regulations for the Employment of Foreign Teachers and Others and Their Expenditures while in Japan" (Gaikoku kyōshi nado yatoiirekata oyobi zairyūchū shohi kisokusho), issued September 28, 1873 (Appendix 2).

These regulations encompassed each point of contact with foreign employees. Emphasis was placed on obtaining prior clearance by the Foreign Ministry for an employee's engagement, on responsibility of the Japanese official handling the contract procedure, on clarifying modes of selection when foreign go-betweens were used, and on fixing lengths of contracts (General Instructions, Articles 1 – 5). Japanese officials recognized the need on occasion to allow salary advances to employees (6) and to attend to housing problems (7 – 8). The necessity of maintaining salary standards (9), with exceptions being made for persons of learning and achievement (10), was noted and the need for care was stressed (11). To avoid yatoi criticism, more allowance was made for adjustments by foreign head teachers or directors than for changes by Japanese officials. Every exigency for travel and baggage allowance was covered (12 – 22). The leisurely pace and nostalgic modes of transportation place this era of feverish construction in its nineteenth-century context, if only for a moment.

The approved bases for special treatment of foreign employees were asserted to be merit and achievement, but good work was expected as a matter of duty (23). And in the attention accorded foreign employees who died in service, Japanese concern to prevent future claim suits is evident (24).

In November, the Foreign Ministry clarified several points. It would in fact be necessary to give three-months notification of intention to dismiss an employee before his contract's expiration and to pay three-months' salary even if the employee were dismissed within the first three months of his engagement (Contract Model, Article 10, par. 2) and even if he were dismissed for negligence (Article 11). Foreigners must have taken umbrage at the procedure under Article 24 of the General Instructions, in which Japanese officials were directed that in the event of a foreign employee's death, his body was to be placed in a strong coffin and delivered to his consul, but no request was to be made of the consul to recognize the day of death as the day of discharge because this caused "unpleasantness."[12]

In actual fact, obtaining prior approval for licensing and adhering to the six-month initial probation period proved to be difficult. Communications were slow and often immediate decisions had to be made. Regional offices found it hampered them to wait for Foreign Ministry clearance. As early as 1871, the ministry had been obliged to condone the issuance of temporary work licences, at first by local offices and then by other offices.[13] An implication in vogue at the time was that Foreign Ministry clearance for temporary employees was not essential. For example, in March 1873, imperial household officials inquired whether contracts for regular employees could be made for a year or more while suggesting that temporary employees should be restricted to six months. And further, was not each ministry free to decide which employees were regular and which were temporary?[14] The 1873 Regulations were intended to put an end to loose interpretations, but the Foreign and Finance ministries continually had to address irregularities. All offices employing foreigners were supposed to submit fiscal reports every six months. By 1874 ministries were ordered to submit reports whether or not they were currently employing foreigners because of the high incidence of foreigners being used and paid without records being entered.[15]

However, officials still found employment and renewal procedures tedious. On November 24, 1874, Public Works officials complained directly to the Council of State that the need for many more employees from abroad was urgent; the acquisition of foreign learning and technology was essential. Unduly constrained by procedural paperwork, they needed to be able to settle details directly. On December 27, the Council of State authorized Public Works officials to circumvent procedure in contracts signed abroad.[16]

Foreign Ministry officials continued to face complaints from foreign employees through their foreign representatives over contract stipulations. The medium of payment was a major bone of contention. However, the formulation of uniform standards steadily progressed. By 1877 (February 3, Council of State decree no. 19), the Foreign Ministry no longer had to screen draft contracts, and detailed applications for permissions were reduced to simple reports of employment and dismissal (March 6, Council of State decree no. 27).[17] By 1881 each ministry administered its own employees.[18] However, two years later (August 3, 1883), the Council of State was obliged to modify this permission. In the interests of economy, prior permission of the central government was necessary to engage, re-employ, or increase the salaries of yatoi.[19] These administrative changes coincided with major reductions in the employment of foreigners, but they also demonstrate the growing expertise of officials. From the mid-1870's contract disagreements were rare.

From 1881, directives no longer involved the Foreign Ministry. With the transition from the Council of State to the Cabinet era, the latter assumed from 1886 most of the administrative responsibility for foreign employees, because yatoi were still viewed within the diplomatic framework. By a Cabinet directive of April 25, 1890, all areas of government were required to report to the Cabinet the employment, dismissal, or re-employment of foreigners.[20] Success in the establishment of employment standards meant that Western government representatives no longer had grounds for complaints. The co-ordinating role of the Foreign Ministry, so essential in the first decade of the Meiji period, proved unnecessary in the second. This progress bears a direct relationship to foreign employees themselves; by the second decade the majority were professionals.

By the end of the first decade, all contracts were in correct legal form. Several early lawyers and general advisers prepared their own contracts, and it is reasonable to suppose that others did as well. Yet, while providing themselves with handsome fees, they did not incorporate into their contracts contentious, ambiguous, or excessive demands. Lawyers recognized the employer role of the Japanese government by accepting direction by multiple superiors and by acknowledging that they could be summarily dismissed without argument for contract infringements.

The Western concept of legal contract was thus introduced to Japan, and Japanese officials learned that written documents could work for them as well as against them. Previously they had been aware only of the latter. The Japanese thus successfully clarified their employer role. Also, with the help of foreign legal advisers, Japanese officials addressed themselves to the question of legal jurisdiction over foreigners in government employ.

CONTROLS

From the early through the mid-Meiji period, Japan's diplomatic efforts were directed towards equalizing relations with foreign countries. From the 1850's, foreign powers entered into a series of treaties with the bakufu by which certain ports were opened to foreign intercourse and areas within those ports conceded for foreign residence and trade. Tariffs were fixed at a flat rate, and legal jurisdiction in the open ports was placed under the consular courts of the various foreign powers. This entire chain of concessions to foreign nations is known as extraterritoriality or extrality. In practice it meant that foreign powers assumed to their own jurisdiction areas on the soil of an otherwise sovereign nation. In Japan the system operated differently from other areas such as the Middle East or China in that walls were not erected around foreign compounds; foreign powers feared isolation such as occurred with the Dutch at Deshima in the earlier era. Nor were concessions of areas made to specific foreign powers; the powers decided not to separate themselves, in order to prevent the bitter controversies they had experienced among themselves in China.

The initial arguments advanced for extraterritorial rights in Japan concerned the safety of foreigners and the inequities of Japanese law. Special residence areas (*kyoryūchi*) where foreigners could, under the treaties, lease land, purchase buildings, and erect dwellings and warehouses were delineated in the open ports of Yokohama, Nagasaki, Osaka, Hyogo (Kobe), and Tokyo.[21] Foreign residents, including foreigners employed by the Japanese, were protected through their national representatives under the laws of their country of origin. Law instructor Georges Bousquet commented in the 1870's that "no European concerned for his dignity would wish to place himself under Japanese law in its present state."[22] This remark represented the foreign consensus of opinion.

The Meiji government soon began preparation of legal codes, but first it set about removing grounds for the foreigner's fear about personal safety.

The danger was real; random but serious attacks on foreigners were many.[23] The common people, as well as masterless samurai (*rōnin*), had equated over-throw of the bakufu (*tōbaku*) with expulsion of foreigners (*jōi*). For example, when the outspoken advocate of opening Japan, Yokoi Shōnan, was assassinated (Meiji 2/1), popular sympathy was with the assassin.[24]

A special police for foreigners (*bettegumi*), with a complement in the capital of over two hundred men, was reactivated in the summer of 1868. In 1869 it was divided into two sections: one to guard the foreign residence area in Tsukiji and the other to guard legation personnel and foreigners employed by the Japanese government. These guards were authorized to use their swords in any attempted attack on foreigners.[25] The situation was sufficiently grave that early yatoi like Verbeck were sometimes confined to their houses under guard for weeks at a time. Yatoi William Elliot Griffis wrote that Verbeck always carried a small pistol.

As part of the policy of establishing centralized control, the Meiji government issued a series of notices and warnings that attacks of any nature on foreigners would no longer be tolerated. In 1868 these were general in nature, forbidding violence or establishing injunctions against Japanese being rude to foreigners visiting shrines or temples.[26] In 1869 orders were issued that foreigners were to be protected on city streets, and regulations were published in regional domains (han) informing foreigners to report untoward incidents or assaults on themselves to the nearest government office. Han officials, not unnaturally, inquired what action should be taken in the event of misbehaviour on the part of a foreigner. The Council of State replied curtly that they should report the foreigner's name to the local government office.[27] A tougher note appeared in ordinances in 1869. In the event of an attack on foreigners, the guilty party, his head of household or master, and other responsible persons would be punished.[28] In 1870 police control regulations were issued to the three urban prefectures (*fu*) and to open ports. Article 13 enjoined the Japanese people to desist from offences against foreigners because they reflected badly on the dignity of Japan. And again in 1871 a directive ordered punishment not only of guilty parties but of those related to or associated with them.[29]

At the same time, the Japanese government resisted foreign pressure and maintained that punishment fell under Japanese law. In 1871, for example, when the British accused Japanese police of negligence in apprehending the murderer of a foreign employee in the Kaisei school in Tokyo and wished to interfere in the investigation, Ōkubo Toshimichi upheld the rights of Japanese police to act alone, asserting that the issue was domestic.[30] Dissolution of the special police force (*bettegumi*) in 1872 was indicative of progress. Thereafter, Japanese were able to police the hinterland successfully, and foreign police were hired by the Japanese government for foreign residence areas.[31]

Foreign residents in both Yokohama and Nagasaki very early became disenchanted with the taxes levied by their own municipal councils. Residents in the Yokohama settlement brought suit in consular courts with the result that the municipal council was declared to have no right to tax. This was but a symptom of the relinquishing of administrative control by foreign residents, who looked on kyoryūchi administration as a nuisance. While some licence fees and minor assessments continued to be collected until 1874, the Japanese exercised considerable authority from December 1867, when the Kanagawa commissioner and his successor, the Meiji governor of Kanagawa, appointed an American foreign director, E. S. Benson (1867 – 77), and paid him $500 monthly.[32]

The foreign director, as representative of the governor of Kanagawa, supervised repairs, sanitation, and so forth, took charge of yatoi police, collected land rent, and, in the name of the governor, sued foreigners in consular courts for default. By 1877 the foreign directorship was dropped, and administration of the settlement, together with the financial burden, was assumed completely by Japanese authorities.[33]

In Nagasaki, foreign residents proposed that expenses for such municipal needs as lighting, repairs, and foreign police, be borne on a matching basis by the Japanese government rather than entirely by assessment on foreign residents. Japanese officials refused. They demanded full administration of the foreign residence area. They took over the employment and direction of the foreign police and in 1876 assumed full administration of the area.[34] The foreign settlement in the capital, the Tsukiji section of Tokyo, was never significant except as a residential area, despite Townsend Harris's prophecy that 90 per cent of the Japan trade would centre in the capital. In Yokohama, preferred by businessmen, Japanese officials not only provided police protection but administered hotels and inns from the first year of the Meiji era.[35]

Only in Osaka-Kobe did land regulations continue to the 1899 treaty revision. Advance assessments were made on all foreign renters to provide funds for municipal needs, and the Japanese were only responsible in times of disaster to provide half the cost of repairs.[36] However, Japanese officials in Hyogo hired foreign police and employed a co-ordinator to ease the tension between Japanese and foreign officials. At Kobe, foreign police supervisor Alfred Nichol (1873 – 80) was paid first from local Japanese taxes and later from central government funds (Finance Ministry).[37]

By the mid-1870's, all funds for foreign police in each of the open ports were dispensed by the central government—by the Finance Ministry to 1885, the Home Ministry thereafter.[38] The early yatoi police administration, supplemented by the gradual hiring of foreign police experts through the 1880's, provided the base of the training and reorganization of Japanese national police initiated by Ōkubo Toshimichi in the early 1870's. The continuing need for foreigners as police was to keep order among foreigners themselves and to prevent incidents involving Japanese. Inebriated or fractious residents, including yatoi, intimidated native Japanese police, who, under diplomatic pressures, were limited in the actions they could take.[39] By paying for and administering yatoi police, the Japanese government was able to enforce treaty stipulations which were supposed to restrict foreigners to prescribed residence areas and an additional twenty-five-mile radius. With the help of yatoi police and despite continued foreign protests, they were able to prevent unauthorized movements into the interior and control violence, smuggling, and other crimes by foreigners. In particular, with the help of British and Chinese yatoi police, the Japanese were able to circumvent private British and Chinese connivance in the attempt to extend the opium trade to Japan.

Police of several nationalities were hired, full- and part-time. Part-time employees were largely from foreign troop complements stationed in open ports. The pay of sergeants-at-arms varied from $45 to $80 a month, and ordinary yatoi police were paid $15 a month.[40] Their low pay in comparison with the pay of other yatoi was the result in part of the few hours of evening duty required of them. But many were Chinese, and Chinese pay levels, except for court translators, who were paid on a par with Western yatoi, were always closer to those of the Japanese themselves. Chinese enjoyed treaty status and were confined to residence areas as were other foreigners, but perhaps because they consistently outnumbered all other foreigners, there was need for so many Chinese yatoi police.[41] More important would appear to be the attitudes of Westerners, far more favourable towards the Chinese than the Japanese. Certainly Western attitudes were coloured by Japanese efforts to regain legal jurisdiction.

Implicit in the concession of extraterritoriality was the proscription of foreign access to the interior (*naichi zakkyo*). However, the employment of foreigners by the government soon presented a challenge to this restrictive policy. Foreign employees had to take up posts in government offices outside their residence areas in the capital and even in the interior of Japan. Officials therefore took several steps to prevent the movement of foreign employees in the interior from becoming a precedent for foreigners in general.

Tokyo-Yokohama area foreign employees actually brought about the demise of the Tsukiji foreign residence area by insisting on living close to their work. At first displeased, Japanese officials soon perceived advantages in having yatoi close at hand. Special quarters were constructed in school and work compounds, and the revised regulations of 1874 required that those who lived in private housing submit to specific regulations circumscribing their movements and activities.[42]

For all foreign employees, a licence system became a major method of control. Work licences rather like alien registration certificates and special travel or transit licences were issued to government foreign employees (Appendix 3).[43] Permission was soon granted to private Japanese businessmen to employ foreigners who were also licensed by the Foreign Ministry. When travelling, the foreign employee had to produce his papers for Japanese officials, police, innkeepers, and the like. Innkeepers in particular were notorious for their officiousness. The system, however, also worked to the employee's advantage. It ensured careful and respectful treatment.

The system was strictly enforced, and local officials sought top-level clearance for any movement not specifically authorized. Aichi Prefecture officials, for example, informed Home Minister Ōkubo Toshimichi in 1876 that an Austrian doctor in their employ, Albrecht von Roretz, wanted to engage a Chinese servant from Kobe, but Hyogo Prefecture would not issue a transit licence because there was no precedent. Ōkubo referred the matter to the Foreign Ministry, which issued a licence for the Chinese to travel to and stay in Aichi.[44]

The system continued while the unequal treaties were in force, and local officials were reluctant to take any responsibility without receiving clarification from the Foreign Ministry. As late as 1892, Shimane Prefecture officials inquired if a licence permitting travel in or near the treaty ports could be used by a yatoi to travel to Yokohama and back. The reply was a flat negative.[45] Foreign employees were packed off under escort and were even fined for violations.[46] Although by 1877 private foreign employees could apply to live outside foreign residence areas and government foreign employees could easily obtain a local travel licence authorizing transit (*tsūkō*) and temporary residence (*kiryū*) outside the fixed treaty travel area, controls remained in effect until treaty revision was accomplished.[47]

Other restrictions were also placed on foreign employees. Foreign employees living outside the prescribed treaty areas were subject to local Japanese police, court, and tax regulations.[48] All foreign employees were forbidden to engage in trade, as were the Japanese in government. Until the Japanese received tariff autonomy, foreign trade was to be contained in the open ports. Japanese officials displayed consistent animosity towards foreigners attempting to expand channels of trade, and yatoi were obliged to renounce all business connections to avoid any conflict of interest.

Foreigners were also enjoined against preaching Christianity, proscribed until 1873. Although the Education Ministry issued an order to Japanese school officials to avoid hiring missionaries, the need for teachers overrode it.[49] Foreign representatives felt the government policy extremely aggressive, and American diplomats charged that missionaries were in fact hired by the government to prevent their proselytizing.[50] Later, missionary teachers and other foreign employees complained that officials, by making Sunday a work day, were trying to oust them from government schools.[51]

However many restraints with which the Japanese government surrounded the foreign employee, he was still under his own nation's consular jurisdiction. The validity of contracts rested on a letter of consent from the employee's government representative in Japan, and until 1878 many contracts continued to declare the latter an arbiter of any complaint. It was only a matter of time before the Japanese would address themselves directly to the question of the jurisdiction of foreign employees. In the mid-1870's certain appropriate occasions arose.

In 1874 a special office (*Banchi jimukyoku*: literally, Barbarian Land Administrative Office) was established as a temporary organ to handle a punitive expedition against Taiwan because natives had murdered some shipwrecked Ryūkyū islanders and China had failed to take disciplinary action. At least a dozen foreigners were engaged. In the diplomatic dispute over the legitimacy of the employment of American nationals, U.S. minister to Japan John Bingham failed to force their resignation because of varied interpretations of what constituted an American court and consular court jurisdiction. The previous U.S. minister, Charles DeLong, had maintained that a United States citizen in Japanese government employ could not be dismissed except by his conviction in an American court on a serious count.[52]

This interpretation opened innumerable possibilities. When Bingham tried to remove American nationals from the Taiwan expedition, insisting that they had to obey his court order, E. Peshine Smith, American yatoi adviser on international law, rendered the defence incorporating DeLong's position. Americans had to obey American court decisions but a consular court was not an American court. Because United States state and territorial laws were not uniform, the consular court could not represent any American court. On Smith's advice, foreign employees rejected the jurisdiction of their government representative and, to protect themselves (two were former U.S. Navy officers), entered into verbal agreements for the expedition.[53] The British consul in Amoy was successful in preventing newly engaged British subjects from participating, but British yatoi already in Japan joined the expedition.

At the same time, another incident occurred in which yatoi accepted Japanese legal jurisdiction. After cancelling the Oriental Bank contract for the Mint, the Finance Ministry decided to retain a few employees. Three of the five retained were British subjects. Even so, these employees entered freely into new contracts in 1875 which were actually orders of employment (*meireisho*) from the Finance Ministry. They acknowledged Japanese jurisdiction over their employment and rejected recourse to their national representative.[54]

It was also in 1875 that Sir Harry Parkes, perhaps the most vociferous of foreign representatives, met defeat in his defence of a minor yatoi's contract.

Though the case was minor, the result was more significant than any of many incidents in illustrating both the lengths to which a foreign representative could carry a specious argument and the stature attained by Japanese officials. Alexander Pope Porter was a simple sort. In 1871 he was appointed harbour master in Hakodate and had complied with the injunction to disengage himself from private business. Because of the hostility among foreign representatives to British harbour masters, his job was abolished.

He plagued government offices with tales of his declining circumstances and in 1874 finally received an appointment as sailing master. In the 1874 contract he agreed to conform to the laws of Japan and to reject the intervention of any foreign representative or government in any dispute (Article 13). In his dissatisfaction with the new appointment, largely because it was less prestigious than that of harbour master and because attitudes of Japanese officials had hardened with respect to employee obligations, he defaced and returned his contract and sought aid from the British minister. The truculent Parkes took umbrage at the clause rejecting his mediation and charged Japanese officials with nefarious plotting. When he received no satisfaction, he carried his argument with Foreign Minister Terajima Munenori to irrational lengths.

Because Porter's first contract had no fixed term of employment (*mukigen*), Parkes maintained that Porter could consider himself a lifetime employee (*eisei oyatoi*) and that therefore the government had acted dishonestly in abolishing his job. Actually at the time that Porter's first contract was reported, Hakodate officials had been instructed to correct the omission and amend the contract to indicate a specific period of time but had failed to do so. With experience gained in previous confrontations and with his increased knowledge of legal procedure, Foreign Minister Terajima was able to cut Parkes short with the statement that if lifetime employment had been intended, it would have been specifically written into the contract, in accordance with the legal practice with which Parkes was familiar.[55]

Probably the stronger posture of Japanese officials in the mid-1870's was related to the acknowledgement by foreign powers that the Japanese government had brought the countryside under control. Earlier, Japanese officials had worked assiduously for the withdrawal of foreign troops from Yokohama. In 1864, some eight thousand foreign troops and twenty-four warships, half of which were British, were stationed in Yokohama. In 1867 there was a permanent station of eight hundred British army troops and three hundred French naval troops. The Meiji government continued the bakufu policy of providing buildings and maintenance for Anglo-French garrisons.[56] The financial drain, the Japanese fear of foreigners, and the matter of dignity prompted Meiji negotiations for their withdrawal.[57]

In the initial conference on November 26, 1869, for withdrawal negotiations, Iwakura Tomomi showed considerable understanding of the British position. The government recognized that many Japanese still clung to the old idea of expelling the barbarian (*jōi ron*), but the Military Affairs, Civil Affairs, and Justice ministries in conjunction with municipal governments conferred to discuss taking every possible step to exercise strict control over Japanese in Tokyo, Osaka, and Hyogo. Iwakura stated that formal request for withdrawal would be made when this control was perfected. Parkes assented to withdrawal when the safety of foreigners was guaranteed and promised to so inform the French representative.[58]

In the 1870 conferences, Parkes reiterated that unstable conditions precluded immediate troop withdrawal.[59] The French minister to Japan had tried to link the presence of troops to the treaties, but Sawa Nobuyoshi, the Japanese negotiator, rejected this outright.[60] From 1867 to 1870 the numbers of foreign troops had been considerably reduced. At the end of 1871 Kanagawa officials informed the Foreign Ministry that in Yokohama the complement of British marines numbered 301 and that of the French army 200.[61] The personal safety of foreigners had been largely guaranteed since 1872, but the Korean crisis of 1873 and the attendant polarization of intra-government factions (with one threatening war with Korea), had delayed the British withdrawal. Although the rift was not entirely patched up until mid-1875 and would erupt again, Parkes informed the Japanese government of the British intention to withdraw the Yokohama garrisons on January 27, 1875.[62] Britain and France were in fact recognizing that one major reason for extraterritoriality (the safety of foreigners) no longer existed.

The Japanese placed weight on every action and gesture, however small, which promised to enhance their political independence. Little is known of actual steps taken by Japanese officials to negotiate the formal transfer of foreign employees to Japanese legal jurisdiction. But, towards the end of 1875, records reveal at least one such formal attempt. Enomoto Takeaki, Japanese Minister Plenipotentiary, had in May concluded a settlement reached on the Russo-Japanese border question. Later in the year he had occasion to confer with Baron Antoine Jomini at the Foreign Affairs Ministry in St. Petersburg. The lengthy Japanese notes of that parley reveal the importance placed upon foreigners employed by Japan coming under the jurisdiction of Japanese law.

Enomoto pointed out that many foreigners hired by Japan had to travel and work in the interior. However, under extraterritorial arrangements, other foreigners were refused access to the interior. This anomaly caused complaints, and the matter would be greatly simplified if foreign employees were to come under the jurisdiction of Japanese law. Some Americans wished to do so, but Enomoto did not know about the French or English. He then asked directly if the Russian government would consent to Russian employees coming under Japanese legal jurisdiction. While Jomini thought that the wish was reasonable, he replied that Russia would consent only if all foreigners did so. He could not agree that this action should apply to Russians alone.[63]

From this effort it may be surmised that there were others. The approaches at least are consistent. The sounding out of lesser powers and figures is a piece with the quiet Japanese pattern of establishing precedents, "small victories" even if they did not promise immediate headway. The steady weaning of yatoi from their consular ties, the equitable treaty with Mexico, and the treaty in the mid-1870's with the United States fit these patterns. Japanese were well aware that all powers had to agree under the system in order for a bilateral treaty to take effect. While they hoped tariff revision with the United States would sway Britain, the Terajima negotiations aimed at least to establish a precedent.

What became of the Enomoto feeler is not known. But he clearly placed the question of jurisdiction of foreign employees in the broader context of the return of total legal jurisdiction to Japan, just as the whole administrative policy towards foreign employees was viewed in this context. Again, the attitudes and conduct of foreign legal advisers towards the rights of the Japanese government over foreign employees undoubtedly encouraged this approach. Legal advisers appear to have been completely divorced from the current politics and diplomacy of their own governments, and the secrets clause in contracts was professionally observed. Japanese officials took courage as well as skill from that professionalism. In practice, they put up a far better defence against Western expansionism than is sometimes appreciated.

PREFERENTIAL TREATMENT

Directed at foreign employees was a rather shrewd public relations programme, which offered generous moving allowances, and for long-term employees provided various privileges and advancements until the award of severance bonuses or pensions. If they died, proper burial was provided and money allowances often were given to bereaved relatives.

François Coignet (1868–77), a French mining engineer, technically was the first foreigner employed by the Meiji government.[64] As he started into the interior to carry out a survey of silver mines, an order was issued by the Council of State that he not be molested or have his work interfered with.[65] Thereafter, the Japanese were routinely enjoined to treat government foreign employees the same as Japanese subjects.[66]

In practice, this meant that the Japanese government integrated foreign employees, outsiders (*gaijin*) though they were, into the Japanese status system. The result was that even a lowly day labourer enjoyed an élite position by the fact of his special protection, living arrangements, and salary. Injunctions regarding status treatment, from the 1870 Instructions for Hiring Foreigners through the establishment of a formal system in 1886, were part of the age-old recognition that all men are not equal, that different levels in human relationships require differences in treatment. Foreign employees were quick to perceive these differences and to lobby for élite positions. Japanese officials usually pursued the carrot treatment because the stick treatment, possible only occasionally, was less productive.

Until the establishment of the cabinet system and the formal revamping of the Imperial Household Ministry by 1886, there was no set formula for the rank or treatment of foreign employees. Yet a pattern evolved which illustrates official concern to standardize status treatment on a qualitative basis. In 1869, the new government established three principal categories with gradations by which to rank Japanese officials.[67] Prestige, precedence, and salary were certainly prime considerations. Other areas of consideration were living arrangements, gifts, cash awards, decorations, pensions, receptions, palace ceremonies, honorary positions upon retirement, and various privileges connected with daily work. Foreign employees were drawn into this élite situation.

Although it is true that traditional class and rank consciousness pursued the Japanese into the Meiji era, foreigners also were acutely status conscious. They came to operate on the presumption of a most favoured yatoi clause— which was the most favoured nation treaty clause writ small.

Some foreign employees refused to obey Japanese officials inferior in rank, and there was considerable rivalry among yatoi themselves. Japanese officials felt that some of these problems were the result of unclear definitions of employee status. In the Mint dispute, the Japanese were chagrined because foreign employees distinguished themselves by affixing gold crests (*mon*) to their hats. Unfortunately, the gold chrysanthemum was an imperial symbol, and the Japanese were offended. Officials felt that this kind of display would be avoided if a system of ranks were devised. In 1873, Major Thomas W. Kinder, the director, was given rank four, and the other yatoi were given ranks five through eight.[68] For Japanese officials, ranks four to seven were *sōnin*, the second highest level of the new civil service, and rank eight was the highest grade in the third level of civil service (*hannin*). In military terms, ranks four to eight corresponded to titles ranging from colonel to second-lieutenant. Later, when these civil service designations came to be applied officially to foreign employees, remaining Mint yatoi in ranks six and seven were designated *sōnin*.[69]

But even earlier than the application of ranks in the Mint, Japanese officials were using Japanese civil service ranks for yatoi. Numerous questions arose about how rank should be determined. Gradually, officials decided that the level of work performed was a sounder index than salary.

On December 23, 1875, the Tokyo city government requested that the Foreign Ministry permit Charles J. Manning (1875 – 81) to receive treatment at the second level of civil service (sōnin) in order that he could attend the New Year reception given by the emperor. The letter of request referred to an earlier Council of State directive which gave this privilege to sōnin and above. Because he was a lecturer in the medical school and a doctor in the Tokyo-fu hospital with a salary of $310 per month, Tokyo authorities considered him sōnin. The Foreign Ministry in reply the same day argued that E. Peshine Smith was employed with a $10,000 annual salary and so was entitled to be received by the emperor, but Peyton Jaudon (1873 – 86), a French- and English-language teacher and translator with a salary of $350 a month would not be received. Therefore the Tokyo government was asked to reassess Manning's status.[70] The next day, December 24, the Foreign Ministry was obliged to acknowledge that Jaudon's position had been rechecked. He did indeed have sōnin status and therefore could attend the palace reception.[71] One can only surmise that office rumours reached Jaudon and that he was involved in the review of his status.

In an interesting letter from Kanagawa Prefecture, May 9, 1876, the enquiring official wrote that sōnin treatment was to be the same as for *sōninkan* (an official of sōnin rank), and according to a Council of State directive a person of sōnin status could mount and dismount within the gate of each bureau. The question was at what salary level a foreign employee became sōnin?[72] From this excerpt it is easy to conjure up a picture of a yatoi's being given a parking admonition or more likely being obliged by a conscientious guard to dismount outside the gate and tramp in on foot, proceeding immediately to a Japanese official with his grievance. The official in turn sought a simple solution, perhaps voicing the yatoi's own question: at what salary level did one become sōnin?

The Foreign Ministry (May 15, 1876) replied that the answer had not yet been determined. Because the relationship between status and salary was undecided, bureau chiefs should think of the personality and position of the employee and consult further with Foreign Ministry officials.[73] But, by the end of the year, as the annual palace reception drew near, the Home Ministry solved the problem for the Council of State (December 22, 1876). In the absence of standardized regulations for the status treatment of foreigners, persons with a monthly salary of 350 yen or more were regarded as quasi-sōnin and were recommended for the reception. However, in the view of the Home Ministry, determining status by salary alone was unsatisfactory. (The

Home Ministry employed several distinguished yatoi at salaries of $300 and below.) Rather, the type of work regardless of salary was a preferable basis for determining status. These officials wished clarification before the coming new year. A general order was issued on December 25 announcing that the actual level of work should determine the status required for attendance at the imperial reception.[74]

As time went on, further clarification was sought. On September 26, 1878, for example, the Justice Ministry sent an enquiry to the Council of State secretary. Justice officials pointed out that as yet there were no general regulations, but that they wished to be advised of the usual practice. They asked if they might make status designation in accordance with the 1873 Decree no. 207—distinguishing sōnin by salaries of more than 350 yen and hannin by salaries of more than 30 yen.

In a review of the situation, the Council of State correspondent (September 30, 1878) pointed out that the 1873 decree provided entertainment money to persons of sōnin and hannin status based on the salaries of those ranks. However, the privilege had been abolished by the 1875 Notice no. 175. Likewise, the 1874 Notice no. 71, which used salary as a basis for designating sōnin and hannin status of government personnel accused of crimes (and therefore determining penal treatment), was also abolished by the 1876 Notice no. 14. The Council of State correspondent concluded that no general rule existed for determining status treatment of foreign employees.[75]

Yet ranking continued not only for the purpose of determining yatoi privileges but for disciplining them as well. In 1879, for example, Kanagawa Prefecture inquired about the treatment of criminals who had received imperial awards. The Justice Ministry replied that foreigners and Japanese were to receive the same treatment according to rank.[76] It was not, however, until 1886 that status treatment of foreign employees was formally resolved.

At the behest of the new Imperial Household Ministry's Bureau of Ceremonies (Shikibushoku), the Foreign Ministry on February 12, 1886, requested all offices to submit a report on the status of each foreign employee. Foreign employees were to be included in the civil service rank system, and the Bureau of Ceremonies was to implement a new court precedence system for Japanese officials, foreign representatives, and foreign employees. Each ministry, with Foreign Ministry approval, was to determine the rank of each foreign employee based on his social position in his home country (nobility, profession, and so forth) where it could be estimated and/or based on awards and decorations received from the home country and from Japan. Japanese decorations were awarded according to achievement and seniority in service.

In 1886 correspondence reviewing the positions of yatoi, the above criteria and the nature of the actual duties of the employee were included in the evaluation. Short forms were provided for each employee. The level of work was clearly the salient criterion. For example, on the form for Heinrich Mänz (1886–88, or 90), a German listed as an architect and construction assistant for the Home Ministry at $300 a month, "no title" "no decorations" were scrawled across the form and specific items were left blank. He nevertheless was assigned sōnin treatment. Nor was salary any longer a determining factor, as illustrated by a March 19, 1886, Foreign Ministry report listing legal advisers and translators.[77]

Prior to 1886, almost all yatoi had received at least hannin treatment (salary basis), many received sōnin treatment, and General Horace Capron, adviser (komon) for the Hokkaido Development Commission, had received chokunin treatment. But, from 1886 the Japanese civil service status of foreign employees was clearly demarcated. They were included in the Japanese official status system. Letters of appointment assigned to a foreign employee a title that was "commensurate with such and such a rank," *sōninkan santō ijo sōtō, sōnin ijo ni junzubeki mono, chokunin ni junji, chokunin toriatsukai.* Thus foreign employees were quasi-civil servants.

This is true notwithstanding continued foreign criticism of the designation "yatoi." For example, as reported in the *Japan Weekly Mail* (July 30, 1892), "all persons in the service of the Government who do not possess official rank are yatoi . . . a term often resented by foreigners as a rudeness." Men of distinction "are in Japan reduced to the level of the lowest semi-official in a Department." Lower levels of Japanese officials were also called yatoi. Significant is the fact that the same qualified expression that invariably applied to foreign employees ("commensurate with such and such a rank") was also applied to Japanese bureaucrats when they were given quasi (*jun*) status; some Japanese bureaucrats held quasi (*jun*) status for many years and sometimes for their entire tenure. Clearly, foreign employees were treated as, and in fact became, quasi-bureaucrats.

Of course, chokunin treatment was the most highly coveted; it drew the foreign employee, as regards his treatment, into the highest circle of Japanese officials, the prime minister, the Privy Council chairman, the Home minister, the Imperial Household minister, field marshalls, and admirals of the fleet.[78] Foreign employees were not adverse to lobbying for élite positions, and on occasion an amusing note was struck.

William Montague Hammett Kirkwood, Justice Ministry legal adviser between 1885 and 1901, provides an example of rather genteel pomposity. In establishing ranks, officials had solicited information from yatoi. Kirkwood replied that in England he was an esquire, barrister, and crown advocate; and, in fact, during his employment he continued as crown advocate with the British Embassy. He was awarded sōnin treatment in 1886. Kirkwood, apparently a stickler for precedence, chafed under this for some years. The son of yatoi Francis Piggott has noted the "good humoured difficulty" at public meetings over precedence, Kirkwood being adviser to the Justice Ministry, and Piggott being adviser to the prime minister.[79] But in 1898, Kirkwood was asked to submit to the Imperial Household Ministry Bureau of Ceremonies a long list of court precedence in Britain. He appended a note suggesting that Japanese officials find his true position on that list. As a result he was awarded chokunin treatment.[80]

Kirkwood's promotion was tied to his position with the British Embassy. In the 1870's and 1880's, there had been several yatoi who had continued as legation employees, but, perhaps to protect themselves from further claims from esquires, barristers, and crown advocates, Japanese officials added a note to the appointment. Embassy employees and employees in the Japanese government were actually separate entities bearing no relation to each other.[81]

In the overall conferring of status and decorations, merit became the basic determinant. In the 1886 revision, the Order of the Rising Sun, with various degrees, was awarded for achievement, and the Order of the Sacred Treasure was awarded most often for length of service. Other decorations were established, including one for women. In January 1888, the Order of the Rising Sun, First Class with Paulownia Flowers, was designated the epitome of Japanese honours save that of the Order of the Chrysanthemum (the latter being a personal award of the emperor to heads of major states).[82] Although many honours and awards designated foreign employees as an élite, chokunin status treatment, unless conferred because of the employee's noble birth or high public office at home, was reached arduously through achievement and seniority, as for native Japanese civil servants. And although decoration of foreign employees often occurred, particularly on resignation, the upper two degrees of the Orders of the Rising Sun and of the Sacred Treasure were parsimoniously bestowed.

When one notes that even such long-term and distinguished advisers as Boissonade (twenty-three years) and Roesler (sixteen years), both with chokunin status, were never accorded decorations above lower rank generals, and that not a handful of other yatoi received this distinction, it is evident that Japanese officials were selective. It was not until 1896 that the respected legal adviser who gave half his life to Japanese government service, Henry W. Denison, was awarded chokunin treatment because of his achievement (Order of the Rising Sun, Third Class, 1888; Second Class, 1894) and length of service (Order of the Sacred Treasure, First Class, 1895). Shortly before his death in 1914, after thirty-four years of service, he alone of all yatoi was awarded the Order of the Rising Sun, First Class with Paulownia Flowers, the highest award for which Japanese and foreign heads of small states were eligible.[83]

Though a sophisticated selectivity operated in the conferring of special awards, officials dispensed hospitality lavishly. Receptions, parties, and entertainment paid for from government funds were constant. Ministries had entertainment expense accounts for yatoi and Japanese civil servants. The distribution of annual thanks money (*orei*) was fairly routine. Japan's is a gift culture, and no foreign employee was honorably separated from service without receiving gifts of Japanese silks, lacquerware, damascene, cloissoné, and the like. Often words of thanks from the emperor (*chokugo*) were bestowed. Cash awards varied from 100 to 5,000 yen, silver or gold. In the event of a yatoi's death, officials arranged funeral expenses, Christian burial services, and interment in well-kept cemeteries in Yokohama, Tokyo, and Kobe on land set aside by the state (some are still cared for today). Grants were sometimes made gratuitously to the family of the deceased, quite apart from any ground for claims. There were numerous cases of life annuities of 1,500 to 2,000 yen, silver or gold, paid to distinguished foreign employees on their retirement.[84] Professors who had extended tenure in the university were named honoured professor or professor emeritus (*meiyo kyōju*) upon retirement, a title which carried a life pension.

Besides offering special allowances, housing, paid vacations, and free medical care by European doctors, the government established rest centres. At the behest of Dr. Erwin von Baelz, the hot springs resort of Atami was purchased and developed by the government in 1890. Baelz actually felt that Japanese officials required such facilities and had encouraged development of hot springs rest centres for government personnel since 1879.[85] He and Dr. Julius Scriba (1881 – 1901), another special physician to government officials and the imperial family, sought and brought to government attention major hot springs areas such as Kusatsu. They also analysed the various properties and designated the cures.

Travel for health reasons became a standard privilege. Employees made wide use of it: in the summer of 1874 two-thirds of all yatoi in the Navy Ministry applied for such travel.[86] The device was probably necessary because employees also complained of difficulty in negotiating time away from work. Signed medical excuses from authorized foreign doctors were the order of the day. The climate was hard on many yatoi; some succumbed to tuberculosis and alimentary ailments, so it would seem that health care was essential.

The Japanese civil service provided the good life for yatoi, not the least in terms of social status. By the mid-1870's, attendance at imperial audiences and palace receptions had become a coveted status symbol. The fact that the emperor, with his increasingly heavy social obligations, might be indisposed or travelling did not prevent vociferous complaints from yatoi who expected to be received on departing for extended leave or upon resigning. Officials had to take the matter in hand. By 1877, refusals were given even to respected employees, and personal letters of regret sent out. By 1881 the Council of State declared that despite the fact that it had become usual to receive foreign employees, especially prior to their return home, audience would thereafter be granted only at the convenience of the emperor. And, in 1882, the decision was reinforced with the statement that the reception of foreign employees was not very important.[87] Official attitudes thus altered from promiscuous generosity to selective propriety.

The long tenure of many foreign employees speaks to the viability of this administrative policy. The overall average length of service for the yatoi examined in this study was about five years. But of 170 yatoi who received monthly salaries of $500 or more or who from 1886 were formally appointed to sōnin or chokunin status, the average length of service exceeded nine years. Of these, for 62 in this group who served ten years or more, the average was eighteen years. Among all the yatoi, almost 100 served twenty years and at least 13 celebrated a twenty-fifth anniversary. A few others served even longer.[88]

As the administrative policy towards foreign employees was increasingly articulated, problems related to their employment were reduced, and employees themselves came to accept without demur the channels delineated by their official employers for their services. The Japanese had succeeded in applying their concept of preferential treatment. In the establishment of standards and the application of merit critieria, in efforts to obtain legal jurisdiction, in the delineation of quasi-civil servant status, and in the length of service of many foreign employees, the Meiji administrative policy towards yatoi created a foreign quasi-bureaucratic corps parallel to the Japanese bureaucracy.

4

The Yatoi Self-Image

In the phenomenon of the expansion of the modern West, the missionary urge was expressed in symbols which ranged from the god, gold, and glory of the Portuguese and Spanish to the queen and country of the British. This subtle mixture of Christianity, nationalism, and profiteering was expressed in colonialism, in the bearing of the white man's burden. Western expansion into East Asia, however, took a different pattern because China and then Japan were nations with dynasties which had at least fair title to control of the entire country. The colonial pattern was replaced by one of concessions obtained from titular governments.

From this ideological milieu, it is not surprising that many Westerners would see the Meiji policy of hiring thousands of foreigners from more than two dozen countries as a literal implementation of the 1868 Charter Oath injunction to seek knowledge throughout the world and would see that they, the foreign vanguard, were called upon to lay the foundations of modern nationhood. The fact that the Japanese issued no such call to aliens and that the leaders intended to shore up existing foundations rather than lay new ones introduced an immediate anomaly in relations with foreign employees.

However, the values of a society are borne consciously or unconsciously by its members, so that foreign employees were in large measure culture bearers of late nineteenth-century Western society with its peculiar mixture of profiteering and philanthropy. In a sense this was true of Filipino and Chinese yatoi as well. Many of the foreign employees, especially the better educated, were responding in some sense to the mystique of a call. They saw themselves variously as adventurers in Lotus-land, creators of the New Japan, part of a foreign civil servant corps, and professional collaborators with Japanese bureaucrats. For some employees, some or all of these self-images were present at once.

Foreign employees and Japanese officials, dissimilar in cultural temperament and world view, lived together to their mutual advantage in close and
sometimes prolonged association. Taking part in such a challenging enterprise afforded both of them unique opportunities and evoked various responses from the yatoi. Consciously and unconsciously, they assessed their
own role in this symbiotic experiment, their self-image conditioning the
symbiosis.

SOJOURNERS IN LOTUS-LAND

Yatoi Basil Hall Chamberlain (1873 – 90), angered by the instant views
and instant conclusions of travelling journalists, commented:

There is nothing picturesque in the foreign employé. With his club,
and his tennis-ground, and his brick house, and his wife's piano, and
the European entourage which he strives to create around him in order
sometimes to forget his exile, he strikes a false note. The esthetic and
literary globe-trotter would fain revel in a tea-tray existence for the
nonce, because the very moment he tires of it, he can pack and be off.
The foreign employé cannot treat life so jauntily, for he has to make
his living; and when a man is forced to live in Lotus-land, it is Lotus-
land no longer.[1]

Meiji Japan became a land of opportunity for the ambitious foreigner, for
the man of wit, skill, broad learning, professional specialization and for the
day labourer as well. It became a refuge for the disenchanted and a temporary
haven for the inept. The aura of Lotus-land, with its opportunities for employment and its different mode of life, lingered long into the next century,
when traces of yatoi were being erased, and it revived with the alien corps
which came to design the present New Japan.
    A hundred years ago yatoi Georges Bousquet wrote:

Young students of fine arts build palaces, bank clerks handle large
credits, army captains perform duties which would weigh heavily on
the shoulders of a general, serious counselors with light beards are
called legislators. . . . But it is not only the reign of young people,
the mature also see their sphere of activity enlarged.[2]

Undoubtedly, as the news spread that a nation was being built, the opportunity and challenge of aiding the endeavour drew thousands of foreigners to Japan for trade and employment. The initial years of development were marked by the appearance of the dregs which silt any seaport and of adventurers and ne'er-do-wells who had exhausted the China scene. Kobe resident and local history buff Harold S. Williams has commented delightfully on "instant professors," in quoting from F. V. Dickens's *The Life of Sir Harry Parkes* (1894):

> It is an unalloyed truth to say that the majority of the "Professors" in the schools of Tokei were graduates of the dry-goods counter, the forecastle, the camp, and the shambles, or belonged to the vast array of unclassified humanity that floats like waifs in every seaport. Coming directly from the bar-room, the brothel, the gambling saloon, or the resort of boon companions, they brought the graces, the language and the manners of those places into the school room. . . . Japanese pride revolted . . . after a report had been circulated that one of the professors was a butcher by trade.[3]

But these *ikasama* (honourable frauds) were sifted out as the Japanese gained experience and as standards and regulations were devised. Continued vigilance was required. As William Elliot Griffis has remarked, with some yatoi the Japanese "had their hands full."

The hypnotic lure of silver and gold glittered in the high salaries and fringe benefits provided. When Edward S. Morse urged his friend Ernest Fenollosa to take service with the Japanese government, he explained that with regard to time or money there were no disadvantages. One could save half the salary, enjoy a high standard of living, the contract was renewable, and, afterwards, lectures in the United States would be remunerative.[4]

Yatoi found it possible to bargain with Japanese employers for more than they originally offered, especially in the early years. Any precedent set for another yatoi in service in the same line of work could be claimed. The power of national representatives could be drawn on when necessary. And, even later, professionals pressed for advantage. In the 1880's, the German architect for state buildings, Baurath Boeckmann, in addition to preparation and travel allowances, initially agreed to 60 marks a day compensation for business losses while away from Germany, but as negotiations proceeded the emoluments grew to include a food allowance, then all expenses.[5]

Socially as well as monetarily, service with the Meiji government assured special status as an alien élite. For the educated and able, the mystique of challenge was dominant. Doors closed at home were open in Meiji Japan. The Japanese were avid seekers of information; it was the heyday of the informant. Some yatoi were specifically hired as advisers (komon), but all were invited—in the words of a minor yatoi's contract—to "speak without concealment all . . . [that was] useful and favourable for the Japanese government."[6] Speak they did. The Ōkuma Shigenobu papers are a formidable collection; more than half, in a sense all, consist of information gathered from foreigners in Japan, principally foreign employees and is a major source for yatoi opinions and proposals. Many such collections are extant in government and university library holdings. Every yatoi was expected to be an informal adviser and thus they were encouraged to give full play to their ideas.

Yatoi did not hesitate to address the highest officials or even the emperor himself. Thus, there are available innumerable letters, reports, tracts, books with concrete findings and proposals on subjects ranging from agricultural and industrial development to social and legal institutional revision, and from fish breeding to spying and territorial expansion to appeals for imperial protection of the custom of mixed bathing. Recommendations for private enterprise were included in the geological surveys of Hokkaido by Dr. Benjamin S. Lyman (1872 – 79), in the mining development critiques of Dr. Curt Netto (1873 – 85), and they were implicit in the pioneering of vocational education and the encouragement of local commercial manufacturing by Dr. Gottfried Wagner (1868 – 88). Recommendations for social welfare assistance were included in studies for the improvement of agriculture by Dr. Max Fesca (1882 – 94) and in the dozen books on fire and home insurance and aid to the poverty-stricken farmer by Dr. Paul Mayet (1876 – 91). Many shades of socioeconomic and political views were presented. In this library-building milieu, yatoi could feel they were taking a real part in the new nation. If their advice was ignored, they had the satisfaction of warning high officials of their peril.

Research opportunities abounded. John Milne (1876 – 95), honoured professor at Tokyo Imperial University, was a world pioneer in seismology. William Ayrton (1873 – 78) brought the new field of electricity to Japan. Erwin Knipping (1871 – 91) pioneered weather observation. Research in pharmacology, public health and sanitation, chemistry, physics, and natural science was pursued so diligently by some yatoi and their Japanese students that the Engineering College and the laboratories in many offices were intensive experimental research centres. Opportunities were immediate for improved and experimental techniques to be demonstrated in irrigation and waterworks; in bridge, tunnel, and other construction; in manufacturing; in engraving; and in printing. There was freedom to employ new architectural and engineering designs in the reconstruction of the Ginza area of Tokyo and in public buildings.

In the first decade professional yatoi were, on the average, in their mid to late twenties when they came to Japan; some were fresh from university and some had a few years work experience. Rising to the challenge of building the New Japan, they matured and carved reputations for themselves in academic and other professional fields. For example, Paul Mayet, long-time assistant to Ōkuma and later to Yamagata, earned a doctorate from Tübingen University in the process, his dissertation being an outgrowth of practical work in Japan. Mayet's career is an example of how the Meiji government used yatoi in diverse multiple capacities.[7] His fortunes clearly rose and fell with his first mentor, Ōkuma, and rose again under Yamagata. Yatoi fortunes were sometimes tied closely with those of officials who sponsored them.

Much study is required on individual yatoi; not many appear in national biographies illustrating their later rise to prominence in their home countries. But those who became Tokyo University professors displayed a high degree of competence. Among naval and military yatoi, some later rose even to the high ranks of admiral and general (Douglas, LeBon, Meckel). Others became leaders in government and finance circles at home (Cargill, Williams, Shand). Many used their experience in government service to find other career opportunities in Japan. Captain Frank Brinkley (1867–80), a government and, later, a private employee, became a journalist and editor (*Japan Mail, Yokohama Mail*). The *Japan Mail* he began with a Japanese government subsidy, and that newspaper provided a vehicle by which the Japanese government viewpoint could be presented to the foreign community.[8]

Experimental opportunities and challenges were not limited to the area of technology. Social, educational, and institutional theories not yet accepted in the employee's own country found a home in Japan. Edward S. Morse's teachings on Darwinian evolution and Hermann Roesler's theories on social constitutionalism are two examples of such theories. Morse's teachings not only laid the basis for physical anthropology studies in Japan and account in part for the continued emphasis until recently on the physical rather than the other fields of that social science, but also influenced political theory as well. Morse's ideas also affected zoological and archeological studies. Respected teachers—such as German philosophical idealists and doctors from the German school of medicine—strongly influenced Japanese intellectuals. Western literature and law continued to be pluralistic disciplines. Yatoi such as Chamberlain, Aston, Florenz, Fenollosa, and others revived interest in native classics and art, which, in the midst of foreign borrowing, again became valid fields of study. But endeavours in social reform (of prisons and mental asylums and in women's education) made less progress. It was, however, in the field of political law, and especially international law, that innovation was greatest. Young lawyers and more experienced lawyers brought all their abilities and ideas to bear in interpretations, first in defence of and gradually in the extension of Japan's sovereignty.

A sense of adventure was inherent in the challenge, and on occasion this sense literally surfaced, as in 1874, for example. When Ryūkyū islanders shipwrecked on Taiwan were murdered by natives, no redress was received from China. Resentment was high, and a coterie of Japanese officials, contrary to conservative official policy, undertook military action against the Taiwan natives. The adventure had portents of Japan's awakening interest in its neighbours, an interest which was accelerated by yatoi and manifested in the employment of yatoi down to 1945.

General Charles LeGendre, a Swiss who was a naturalized American, a commander in the U.S. Civil War, and a former U.S. consul in Amoy, came into Meiji service under Ōkuma Shigenobu through the recommendation of U.S. minister Charles DeLong. LeGendre was a general in search of an army, and he found kindred adventurers among Meiji leaders. The punitive expedition against Taiwan could not have taken place if Foreign Minister Soejima, Ōkuma, and the younger Saigō were not of a similar mind. Ōkuma conducted the special office, and LeGendre and Captain A. R. Brown hired the necessary foreign employees.

For the yatoi it was a tragi-comic adventure replete with a code list for espionage against China (Emperor Meiji was codified as "Young America"). Amid charges of corruption in the hasty purchase of steamers such as the S.S. *Kuroda*, which was "no more seaworthy than the sampan that took him [Cassel] to her," yatoi sailors were sworn to be sober, diligent, and obey the orders of the captain. Disease decimated seamen and soldiers, and Japanese conscripts did not share yatoi enthusiasm. After the expedition, yatoi were paid handsome stipends; in Commander Douglas Cassel's case the stipend was paid to his heirs. LeGendre and other yatoi participants had been harried by the British and American ministers for joining the expedition and had rejected their jurisdiction. After the adventure, LeGendre received from a friend in the Bureau of Navigation of the U.S. Navy Department a congratulatory message which concluded:

This should make the "diplomatists" who opposed their going to Formosa ashamed of themselves. The expedition to Formosa was capital too, as a school of instruction and will be most useful if an expedition is designed against Corea. I feel sure Mr. Bingham received instructions to have in his horns in relation to you and our countrymen not actually in our Military or Naval services.[9]

For Terajima and the majority of Japanese modernizers, the venture was both premature and a diplomatic embarrassment, but for the Japanese and yatoi participants in the expedition, it was an ankle-deep dip into adventure. One of the translator-interpreters hired for office duties summed up the esprit de corps when he wrote Ōkuma that he quite understood the office being closed, but he was "in time of peace as in time of war a person entirely devoted to the Japanese government."[10] Gaston Galy was soon after hired by the Seiin. LeGendre became Ōkuma's private secretary, and most other yatoi returned to their mundane contract duties in the shipping bureaus.

Growing out of the expedition was the long relationship of an American, E. W. House, with Ōkuma Shigenobu. House, acquainted with Ōkuma from the early 1870's, accompanied the expedition as secretary and reporter. His interest in Japan never abated. His precise relationship with Ōkuma is yet to be determined, but his reports were sent to Ōkuma from all the countries in which he had journalistic and diplomatic entrée. In effect he became a free-lance adviser, apprising Ōkuma of attitudes abroad about Japan, praising those with pro-Japanese positions, blaming those impeding Japan, and conveying scraps of gossip from inner circles of government.[11] House well illustrates a distinct type of yatoi, many in number, who were emotionally committed to Japan's nation-building.

Coinciding with events which triggered the 1874 expedition and its international repercussions, reconnaissance of Chinese diplomatic and strategic operations was necessary. At least from the mid-1870's, there were a half dozen yatoi who, in addition to their regular work, were paid to spy in China and in other foreign embassies. Iwakura, Ōkubo, and Ōkuma were among the officials who made these arrangements. Persons from the foreign business and diplomatic community were used most often. Among yatoi, those who can be identified by name are Francis Elgar, a Navy employee and John Pitman, a Finance Ministry employee.[12]

Challenge and opportunity attracted the yatoi, but once in Japan other factors became dominant as well. One can only guess at the motivation for one yatoi's going to Japan, taking along a stout coffin for harried officials to store in a "safe" place because he was going to stay in Japan until he died, but social tolerance and cultural enchantment were other attractions of Lotus-land. Japanese society then as now was far more tolerant of social excesses, such as over-indulgence in wine and women, than the home countries of late nineteenth-century yatoi. Drunkenness was routinely accepted unless the condition totally incapacitated the yatoi for duty. Navy officials, loathe to lose a single yatoi, protested Commander Douglas's dismissal of seaman Timothy Cripple for drunkenness and relented only after a thorough explanation of the danger to discipline.[13] The chronic alcoholism of Major A. G. Warfield, a railway engineer in Hokkaido (1871 – 72), was tolerated because he was competent and well-liked when sober, but Hokkaido Commission officials were forced to take action against him when he became violent.[14]

Prostitutes and mistresses were readily available. Prostitutes, however, were not to be brought into living compounds. When two Kaisei school instructors who maintained a male Japanese procurer in their quarters were attacked by samurai while strolling outside the compound with prostitutes, one of them, Charles H. Dallas, was able to retain the current lady during convalescence. While the fate of the other instructor, whose surname was Ring, has not been learned, Dallas was transferred to Yonezawa Prefecture and continued to be employed despite the fact that he brought the attack on himself by violating rules for his personal safety.[15] To keep Japanese mistresses, the permission of government officials was necessary, and those officials in turn reported to the Foreign Ministry whether the yatoi had a wife or children in Japan.[16] Foreigners desiring to cohabit with Japanese women were advised by local procurers to trim their beards because of the Japanese distaste for hairiness. Early newspaper reports suggested that a man's morals could be judged by his hirsuteness. An American naval officer with Perry had made the same comment, but photographs of Itō Hirobumi, for example, argue against the suggested handicap.

Some yatoi, and foreigners in general, became enamoured of this greater social freedom. Erastus Peshine Smith cut a flamboyant figure, indulging in both wine and women. Not all officials were pleased; there is also a sedate and decorous streak in many Japanese. Terajima Munenori, for example, was mortified at the sight of the elderly Smith on horseback clasping his young mistress to his bosom. The lady's being clad in a bright red *hakama* (trouser-skirt) made the picture more spirited. Smith also wore samurai dress and the two swords even though Japanese officials had already foregone them. Smith's outspoken castigation of the foreign community caused him to be ridiculed—he was labelled a "crapulous dotard"—in the English-language press. On one occasion, he was hauled into the U.S. Consular Court, under his successor, Sheppard, for his failure to register as an American citizen. His flippant responses and refusal to admit citizenship earned him public disgust among foreigners, and his "malign influences" in Japanese foreign affairs were decried.

Yet it was this Smith who in 1871 was enjoined by the emperor (*chokugo*) to clarify the course of Japan's future relations with foreign countries, which he did with élan. It was his criticism which prevented the hasty treaty revision in 1872 which would have given concessions to the United States with inevitable ramifications within the treaty system. It was he, among other yatoi lawyers, who defended the Japanese position on the Taiwan expedition. He was also responsible for at least three major treaty revision drafts and clear statements on the quid pro quo in international law. His enthusiasm on Japan's behalf moved a Japanese official to remark to Iwakura Tomomi that he would like to see Japanese officials imbued with Smith's spirit. Smith, he commented, worked hard, was always helpful, and had confided that he would work for and die in Japan. However, at the end of Smith's five-year contract, Terajima replaced him with a more sedate yatoi.[17]

There were many yatoi whose identification with Japan was, in various degrees, deep and permanent. Many, like Alfred Roper a seaman who had been taken on for the Taiwan venture, married and settled in Japan. Roper wrote Ōkuma for another job because he had purchased a home in Nagasaki and had chosen Japan as his adopted country.[18] A fascinating character, named James Matthew James (1872–86), a British navigator, appears in innumerable Public Works, Navy, and later shipping bureau records and is listed sometimes as *Saru* (monkey) James and sometimes as *Shinagawa* James. He was given sōnin status treatment in 1886 and was very popular with the Japanese whom he trained. There are frequent allusions to him in newspapers and memoirs of the time as a Nichiren Buddhist, active, laughing, with a *juzu* (a circlet of prayer beads) on his wrist.

A paternal kindness still observable in Japanese social relations on occasion moved the Japanese to acts of kindness towards former yatoi remaining in Japan, especially elderly teachers. Even Alexander P. Porter, the former Hakodate harbour master who caused such a furor in 1875 by tearing up his second appointment contract and appealing for redress through the British minister, was aided financially. Porter unsuccessfully tried various ventures over the years and in his declining years, Japanese businessmen and officials arranged to pay his back taxes and other debts.[19]

Japanese laws on mixed marriage were modified, and some employees married their Japanese wives, a few even in Christian church services. A very few did the totally unprecedented and took their Japanese spouses back with them to their home countries. The sculptor Vincenzo Ragusa was virtually unknown when he came to Japan, but he returned to Italy and later became famous for the Garibaldi statue in Palermo and the San Carlo Opera House figures in Naples. His striking busts of Japanese fishermen and farmers in the Naples Museum illustrate his genius and his love for Japan. His Japanese wife was also a talented painter. Ragusa requested and obtained government service again at the beginning of the Taishō period. After his death, his wife returned to Japan.

Dr. Erwin von Baelz took his Japanese wife and children back to Germany on his retirement. Baelz, as his diary and his son attest, made a sincere effort to understand cultural disparities and stressed the necessity for language study and for living abroad a long time in order to change oneself. Anything thought strange or ridiculed in another culture reflected one's own lack of understanding.[20] Baelz's approach to Japanese society and culture was intellectual, but his meeting with Japan was an emotional experience. Among the yatoi he perhaps came closest to desiring the wedding of cultures.

Total cultural identification was achieved by some yatoi. Ernest Fenollosa (1878 – 90) is the most well-known example. Whereas yatoi as a whole were culture bearers, Fenollosa became a culture preserver. Responsible yatoi, in responding to the challenge and allure of Japan, desired to bring the best of their own culture and preserve the best of Japanese culture. They cautioned the Japanese against losing their cultural identity in the inundation of foreign borrowing. Some, such as Fenollosa, emphasized preservation over importation.

As commissioner of fine arts for the Education Ministry, he had courses in Japanese art and painting reinstituted in schools and opposed the unselective introduction of Western art and manners. By 1884, the government was made aware through his efforts of the importance of safeguarding Japan from the utter depletion of its works of art by foreign collectors, many of whom were yatoi. He was even instrumental in getting some items returned, but major Western collections date from the early Meiji era. Though Fenollosa died on a trip abroad, his ashes were returned to Japan the following year and interred in Miidera.[21] His activities coincided with a reaction by conservative elements in Japanese society against extreme Europeanization. So, at a crucial time, Westerners like him helped reinforce the swing of the cultural pendulum from an alien to a native institutional emphasis.

Japan's hold on yatoi was multifaceted. There was in Japan the challenge of service, the experience of an alien culture, and the employment opportunity unavailable at home. There was the cosmopolitan life of the foreign community as a separate society—the semi-colonial social syndrome. There was the simpler life with a Japanese spouse in the local native community. For the yatoi, in terms of income and status, the latter alternative was no less élite than the former; both were very different from the prosaic life at home. Judging from the length of time some yatoi remained, one can see that the hold exercised by Japan was strong, and many continued association with Japan on their return, becoming self-appointed interpreters of Japan to their own countries. For many, whatever their self-images, Japan was indeed Lotus-land.

CREATORS OF THE NEW JAPAN

In the early Meiji period, an Englishman so frail in health that he could not complete a formal university programme took a sea voyage to Japan. There in the feverish activity of nation-building Basil Hall Chamberlain (1873 – 90) found his niche and his health. He was first taken on as an English teacher in the Navy school, but he showed such remarkable proclivity for the Japanese language that later (1886) he moved to Tokyo Imperial University as a lecturer in Japanese language and linguistics. In 1891 he was named honoured professor. His studies of early Japanese society and his translations of classical texts are still distinguished today. In one of several books about things Japanese, Chamberlain commented: "From that time [1850's and 1860's] dates the appearance in this country of a new figure—the foreign employé; and the foreign employé is the creator of the New Japan."[22] This hypothesis was not unique to Chamberlain. Many yatoi saw themselves as emissaries of their national culture. As might be expected, they were intelligent, well-educated, and for the most part possessed solid background experience. Some with this self-image, perhaps with a sense of their own importance and more than a touch of their own cultural pride, literally boasted that they had come as "creators of the New Japan."

From the Japanese viewpoint, foreigners were employed as "tutors," by and large, even when in their contracts they were given the title "adviser" (komon) or when as heads of construction projects their contracts conferred the title "director" (*shuchō*) upon them. The service of some was marked more by conflict than by the accommodation one would expect of a tutor. Yatoi placed in administrative charge of other yatoi were usually competent and sincere in getting the job done, but the attitudes and methods of some were more like some kinds of prefects and senior monitors in the British public school system.[23] The analogy has a factual basis, since most foreign employees were products of a British education and society, though not necessarily of the public schools. Prefects, according to Rupert Wilkinson:

> ran house activities and helped legislate rules; they kept order, judged offences, and often did the punishing themselves. They were, in short, an administration, a judiciary, and a part of the legislature rolled into one. . . . Nominated by housemaster, headmaster, or their own number, prefects enjoyed a tenure of office that was virtually unshakeable.[24]

The thesis Wilkinson develops is that the public school ethos of restraint and conformity, based on a sense of class and common educational background, brought to public offices generation after generation of persons of the same pattern. In particular, he discusses British civil servants in India, among whom the concept of national glory was coupled with philanthropy. The ideal was "tactful management, the light touch and a background hint of force." If the civil servant "dedicated himself to his subjects, he usually did so as a superior being," and there was a "marked tendency to equate cultural differences with difference in status."[25] While the analogy ought not to be pressed, there were yatoi to whom these remarks apply, especially among heads of missions. The expansionist and colonialist spirit was still strong and influenced many yatoi.

In the bakumatsu era, François Verny was one of the first foreign employees to be invested with the title of director (shuchō). A French naval officer and marine engineer with solid experience in shipbuilding and repair in the Shanghai dockyards, he was selected by French minister Léon Roches in the arrangement made with the bakufu to erect dockyards and a foundry modelled on that in Toulon (two-thirds its size). According to the written agreement, the French were in charge, and bakufu officials only made amendments in the area of finance. Literally, only the director was to deal with direction. Verny was in charge of the Japanese workers and, initially, of some forty French workers, though the latter had the right of appeal to the French minister.[26]

Bakufu officials, however, did not strike deferential postures in their relations with the French director. Volatile exchanges took place with Japanese officials, and Verny made many protests to Roches. Verny maintained that the four ranking Japanese officials fiddled accounts, absented themselves from important duties without consulting with him, contravened work orders, and instigated disobedience among the Japanese workers. When, on occasion, Verny exercised his right to dismiss Japanese officials for insubordination and malpractice, they refused to accept his decisions. Verny begged to employ persons of lower rank who were amenable to instruction and the transfer of high-ranking officials to duties more worthy of their status.[27]

The French minister supported Verny's position and hinted he might "put an end to the mission of M. Verny and of all the French employees in the dockyard." As administrative problems continued, Roches castigated the "unsuitable attitude of certain *yakunin*" in a letter to senior councillors (*rōjū*). He concluded:

> Prolongation of this actual state of affairs at Yokosuka will leave me with the sad necessity of rendering account to my government and asking the recall to France of the officers which it placed at the disposition of the Japanese government for a mission which the ill-will of subaltern employees has rendered impossible of completion with advantage for Japan and with dignity for their own character.[23]

The Roches correspondence, which illustraes the foreign pressure generated, evoked assurances from bakufu councillors that these problems would be resolved. These personnel and administrative problems reveal a bifurcation of attitudes between governing officials and administrative bureaucrats. The latter found it difficult to accommodate native pride and class orientation to what had been intended as a new learning situation. Verny, for his part, rejected interference in his legally defined sphere; he was apparently as strict with French workers as with the Japanese, but he had a reputation for fairness. The transformation in attitudes undergone by Verny in the early Meiji period was due largely to Terajima Munenori and a new breed of modernizers. Verny was quite willing to accept a reduced administrative role when the legal contract was altered to that effect.

In the Meiji era there were other yatoi who experienced similar tensions. Richard Henry Brunton engaged for lighthouse construction and the coastal survey, had been a railway engineer with five years' experience. After being selected for the position in Japan, he spent some time with the Scottish Lighthouse Board in preparation. He then proceeded to Japan with two assistants, the number of whom soon rose to twenty-five.[29] His contract designated him chief of lighthouse construction (*tōdai shuin*).

From the outset, although Brunton admired Itō Hirobumi and Ōkuma Shigenobu and sought them out, there was friction between him and the Japanese officials with whom he was supposed to work. He clearly identified himself with his superiors and not with his peers. In a manuscript record of his experiences, Brunton reveals the tension faced by many yatoi in administrative positions:

The conscientious and efficient conduct of new work in Japan was a task which presented the most perplexing difficulties both to employers and employed. Their high pay, their different mode of living, their want of disciplinary power, and the knowledge of the Japanese that foreigners were more or less indispensable to them, rendered their European assistants most impracticable and difficult to deal with. Resignation, insubordination, absence from duty, drunkenness, and other aberrations of conduct among Europeans employed in the Japanese Government service, became frequent, and distressing. On the other hand, the semi-ignorance of the native servants of the Emperor, and the self-esteem, untrustworthiness, craftiness and corruption of the Japanese underlings rendered cooperation by an honorable foreigner with them extremely irritating.

In dealing with the Japanese officers who considered themselves my employers, it soon became apparent that I must perforce choose one of two lines of conduct.

The first choice, which promised quietude and repose, was to let things take their course, give advice when asked for, feeling undisturbed if this was neglected, and to become imbued with the Oriental estimation of the valuelessness of time, allowing nothing that hinders progress to perturb or annoy. Such was the method in the seventies, by which the European could become a favorite with his Japanese employer; and such, it is to be feared, was the mode adopted by most of these entering the Government service, with the natural result, that much of the early work done caused scandal and opprobrium.

The other method was an insistence by the European official employed, of a due enforcement of his directions; he being, from the position in which he had been placed, responsible for results. While such a line of conduct would go far to ensure the execution of the appointed work, according to the ideas of the person in charge, it was almost certain to create friction, ending possibly in rupture of relations. It was evident that the Japanese had made up their minds to make what use they could of their foreign servants, but in no case to have them become masters, or to invest them with any power. They would hold them in the position of advisers and instructors only, without the authority to direct.

Besides feeling the indignity of remaining in such a position, I formed a clear opinion that it would certainly tend to an unsatisfactory execution of work. I came therefore to a decision, that, at whatever personal discomfort and self-sacrifice, I should assert my position as the responsible conductor of operations.

A further consideration presented itself to my mind, viz.:—that while other works undertaken by the Japanese Government may have been their own domestic concerns, the construction of lighthouses, which had been intrusted to me, was a work covenanted for in solemn treaties, and was in the interests of humanity at large. I felt myself therefore responsible to foreign Powers as well as to my immediate employers.[30]

Sincerity, dedication, and pride are evident in the above excerpt. Brunton intended to run activities, to legislate, and to judge. His first loyalty was to his headmaster, British Minister Parkes, who nominated him. His brusqueness and authoritarian manner alienated his British as well as his Japanese associates, and most of the original crew found positions in other bureaus of the Public Works Ministry.[31] Brunton also had genuine problems to contend with over and above those caused by his own personality. During his stay in Japan, there was a change of officials about every six months in the Lighthouse Bureau. This lack of continuity, combined with the fact that he was kept ignorant of finances, impeded his work. At times his legitimate work orders were countermanded, and on occasion he was obliged to withdraw directives he had issued without permission from Japanese officials. His efforts to establish an efficient operation and his attempts to adhere to a time-table met with frustration, and he commented with chagrin that "The complete indifference to time and to the exigencies of circumstances which at this period was so characteristic of Japanese in all their dealings did not seem to be much interfered with by the French yatoi, or 'hired' foreigners."[32] It took Verny several years to reach a modus vivendi, but Brunton never came to terms with the Japanese.

As Brunton attempted to assume a director's prerogatives and as Japanese officials asserted their managerial function, friction was inevitable. At last Brunton did get one of the new bureaucrats as bureau chief—the able Sano Tsunetami, who had studied abroad. Sano was co-operative and Brunton recognized him as a gentleman. Brunton, however, mistook Sano's reserve and quiet manner for weakness and at length discussed the "foibles of the man." Actually, Sano simply refused to react to Brunton's aggressiveness. He was understanding because he worked under the same limitations as Brunton in his efforts at co-ordination with other government offices.

In other offices as well, there were open conflicts with foreign directors. Major Thomas W. Kinder, director (shuchō) of the Mint, was a metallurgical engineer with considerable experience. He, too, considered himself in full charge and was a hard taskmaster for Japanese trainees. Over and above the routine constant transfers of Japanese officials, he literally fatigued a series of Japanese bureau heads and intimidated foreign employees as well.[33]

The type of temper exacerbated by frustration so evident in Kinder was seen also in Commander Archibald L. Douglas. His competence was without question. He came to a situation bordering on chaos, where students (samurai) obeyed neither regulations nor teachers, and he revised regulations and established a basic curriculum for modern naval education which included half-time academic and half-time practical instruction. Insisting that future officers undergo the same training as seamen, he instituted regular ocean navigation courses on training ships. Despite the fact that Japanese officials Nakamuta Kuranosuke and Kawamura Sumiyoshi both had been trained in their youth by the Dutch and that both were committed to the use of foreign instructors (Nakamuta at least shared Douglas's stern sense of discipline), these officials balked at Douglas's attempts to involve himself in everything, including ministry administrative decisions, which they reserved to themselves. For his part, Douglas informed the Japanese that they had no right to refuse his advice because the British had not come as mere tutors but to "create" a new Japanese navy. Virtually ignored by and isolated from Japanese officials, Douglas withdrew early from his contract.

Actually, in two years of hard work he made a solid contribution to the foundation of the naval training programme. In later years, when Douglas had risen to admiral and had occasion to receive high officials from Japan, his comments indicated that he was still ruffled by the experience.[34] In a sense, that conflict was one of character: Nakamuta and Douglas were both ramrods. Neither gave in, but neither could avoid having a grudging respect for the competence of the other.

Likewise, when General Horace Capron (1871 – 75) was U.S. commissioner of agriculture he had a good record in agricultural experimentation, but as adviser to the Hokkaido Development Commission (Kaitakushi) he provoked quarrels with his foreign staff, driving most of them to other yatoi jobs. He quarrelled with lower Japanese officials, though he maintained rapport with Commissioner Kuroda Kiyotaka. A lack of administrative coordination was his principal obstacle and it afflicted his Japanese counterpart as well. Capron complained that he was supposed to know everything from the "formation of government to physicking a sick animal," but when he asked a question he was turned away and never informed of how much money was allotted for a project. He charged that he was criticized and made a scapegoat of the Commission's "useless supernumeraries"; money was spent on expensive buildings for these incompetents instead of on soil improvement and other projects as he directed. Yet the successes he outlined were due to his labour.[35]

A brilliant young German geologist, Edmund Naumann (1875 – 85), who taught at Tokyo University until he was transferred to the soil analysis section in the Home Ministry, evoked admiration for his intelligence and industry and fear for his temper and tongue. He did not hesitate to beat Japanese trainees and brawled with other yatoi over women. On his return to Germany he gave a series of lectures about Japan in which he castigated Japan's social backwardness, with respect to the position of women as servants and sex objects, for example, although he availed himself of these amenities while in Japan, and Japan's superficial modernizing. The novelist Mori Ōgai, then a student in Germany, attended some of these lectures and found them offensive. (Sample joke: How is it possible for a Japanese ship to circle around so soon after training was initiated? Answer: The Japanese learned how to start the engine but not how to turn it off.) More than objecting to the ridicule of the Japanese experiment, Mori objected to Naumann's conclusion that Japan's awakening was not the result of Japanese endeavour but of the contributions made by foreign assistants.[36]

Other yatoi, who in Chamberlain's sense of the term styled themselves creators of the New Japan, did so with humility and accommodation— qualities the Japanese appreciate. They viewed themselves as catalysts for the release of Japanese energies and believed their role was to guide those energies with sound advice. From his balanced criticisms of Meiji development,

Chamberlain himself appears to have been one of these catalysts. He recognized that the final responsibility for implementing advice rested with the Japanese. Yatoi of this type were overseas civil servants but in the style of gentleman managers and helpers. With their rational accommodation and their recognition of the Japanese decision-making role, they established fruitful rapport with the Japanese.

William W. Cargill, director of the government railways and telegraphs (in Japanese *sahaiyaku*, or superintendent), was one of these. As the highest paid yatoi, at $2,000 a month, he was obviously a shrewd businessman, able to negotiate such a salary because he was an administrator for the Oriental Bank Corporation in Yokohama which arranged funding, purchasing, and hiring. He was an able and experienced man and on his return to England entered politics and became a member of Parliament.

Ōkuma and others were impressed by Cargill's competence and courtesy. He was a dedicated public servant and is the only employee to have been officially referred to as "indispensable."[37] In 1871, before assuming his duties, he conferred with Ōkuma Shigenobu on the entire operation and then requested the appointment of a Commissioner of Railways; he suggested

a Japanese gentleman of sufficient rank and importance to insure implicit obedience. He will have to deal with persons of every rank in life and should possess good judgment and if possible be able to speak English. He will be required to give prompt decisions on matters not admitting of delay and must therefore possess the perfect confidence of the government. The office will be no sinecure and ought to be well paid and whoever is elected to fill it should now be prepared to begin the duties before the line is ready for opening.

This officer will be wholly occupied with Railway and Telegraph Affairs and cannot take up other branches of Public Works which will require a separate Commissioner and he will I presume communicate directly with the Public Works Minister.[38]

The very capable Inoue Masaru was appointed. Having studied abroad and being proficient in English, Inoue worked well with Cargill and the administrative liaison (manager) with the Oriental Bank, John Robertson. Cargill was clearly director only of the foreign staff. Inoue gradually assumed direction of them as well, but he suffered the same frustrations that befell Wilkinson's prefect-type yatoi and resigned to protest the lack of Japanese official co-ordination and the lack of support of higher officials. He informed Cargill of his decision as follows:

Railway Office
Tokio June 1873

Dear Sir,

I beg to announce to you my having this day forwarded to the Imperial government my resignation for the official position held by me as Chief Commissioner of the Imperial Government Railways which no doubt will be accepted when further notice of change will be sent to you. Meanwhile you will consider that office as no longer mine and for the present vacant.

Although with great reluctance, I have deemed it necessary to resign in the hope that this department may be placed in charge of some able officer who knowing the onerous and important position he holds may be able to show and carry out the changes so necessary at present in bringing the body of the executive staff in closer and direct contact with such high officers of the government entrusted with full powers to exercise their discretion and decide without so much loss of time, the many and varied requirements of this most important national undertaking.

During my tenure of office, it has been a source of great pleasure to observe with what confidence and good will the managers and yourself as Director have invariably assisted the government, a similar spirit having been invariably displayed by the gentlemen of the foreign staff. Their unanimous support has bestowed on me merits which otherwise I could not have had the fortune to deserve, begging you to accept my sincere thanks and to convey the same to the gentlemen of the Foreign Staff.

I remain, dear Sir,

Yours faithfully,
Enoye Masaru

To: W. W. Cargill, Esq.
Director of Railways, etc.[39]

On hearing of Inoue's resignation, John Robertson of the Oriental Bank wrote to commiserate with him (July 2, 1873):

I am unwilling to criticize the action of your government, but I cannot help saying that the changes of officials after they have become acquainted with a department is most perplexing and in my opinion a great loss to the country.

I have observed in your countrymen what without doubt is extraordinary ability and keen observation but chiefly however as regards theories. In the practical test they fall short and in their haste and ambition they commit the most serious blunders.

It is this that makes me dread any changes in the Railway and if I were your Master I would not accept your resignation but would let you have full swing in a work of which I know you are fond and well qualified to perform.[40]

Cargill also responded to Inoue:

The admirable manner in which you have hitherto discharged the duties of your office, the spirit you have infused into different branches of this important Department, the discipline and regularity you have established among the Japanese officers and employees under your charge, and the good feeling you have at all times displayed in your intercourse with the Foreign Staff have not been unappreciated and I beg to assure you that in my opinion, the very satisfactory working of the open line is entirely due to yourself and to qualities you have displayed in guiding and instructing those under you.

This, I may be allowed to add is a matter of no ordinary importance looking at the Railway as a means of training the habits of those employed on it as well as those who use it, and so successful has been the result that the Tokio and Yokohama Railway will bear a favorable comparison with any similar line in any part of the world.[41]

In his resignation protest, Inoue sought and received the support of the foreign advisers. The resignation was not accepted, and Inoue redoubled his efforts, though a strain in relations with Home Minister Ōkubo Toshimichi was apparent. Cargill restricted his control to finances as Inoue made steady inroads in the supervision and reduction of the foreign staff. Technological and administrative problems continued, with attendant criticism. Yatoi Brunton declared: "The main cause for this somewhat deplorable condition of affairs [poor quality of construction, delays, and excessive costs as described by Brunton] was that the European staff engaged to direct operations, headed by Mr. Cargill, supinely permitted the interference of the native officials with their operation."[42] But yatoi engineer Edmund G. Holtham, who advanced to head of the Tokyo office after being assigned to field work, assessed both the railways and telegraph projects successes; all other projects he saw simply as a transfer of public funds to private pockets. He had great admiration for Inoue, not only for his leadership but for his strict financial accounting.[43]

Cargill's grasp of the workings of government administration and bureaucracy enabled him, as an administrator-adviser, to work with rather than against the bureaucratic tide. Another like him was reference-adviser George B. Williams (1871 – 75). Formerly deputy commissioner of Customs in Washington, D.C., and a banker, Williams was employed in the Finance Ministry and worked closely with Ōkuma Shigenobu. Some thirty-three folios of his reports are extant. He contributed much to the modernization of the coinage system, banking laws, and the patent structure in Japan, as well as participating in loan negotiations for the Japanese government.[44]

Yatoi were looked upon as a brains trust of Western knowledge, and research yatoi such as Williams provided information on topics as diverse as the mixed court system in Egypt, American companies which had declared bankruptcy, Russia's 1875 budget, and American internal revenue laws.[45] Williams, like some other yatoi (especially Americans in the 1870's) brought to Japan a fresh perspective of the international scene and encouraged the Japanese to assert their sovereignty within their own borders. Williams, like other yatoi of the time, was criticized for this position by both foreign representatives and some other yatoi. He nevertheless appears to have been a professional person in every sense.

Yet another yatoi in the position of practical instructor-adviser made a solid contribution in banking development. Alexander A. Shand came to Japan as a secretary with the Oriental Bank; in 1874 he was engaged by the new Bank Bureau in the Japanese Finance Ministry. Shand taught practical banking procedures and edited many books for the use of Japanese trainees. Quiet in his personal relationships, he worked conscientiously to establish sound banking principles and methods and to train the Japanese. Takahashi Korekiyo, later Finance Minister, was one of his most able students. Shand worked with Shibusawa Eiichi to establish a new banking system and in later years as a bank director in England he continued his assistance by making loans to Japan.[46]

Whereas the Wilkinson prefect-type yatoi failed in tension management, the tutors—administrative, research, or practical instructors, whatever their designated positions—provided a professional civil servant touch, "tactful management" without "a background hint of force." The Japanese were quick to react to even a hint of intimidation.

It is interesting in this civil servant context to consider a yatoi, who after his service, designated himself a yatoi historian and an interpreter of Japan and the Japanese to the rest of the world. Returning to the United States after his employment as a science teacher in Fukui and Tokyo, William Elliot Griffis became an avid collector of information about yatoi.[47] He circulated a printed postcard addressed to yatoi to solicit information about their activities before and after their service. His notes were never organized and are far from complete, but they provided live material for his many writings and offer a patchwork quilt of insights which reveal perhaps even more about Griffis himself than about the yatoi phenomenon as a whole. A recent biographer has presented Griffis in his role as helper in the educational milieu of the early Meiji era.[48]

In 1877 Griffis aired his views on the role of foreign employees:

> In accordance with the oath of the mikado in Kioto, in 1868 . . . about four hundred foreigners from many countries, have been in the Civil Service of the Government. All these with but two exceptions, are simply helpers and servants, not commissioned officers, and have no actual authority. To their faithful and competent advisers they [the Japanese] award a fair measure of confidence and cooperation. To the worthless, nepotic, or those who would play the lord over their employers, they quietly pay salary and snub.[49]

Later, in 1919, he defined a yatoi as a "salaried foreign expert"; perhaps hindsight refined the image.[50] Griffis considered himself one of the "first of 5 or possibly 6000 of the yatoi (1869 – 1919) called out from a foreign country under the imperial oath to serve Japan, and the only one from America to go into the interior and live within the mysteries of feudalism . . . ." He then describes the yatoi:

> Then followed in quick succession the vanguard of . . . yatoi. They came as individuals, by groups, and in large commissions. To meet, welcome, and make comfortable and set these aliens to work, the Mikado's advisers and statesmen mostly young men of amazing energy were soon very busy. With some temperaments and characters they had their hands full.
>
> How did employers and employed get along with each other. Surely there is no finer art than that of living together. Not a shred of political power was given the foreigners, but all were paid well. Those aliens who tried to be masters failed miserably . . . . Those who accepted their work fully, honestly and in the spirit of brotherly help (servants) succeeded so they became masters even of their employers.
>
> It was in fact easy for the quiet, modest, discerning and forceful man

to see into and through the Japanese system which so puzzles outsiders, and especially the ultra-egoists, even today.[51]

Both comments, written forty years apart, illustrate Griffis's conviction that foreign employees had been called out under the Charter Oath and that the respected ones had answered the call in a spirit which made them masters of their employers. Chamberlain, of course, had correctly noted the advent of the foreign employee in the bakumatsu era. How much the self-styled modest and forceful man entered into the spirit Griffis describes is difficult to ascertain.

He was a fine tutor in Fukui, but despite the fact that his memory is very much alive in Fukui, surely due in part to his return visit in the 1920's just before his death, his sojourn in Tokyo was marred by conflicts in teaching, caused by his temper and his ready hand, and in contract negotiations. Of course, there is a definite theme perceived in yatoi accounts of the different atmosphere in the countryside (enthusiasm, receptivity, a slower pace) in contrast to the hectic capital where foreigners were more numerous and officials and students more self-confident and sceptical.

Griffis's broad interests and commitment to teaching were typical of most yatoi teachers. Perhaps in the overview these lesser-known yatoi contributed more to Japanese social and academic development than did the major advisers. The base of contact of the former was more personal and less subject to official alteration and obliteration than was the work of some advisers. If one looks at short-timers, one should consider the effect of William S. Clark's nine months in the Sapporo Agricultural School. "Boys Be Ambitious" is a phrase still known to every Japanese today, and the Sapporo band of Christians exerted its influence. Edward S. Morse served only two years and two months, but his name and influence remains. In America their academic reputations were not very different than that of Griffis.

Like most foreigners, Griffis was fascinated by the rapid changes transforming Japan. He was active in the group of Meiji intellectuals attending the Meiji Six meetings (*Meirokusha*) and in the Asiatic Society of Japan, in which early studies of Japanese culture and society owed much to yatoi membership. However, in his papers one cannot miss the implications of Griffis and other foreign employees that yatoi contributed more to the New Japan than would have been admitted by Meiji officials who relegated them to a role as servants. Yatoi were fond of titles for short essays that included words like "Makers" or "Creators" of "New Japan."

Although an admirer of Samuel Robbins Brown and Guido F. Verbeck, both of whom were missionaries and fairly long-term yatoi, Griffis had little patience for the usual gospel minister in Japan. He had that touch of secularism which was already congealing the edges of protestant evangelism in the late nineteenth century. Like most yatoi, though very moral in his personal life, he valued his own "broader" outlook. Yet in his grasp of the role of the yatoi, a sense of mission was implicit. He was a product of his times, in which an evangelical element permeated political philosophy, so blatant in end-of-the-century manifest destiny doctrine, for example. Griffis was in many attitudinal ways typical of a host of yatoi who were conscious culture-bearers. They left both tangible and intangible contributions which should be pursued in depth for a better understanding of the Meiji experiment.

COLLABORATORS FOR THE MEIJI STATE

All yatoi were tutors. Even when they were moved to offer adverse critic-ism of policy, those who saw themselves as professional civil servants never questioned the Japanese official function and right to make final decisions. Those in responsible positions in education, technology, and government fulfilled significant "sub-leadership" roles. While the sub-leader appellation should perhaps be reserved to Japanese bureaucrats, by presenting the options and often by channelling the preferred option, yatoi conditioned the deci-sions of Japanese bureaucrats.

In technology, some officials who were enthusiastically receptive to foreign importation were also remarkably willing to experiment and innovate. Over-all, the emphasis placed in areas of economic development served the in-terests of national sovereignty. A somewhat narrow response may be noted also in formal academic education, perhaps the most difficult area of foreign borrowing, involving as it does cultural assumptions and theoretical bases. In government and finance, any plan or policy had to have promise of en-hancing political independence, but innovation was sought and expected. In summary, whereas trusted yatoi bureaucrats were without question decision-conditioners, Japanese bureaucrats defined the framework of decisions.

These yatoi saw themselves as co-operators with Japanese bureaucrats. Some were able so to respond to the Japanese because of temperament, com-petence, and position that they enjoyed a special relationship with certain Japanese officials. Some were designated consultants or advisers. But this designation as "komon" was not essential and varied in significance. After the débacle in personnel relations in the Mint, Edward Dillon, William Gow-land, and Robert Maclagen were promoted to komon, which meant that in addition to their own work each took on several other sections. It would ap-pear that in technology, if one defines an advisory role as one which provides the overview and designs the specifics therein, other than General Horace

Capron and several outstanding yatoi in agriculture, there were no genuine advisers. This circumstance may indicate the limitations in the Meiji industrial technology programme. Foreign advisers in industry and in technological administration, however successful in specific operations, appear to have been unable to expand the parameters of their role. In education the term komon was not applied, but David Murray, in revising the national education system, and Ernest Fenollosa, in co-ordinating fine arts education, both of whom were called commissioners in English and supervisors in Japanese, were genuine advisers as were a hundred or more in agriculture, finance, and law.

On a conceptual level, all yatoi, whatever their function or education, may perhaps be separated into two broad groups—informants and advisers. Advisers were an élite within an élite. For many yatoi this position was an extra-contractual commitment. Advisers were asked not only to provide factual and theoretical advice and written proposals but also overviews of their area of expertise. They were to call attention to omissions in the area in which they were consulted, and they were also expected to bring attention to potential problems. Perhaps those advisers dealing directly with government matters best illustrate an élite even among the co-operators. Some of them actually saw themselves as collaborators for the benefit of the Meiji state. These were of two categories: early general advisers and later legal specialists.

The activities of the Meiji government during the Council of State era (Dajōkan *jidai*) encompassed a broad range of objectives. It is not surprising then that this formative period was also an era of general advisers, men who, in the words of Griffis, "stood to the new government in the place of the great corps of legal advisers which were afterwards assembled."[52] Of several general advisers (others such as Percival Osborne were in prefectural government employ), the two most well-known were attached to the central government—the Dutch-American missionary Guido Fridolin Verbeck (1864 – 78) and the French infantry lieutenant, later captain, Albert Charles Du Bousquet (1867 – 82). Both had been bakufu employees and early on were employed by the Meiji government.

Verbeck graduated as an engineer in Holland before studying for the Dutch Reformed ministry in the United States. Christianity was still proscribed when he arrived in Japan, so he turned to the study of the Japanese language and, later, to teaching. From 1864 to 1869 he taught in the government language school (Seibikan) in Nagasaki, during which time fifteen future Meiji leaders studied English with him, using the Bible and the Constitution of the United States as texts. Along with Dr. Samuel Rollins Brown, Verbeck was instrumental in sending many Japanese students abroad with the help of John M. Ferris, head of the Dutch Reformed Church of America. Through these early contacts with future leaders he was called to Tokyo, where he served in the Education Ministry from 1869 to 1873 as head teacher (*kyōtō*) of Nankō, which later became part of Tokyo University.[53]

In words from the emperor (*chokugo*) in 1871, Verbeck was praised for his talent and broad learning and his years of effort in teaching and guiding students and was encouraged to continue to work with all his strength to make learning prosper.[54] With other yatoi he helped improve teacher standards and curriculum patterns and had a central role in establishing employment standards for foreign teachers, including the issuance of regulations by the Education Ministry in 1872.

Verbeck was not only a respected associate of several Meiji leaders but also an intimate friend of Ōkuma Shigenobu and Iwakura Tomomi. In Nagasaki, he had counselled Ōkuma in the dispute with foreign representatives over government policy towards Japanese Christians.[55] In Tokyo, Iwakura discussed many sensitive government matters with him, as Griffis records in his biography. Verbeck's opinion was elicited also on the choice of models for the new army and on the advisability of introducing military conscription. His comments influenced officials opposed to conscription ("Peace is the dream of philosophers and the hope of Christianity but war is human history").[56] Also, his proposal that a major observation team be sent abroad entered into a plan of Iwakura's which materialized in 1871.[57] Even though he himself was Dutch, and Dutch doctors were prominent among yatoi, Verbeck pointed out that Germany and Austria had become the most advanced in medical studies. Late nineteenth-century Westerners were flocking to the German medical schools for further study. It was on his recommendation that German medical studies were introduced and became the dominant pattern upon which Japanese studies were based.

In 1873, an education specialist, Dr. David Murray, was hired, and Verbeck was displaced. Being a man of broad learning rather than a specialist, he was no longer needed in education.[58] He himself had recommended the hiring of a specialist. Ōkuma acknowledged Verbeck's proposal for revision of the national education system. His views had long been sought on a variety of subjects and he had earned the confidence of many officials. Thus, he was recommended to the Central Chamber (Seiin) of the Council of State as supervisor of translation and as informant-consultant on foreign matters.

After the withdrawal of the French military mission to the bakufu, Du Bousquet remained in Japan, attached to the French legation as interpreter. In 1870, he became adviser to the Military Affairs Ministry, providing reference materials and opinions on Western military systems and their adaptability to Japan.[59] In 1871, Du Bousquet entered into a contract with the Left Chamber (Sain) of the Council of State, where he served until 1875, then with the Central Chamber (Seiin) in 1875, and finally with the Senate

(Genrōin) from 1875 until his death from tuberculosis in 1882 at the age of forty-five.

He was employed for "various researches" and in fact served these legislative and administrative offices as interpreter, translator, and consultant.[60] One of his varied duties was to co-ordinate the administration of expenditures related to foreign employees.[61] Acting as interpreter for the Justice Ministry's first law instructor, Georges Bousquet, with whom he has often been confused, and later for Boissonade, he acquired legal knowledge advantageous to his work.[62] He contributed numerous opinions on the mixed court system and other legal matters. Du Bousquet recognized Japan's right to independence but also held that foreign powers were responsible for their citizens in Japan in the unsettled early years of the Meiji era. The importance of his research on treaty revision is only beginning to be recognized. His research was done at a time when no solution was acceptable to all parties, but he provided a great deal of significant reference material for the future.[63]

Both Verbeck and Du Bousquet were highly respected by Japanese officials, although there was always latent hostility in employing any foreigner in offices associated with the Council of State. Du Bousquet, for example, was enjoined, under pain of dismissal, not to discuss his work "large or small points" with either Japanese or foreigners.[64] Although his contract cited French government permission for employment, conditions and revisions in both contracts were matters between Japanese officials and the employee only. In most official correspondence there is a faint critical undercurrent, although Verbeck emerges as the epitome of a trusted yatoi.

Japanese official attitudes about these employees and their employment in central offices are clearly revealed in inter-office correspondence especially in Verbeck's case.[65] In October 1873, the head of the Seiin Translation Bureau appealed to Prime Minister Iwakura and Councillors Ōkubo, Ōkuma, Ōki, Itō, and Katsu to employ Verbeck. He mentioned that the Education Ministry no longer required Verbeck's services, but that the Seiin would like to hire him as "superviser of translation and consultant to each bureau on matters relating to foreign countries," since such work recently had increased. Because Verbeck had been in Japan a long time, he understood Japanese conditions. He was also skilled in Japanese and several Western languages, and was gentle, friendly, and honest. Other officials added lengthy comments in support of the application. For example, finance section officials wrote that much thought had been given to the advisability of employing a foreigner. Verbeck was of outstanding character and the finance section needed a foreign assistant. They promised to economize on other expenditures and urged Verbeck's appointment, adding that they were aware that it might seem inappropriate to hire a foreigner in the Cabinet because many matters were secret. Yet, these officials argued, such an appointment was indispensable for the office work, and there would be no impropriety in hiring a person of splendid character.

Included was a dissenting opinion signed by other officials. They wrote that problems had already arisen between Japanese and foreigners in the Sain, and, further, that a supervisor was not required by the Translation Bureau. In continuing correspondence, legislative section officials on November 8 came out in strong support of Verbeck's engagement, noting that when legal translations were unclear they had used informally the services of Du Bousquet in the Sain and Bousquet of the Justice Ministry. These men, however, were unable to help sufficiently because they had so much work of their own. Consequently, they had requested the employment of a legal expert, but permission was not yet forthcoming. While Verbeck was not a legal specialist, he was nevertheless well versed in many fields. Because he understood Japanese conditions and was skilled in the Japanese language, he would be very useful. These officials further noted that if his services to the legislative section were on an informal basis, there would be no difference between this arrangement and the current arrangement with yatoi in the Sain and the Justice Ministry. They asked, therefore, that if Verbeck were employed by the Translation Bureau his time be equally shared with the legislative section.

A petition was then circulated among several offices to hire Verbeck at 400 yen a month for five years. The signed petition was then sent to the prime minister. In a mid-November Cabinet conference, the appointment was confirmed.[66] On December 1, 1873, Verbeck signed a contract with Mizukuri Rinshō, Translation Bureau chief. The contract provided that Verbeck would divide his time equally between translation and answering questions from the legislative section. He would be informed by the heads of those offices when to appear for duty in each. He received the usual housing allowance and accepted the injunction prohibiting his connection with private business. He was given Sundays as holidays, but one-in-six (*ichiroku*) would not be a holiday for him. The agreement could be summarily terminated if he were negligent in his work. He thus continued important consultation.[67]

Verbeck ended government service following this five-year contract. He made trips to the United States and continued in the Christian ministry in Japan. In later years, owing to his long residence in Japan, he knew no home but Japan. In July 1891, some years before the interior was opened for foreign residence, Foreign Minister Enomoto Takeaki issued Verbeck a special passport for himself and his family, under government protection, to move about and reside anywhere in Japan. This unique permission was an official expression of the respect he had earned. After his death a memorial was officially erected.[68]

Such general advisers as Verbeck made solid contributions to Japanese development because they assumed their duties in the same spirit as did native civil servants. They deferred to their superiors and co-operated to the extent of their abilities. Du Bousquet had married a Japanese. Because of his long association with the Japanese, Verbeck lost his taste for the more prosaic ministry and life in the United States. In a sense he cut himself off from his own people. Years earlier he had been criticized for being too Japanese. Dr. Leopold Müller (1871 – 75), head teacher of the university medical school (Tōkō) at the same time as Verbeck was employed at Nankō, referred to Verbeck as the former locksmith who thought only of things to make the Japanese happy, and fellow missionaries viewed Verbeck's government service as compromising to the ministry.[69] Many were envious, too, of his high salary while in Nankō. Because Verbeck was respected, he had no difficulty in obtaining the Sunday holiday even at the height of the dispute. He had none of the truculence displayed by some yatoi.[70]

The description of Verbeck as a man of lofty character, gentle temperament, with an understanding of Japanese conditions and facility in the Japanese language, who was also well versed in many fields though not a legal specialist (all descriptions from official correspondence) also provides a profile of the good general adviser. Verbeck's services ended in the late 1870's shortly before Du Bousquet's services also ended. The general adviser was destined to be displaced in the growing dimensions of Japanese government, and their services terminated in favour of specialists.

Of the legal experts hired by the Meiji government, a small coterie became close advisers. They were especially distinguished by their professional loyalty. Perhaps inevitably, as bureaucratic factions formed and reformed among Japanese officials, foreign advisers became embroiled in disputes. While the ability of long-term adviser Boissonade overrode his volatile personality, for example, he was not above bureaucratic dispute. There was also an element of rivalry among advisers of different nationalities. The French legal orientation of the Justice Ministry was defended by Boissonade against German legal experts in the Foreign Ministry and the Cabinet; as a drift towards German institutions became pronounced, Boissonade reacted strongly.[71] Animosity and jealousy were directed at Hermann Roesler and others. While some special advisers avoided alignments, the fact that they were assigned to particular Japanese offices or officials who sought their assistance and opinions to bolster particular positions involved them in factionalism. However, two advisers who were fairly successful in avoiding association with specific cliques were Hermann Roesler (1878 – 93), despite Boissonade's attitude and the disdain he received from other German advisers, especially Albert Mosse, and Henry Willard Denison (1880 – 1914). Both were loners, as Verbeck and Du Bousquet had been.

Roesler and Denison were quiet to the point of aloofness in social relations, competent, and dedicated. Each had been dissatisfied with his previous situation. Little is known as yet of Denison except memories of him recorded in commemorative gatherings. A native of Vermont and a graduate of Columbia College in law, he worked first in government finance but was transferred to the State Department. He came to Japan in 1874 as vice-consul in Kanagawa. He was involved in several consular suits, but after his vindication in a major one in 1875, he was promoted to consul in Osaka.[72] Following a presidential change he resigned the diplomatic service in September 1878 to practise law in Yokohama. At the time of his resignation, he was listed as vice-consul and interpreter and vice-consul general of Kanagawa. U.S. minister John Bingham entered in the diplomatic registry: "By his resignation the government loses services of a very efficient officer."[73]

Because cases were heard in consular court, private practice palled on Denison. It is suggested that his ability and tact came to be recognized by the Japanese government in his mediation of a dispute between Consul-General Van Buren and the U.S. minister to Japan, Judge Bingham.[74] He was recommended by Bingham to Foreign Minister Inoue Kaoru, and he began formal service with the Foreign Ministry in 1880. Bingham was elated; he felt it boded well for American-Japanese relations.

In ensuing years, Denison displayed remarkable industry and dedication to his work. He clarified the principle of reciprocity for equitable treaty revision: access to the interior required withdrawal of all extraterritorial claims by foreign powers. He argued that foreign consuls had no jurisdiction over foreign nationals abroad, thus denying any basis for the consular court system so grievous to Japan. It was, in fact, the Japan experience and advisers from Peshine Smith to Denison which contributed to the eventual demise of that system throughout the world. Denison also worked on revision of the tariff system.

During the First Sino-Japanese War, he was personal adviser to Count Mutsu Munemitsu and was Itō Hirobumi's adviser at the Shimonoseki peace conference, facing another American, John W. Foster, for the China side. He apparently opposed acceptance of the Tripartite Intervention and was argued down by Foreign Minister Mutsu, who feared greater intervention. As chief counsellor to Foreign Minister Komura Jutarō during the Russo-Japanese War, he won world sympathy for Japan's position and outlined the correspondence, the peace memoranda, and supplementary adjustments with Russia over Manchuria and Siberia. He accompanied Komura to the Portsmouth Conference where, although Japan lost indemnity, it won trade concessions in China and Karafuto. It was Denison who urged a hesitant Inoue Kaoru towards an Anglo-Japanese alliance. As technical representative of Japan at The Hague, Denison promoted the revision of commercial treaties dealing with the whole line of concessions and the return of tariff autonomy to Japan. Throughout his career he trained fledging Japanese diplomats.[75] Denison married an American in 1873, but over the years they often lived apart. She spent her last years in Europe, where she was at the time of his death in 1914. Having received shortly before his death the highest decoration awarded to Japanese with a special *chokugo* (praise from the emperor), Denison was given a state funeral paid for by the Imperial Household Ministry and led by Ōkuma Shigenobu. His pallbearers in Tsukiji Trinity Cathedral included five former Japanese foreign affairs ministers. His tombstone inscription acknowledges that "for five and thirty years he took an important part in the direction of foreign affairs of the Empire, especially rendering signal services during wars with China and Russia, in the conclusion of the Anglo-Japanese Alliance, and in the revision of commercial treaties . . . . For his single-heartedness he was universally admired, and will remain to all generations a pattern of unswerving fidelity."

On July 3, 1933, the twentieth anniversary of his death, some seventeen ranking Foreign Ministry career diplomats who had been associated with him met for a visit to his grave in Aoyama and held a dinner party in his memory. While the remarks were eulogistic, as would be expected, they also add to an understanding of his role. Foreign Minister Uchida said that no one involved himself to the extent Denison did in the important work of making the present Japan. In his opinion, Denison, had prepared the ground for Japan's enhanced position, achieved by the time of the European War (First World War). The liberal statesman Shidehara Kijūrō, who was Denison's apprentice (Denison bequeathed his library on international law to him), discussed Denison's views on Japan's policies, how Denison had worried that Europeanization would overwhelm the Japanese tradition in the Rokumeikan era and how in turn he had feared the reaction led by Tani Tateki (Kanjō). But Denison thought that the two extremes had been reconciled in the crisis of the First Sino-Japanese War (1894 – 95) and thereafter.

In these conversations, various anecdotes illustrated the mutual respect between Denison and many Japanese officials. One participant recalled that whereas foreign employees usually did not appreciate correction, Denison willingly altered his writing exactly as directed. Matsui Keishirō commented that it was Denison's explanation of the contradiction between extraterritoriality and the Japanese constitution which contributed to the formulation of Aoki Shuzō's basic position in the final treaty revision abolishing extraterritoriality. In summary, these officials agreed with Shidehara's assessment that Denison was respected both as a lawyer and as a statesman.[76]

When Denison entered Japan's civil service in 1880, he was engaged as "assistant adviser on International Law to the Minister and Vice-Minister of the Foreign Department . . . subject to the instructions of any of his superior officers . . . and any other person or persons . . . directed by said officers . . . to draft or revise diplomatic and other official correspondence and documents, and generally to perform the duties of such adviser aforesaid." And in Article 6 of his contract, he was bound by a secrets clause:

> The said H. W. Denison hereby solemnly promises and upon his honor binds himself neither directly nor indirectly to divulge or communicate to any other person or persons in whole or in part any matter or thing connected with the official business or concerns of the said Government which shall or may come to his knowledge through the performance of his official duties or by reason of his connection with the aforesaid Department and Government or with the officials thereof.[77]

He could be dismissed without notice and without any financial indemnity from the government for negligence, insubordination, or serious misconduct.

In 1883 the first contract expired. The new contract entered into again with Foreign Minister Inoue Kaoru provided that Denison's legal services would also be required by the finance minister and vice-minister, provided they did not "conflict or interfere with the duties . . . for the said Foreign Department." Article 6 remained the same. In 1887, an amendment was signed by Inoue, renewing his position for two more years, and in 1889, Count Ōkuma Shigenobu, foreign minister, and Denison entered into a new five-year contract in which his services to the finance minister were terminated. With the 1889 contract, Denison received a salary increase for the first time in nine years from 450 silver yen to 600 silver yen a month. Other stipulations in the first contract were maintained. In 1891, Denison also served as adviser to Kanagawa Prefecture, and in 1894 the Ōkuma contract was extended for eleven months by Foreign Minister Mutsu. In 1895 he entered into a new five-year contract with Mutsu. An attached memorandum raised his salary to 2,500 silver yen per quarter (833 per month). In 1900 the contract and memorandum were renewed for another five years by Foreign Minister Aoki Shuzō. No renewal memorandum is found in Foreign Ministry files for the 1905 – 10 period, but a memorandum signed March 28, 1910, by "Jutaro Komura Minister for Foreign Affairs" and "H. W. Denison, Legal Adviser to Foreign Office" provided another five years employment and an annual salary of 15,000 yen.

In these contracts the care of Japanese officials is noted. The first contract was to expire without notice in three years, leaving officials no further commitment, but Denison's value is reflected in the new contract and its renewal. A new contract was entered into on the change of foreign ministers, and in Mutsu's case he preferred a probationary period before an extended contract. In that probationary period in 1894, Denison rendered distinguished counsel which led to his renewal. It seems that the missing memorandum for 1905 – 10 may be significant. For, although most Foreign Ministry files on the employment of foreigners are unorganized, and documentary fragments are lumped together by broad topic and chronology, this was not the case of the Denison files when first viewed, before they were taken away for use in the centennial project on the Foreign Ministry's history. The files were orderly and the contracts were together and in perfect condition, but there were no records for 1905 – 10.

After the Portsmouth trip it appears that Denison planned to retire. Whatever the situation, an informant in London suggested to the *New York Times* (January 18, 1908) that Denison's "retirement" was in retaliation for the dismissal of Japanese servants in the American naval fleet. A contrary opinion was provided by another correspondent, who asserted that "the decision of the Japanese government to dispense with the services of Denison" was really to be expected, "Japan having reached the point in her occidentalization . . . when she believe[d] she [could] continue to progress alone and stand on her present foundation." The correspondent concluded that it was surprising that Denison, the last of the advisers, had been retained so long.[78] On February 2, 1908, in the *New York Tribune* the assertion that the "retirement" of Denison was caused by crisis in United States relations was again rejected. His long tenure spoke "volumes for his tact" and "willingness to efface himself" because of the Japanese "innate aversion, and even disgust for the white man."[79]

In an article published the year of Denison's death, the writer shed further light on the 1908 speculation about Denison's retirement. Denison's services had been sought by the United States, and Denison had been eager to spend his last years there after the long years in which his contacts with other foreigners and lesser officials had been limited because of the confidential position he had held. Denison had tendered his resignation, but the Japanese government had insisted that the relationship remain permanent and had offered him a sizeable increase in salary and a long leave of absence (the 1910 contract memorandum raised the salary from 10,000 to 15,000 yen).[80]

Undoubtedly Japanese officials felt they could not afford to release Denison for employment in the United States. The incident provides an interesting footnote on an important career which requires detailed study, so carefully did Denison preserve his role as the shadow of a succession of Japanese foreign ministers.[81] Shidehara tells us that Denison burned his records on the Russo-Japanese negotiations rather than allow them to be read and published, lest anyone credit him for doing the work of Foreign Minister Komura.[82] Such a stance goes far to explain the confidence Japanese officials had in Denison.

Hermann Roesler, like Denison, was first employed for research on commercial codes and treaty problems.[83] Later, this employment led to his participation in constitutional preparation. He previously had held professional academic posts in Erlangen and Rostok. His very competent biographer, Johannes Siemes, suggests that if his university career in Germany had gone smoothly, Roesler might never have gone to Japan.[84] As a Roman Catholic convert, he lost his university posting under the *Kulturkampf* policy, which barred Catholics from holding public appointments. Roesler served the Foreign Ministry from 1878 to 1885, preparing drafts of commercial law in line with the first phase in treaty revision approach, which was directed to tariff revision. From 1885 to 1893 he served the Cabinet as legal and economic adviser to all offices (*hōritsu komon oyobi ni keizai rizaijo no jikō kakushō komon*).

In 1881, when Ōkuma Shigenobu made public demands for a parliamentary system, other Meiji leaders were already seeking forms which would emphasize sovereignty in the imperial institution. While still in the Foreign Ministry, Roesler worked on constitutional law problems. In the Cabinet, through Inoue Kowashi, Roesler became a close collaborator with Itō Hirobumi. It was the latter who took the lead in seeking countermeasures to the more expansive opinions of those like Ōkuma before the feudal "afterglow" could be dissipated in the modern development that Meiji leaders had set in motion.[85] Roesler participated in all of Itō's important work and brought to this preparation a theory of social constitutionalism which refined the social monarch theories of the Austrian legal scholar Lorenz von Stein.[86]

Just as Bismarck's new laws had been inspired by von Stein, von Gneist, and other theorists, Meiji leaders, searching for a constitutional system complementary to their native imperial institution, were attracted to the concept of absolute monarchy based on social responsibility. Johannes Siemes argues convincingly that Roesler's influence on Meiji leaders exceeded that of von Stein and von Gneist; Roesler's contribution was his presentation of the monarch's importance as social guardian and of the state's responsibility to society. In his revisionist study of Roesler's role, Siemes makes it clear that Roesler should not be credited with impressing the German concept of absolute monarchy on the Japanese; the Iwakura, Itō, Inoue group already knew the basic policy they wished to draft. Roesler's work involved the expression and refinement of Japanese ideas. Roesler's idea of a law-governed state accepting social responsibility was thus refracted through Inoue Kowashi to Itō. Siemes actually designates Roesler a "co-worker."

Inoue Kowashi did alter Roesler's rejection of religious ideology, and Siemes suggests that Roesler's commentaries (now in the Diet Library) were not published because Roesler's clarifications went far beyond a statist interpretation.[87] Siemes comments:

> The most essential feature of his constitutional conception, the stress on the social administrative role of the state, goes beyond the horizon of the authoritarian monarchical constitutions of the 19th century . . . . Above all, the Meiji Constitution owes to Roesler its most distinctive feature, the synthesis of the imperial authority and the rights of the people: that is to say, in consistently carrying through the principle of sovereignty of the Emperor into all functions of government it leaves intact the fundamental principles of a liberal constitution, i.e., government according to laws consented to by the people.[88]

Present scholarship recognizes the conceptual flexibility of the Meiji constitution, but Roesler's role was limited by Japanese officials who altered both the form and the theoretical interpretations he provided. Final decision-making rested with Japanese statesmen. The fact that Roesler was the only foreigner in the intimate circle of drafters of the constitution, however, is indicative of the degree of trust he enjoyed.

Like Denison, by his loyalty and sensitivity Roesler built a special relationship with Japanese officials, and both worked in an atmosphere of reciprocal confidence. Their roles differ from that of Boissonade, despite the latter's fame and his dedicated preparation of legal codes. Denison and Roesler were perhaps the only Meiji yatoi who were not only privy to state secrets (a number of advisers were) but also were drawn into Cabinet-level secret conferences.

Boissonade, moralist and factionalist, was volatile in temperament despite all the worthiness of his character and ideas. As a theorist he was his own man. He did not fit the proper mould of the yatoi bureaucrat, though his long service speaks to the strength of the French legal faction in the Justice Ministry. Nevertheless, it was Boissonade who laid the foundations of legal education and of the judicial system and who initiated the abolition of torture in Japan. He laboured to perfect legal codes, which, although altered drastically in principle as promulgated, manifested his influence in personal affairs and acquisition and ownership of property.[89] He provided much useful advice on treaty revision, but perhaps his most immediate service was as devil's advocate, scrutinizing the interpretations of other yatoi lawyers to ensure that innovations did not create precedents for further foreign intervention. In every way a remarkable jurist, he, in his later work in the Cabinet, may well have been in part a foil against which Roesler could sharpen his objections to French legal premises.

It is significant that the two most intimate yatoi advisers in the Meiji government had background in economics and finance and that neither came into service with established reputations, as did Boissonade and later German legal advisers. As their decorations, eventual appointments to chokunin treatment, gradual salary increases, and title changes indicate—in sixteen years Roesler's salary was raised from 600 to 1,300 a month and in thirty-four years Denison's from 450 to 1,250 a month—they earned their status in Japan's civil service.

It is clear that many yatoi provided techniques, directions, and encouragement for changes in domestic and foreign policy. It is also apparent that yatoi advisers reinforced Japanese official convictions of the need to preserve their national heritage (a "national heritage" that was redesigned or even created by Meiji officials) while acquiring and using modern Western expertise. It is also a fact that yatoi taught the arts of diplomatic self-defence. In so doing and perhaps as a corollary of this instruction, yatoi advisers bolstered emerging expansionist policies of Japan through the early twentieth century. Those yatoi, too, were influenced by contemporary world views. In a very real sense they were collaborators with the Meiji state. As they schooled the Japanese, they were in turn schooled by their students. The practical contributions of general advisers and other yatoi, in giving substantial form to employment standards for the corps of foreign employees, brought into existence a foreign civil servant corps. By negotiating for contract standards, official status treatment commensurate with Japanese bureaucrats, and extended tenure, they moulded this foreign quasi-bureaucracy.

By the 1880's, technical clarification of the non-official status of foreign advisers was achieved. This was before Boissonade's 1887 tirade over the proposal for the use of foreign jurists in Japanese courts. In the light of criticism of the German proposal for naturalization of foreign jurists, it is interesting that this clarification was peculiar to contracts with Germans, perhaps because the later German advisers were themselves officials in the German government. Details of Prussian court magistrate Albert Mosse's engagement were made by telegraph and his contract was prepared and signed after his arrival in Japan. It was made with Chief Cabinet Secretary Major-General Tanaka Mitsuaki (June 12, 1886). Article 2 is pertinent:

Mr. Mosse belongs only to the Cabinet Prime Minister and Home Minister, but by this agreement Mr. [Mosse] does not have the rights and responsibilities of Japanese government officials. Although this agreement is recognized as a civil contract, Mr. [Mosse] by this agreement will serve in the Japanese government diligently and will keep complete secrecy about matters he will handle.[90]

Clauses in other contracts are similar; all legal advisers and all Cabinet advisers were bound to secrecy. They were not Japanese officials, but they clearly functioned on the same level as native bureaucrats: researching problems, preparing directives, proposals, and laws to be ruled on, and conditioning, by their work and consultation, the political decisions of Japanese leaders. All yatoi in sufficiently responsible positions to view themselves as co-workers became in fact, if not in principle, Japanese bureaucrats.

In an amusing letter to Griffis in response to one of his yatoi postcards, John Milne wrote: "*Yatoi* (hirelings and menials) they may have been, but for the full significance of the word dear old Hepburn requires extension. It has led to controversy."[91] "Hirelings and menials" these foreign employees may have been called, but their performance extended the dictionary definition. It was in their tutorial and advisory "sub-leadership" role that their full significance is to be found. The ability of a foreign employee to contribute effectively to the Japanese in the Meiji period depended in large measure on how he viewed his own role, but clearly the yatoi self-image was to a degree sculpted by the Japanese image of yatoi. And in that image is refracted the whole of the Meiji experiment.

5

The Japanese Image of Yatoi

The appellation "hired foreigners" (*oyatoi gaikokujin*) given by Meiji officials to foreigners employed by the government was indicative of underlying attitudes. They were hired help. Yet those who entered into the Japanese pattern of filial relationships were viewed in a filial manner. Japanese officials never lost the awareness of their own identity as hosts and employers. Their views of foreign employees were conditioned by the milieu of constraint in which they undertook modern nation-building, by symbiotic tensions produced in hosting alien organisms, and by the difficulties inherent in modernizing.

THE MILIEU OF CONSTRAINT

Until the latter half of the nineteenth century, international law was a *quid pro quo* applied among Christian nations. But already in international congresses, American theorists in particular were suggesting that reciprocal principles could apply to non-Christian nations if they revised their social and legal institutions.[1] Western powers had learned from the imbroglio in China that a united international front to minimize the hostility among themselves was essential to force trade co-operation from Japan. Home governments had also grown weary of gunboat diplomacy and altered policies restricted the prerogatives of diplomats in the field.

The posture of Western nations towards Japan was, therefore, becoming more circumspect. Profiteering objectives were the same, but government-monopolized trading companies gave way to private merchant houses. Yet moral pressure, to use Ernest Satow's euphemism, was a basic instrument of policy for the field diplomat.[2] Thus the series of unequal treaties entered into since the 1850's made resistance to this moral pressure the principal endeavour of Japanese officials. Because a major motivation for foreign borrowing was a negative one—the recovery of independence—vital energies were sapped that could better have been applied to technological and institutional development. Constraint limited and conditioned the Meiji experiment. Unlike officials in China and the Near East, the Japanese persistently pressed for treaty revision and strongly resisted the extension of foreign privileges. With the aid of foreign advisers their attempts to achieve these aims became more effective. Each foreign power became watchful of any change which might give another nation an inside track in its relations with Japan.

The employment of foreigners was caught up in national rivalries. Japanese officials had experienced this conflict since the bakumatsu era and had shrewdly assessed the intentions of foreign powers. The severity of Japanese injunctions against business activities of employees, against foreigners living together in the same house, against foreigners and Japanese living together without permission, and against foreign purchase of land, were owing in good part to fear of conspiracy and further foreign encroachment.

Without exception, foreign representatives viewed the employment of their nationals as a vanguard to commercial privilege. Despite the initial opening of Japan by Americans, their preoccupation with domestic strife in the 1860's reduced their role there. In the actual course of events, the British acted and the Americans abstained or concurred after the fact. Only after 1863 and the *Pembroke* incident did U.S. minister Robert Pruyn co-operate with the British in taking punitive action at Shimonoseki and in exerting pressure at Hyogo. In Satow's words, the Americans then "partially abandoned the affectation of acting on different lines from the 'effete monarchies of Europe'."[3] The Prussian commercial treaty with Japan was ratified in 1864 and arrangements for German employees and German language study were made with the bakufu by Maxim von Brandt.[4] Nevertheless, preoccupied by political unification, the Germans significantly entered the scene only towards the end of the first decade of the Meiji period. In the bakumatsu era, the Dutch, French, and British were dominant in Japan.

Earlier, British minister Parkes had stressed direct private trade, but during the first few years of the Meiji era, the Americans, following their recovery from the Civil War, made new bids for the Japan trade. The resuscitation of competing American interests helped the British minister to realize the value of foreign nationals in Japan's service. He thus worked assiduously to place British subjects and, when it suited his policy, protested contract cancellations of British subjects.

United States minister Charles DeLong lacked the entrenched treaty port political influence of Parkes, but he hastened to offset his disadvantage. In 1872, two years before the 1856 Consular Act forbidding American diplomats to recommend nationals for service to a foreign nation was rescinded, De-Long was able to report to the U. S. secretary of state: "I have embraced every opportunity that has been offered me to secure positions for Americans that they as quasi-commercial agents for their people might assist in building up American trade with Japan and help our country to overcome as nearly as possible the balance of trade which has been heretofore so largely against us."[5] DeLong's reasoning was based on the fact that the government, rather than private persons, was the chief buyer of goods. He, and John Bingham after him, sought a repeal of the prohibition against recommending nationals. American minister Bingham's correspondence dealt with British intrigue in Japan, and he reported that Parkes denied the allegation made in the U.S. Congress that he attempted to remove Americans from Japanese service in order to make room for his own countrymen.[6] In 1874, the restriction against diplomats recommending Americans for employment by foreign countries was lifted, and comments on the floor of Congress hailed the action as one which would promote trade and would, they hoped, "Americanize the Japanese."[7] DeLong's blunt opinion that foreign employees were quasi-commercial agents of their governments was shared by all the powers, and Japanese officials were fully cognizant of this prevailing view.

The prime position of British trade (Britain had 75 per cent of the trade in the bakumatsu era and 50 per cent in the Meiji era) gave the British minister the deanship of the foreign diplomatic corps in Japan. After the removal of Roches it was the consensus of other powers that Parkes had the French minister literally in his pocket. Thus, overt rivalry among foreigners in Japan moved from the earlier British-French to the British-American polarization in the Meiji era.

For the first decade of the Meiji era, foreign representatives in Japan tried to make the engagement of foreign nationals contingent on commercial arrangements for projects and were personally involved in the hiring process. Team projects in particular bore national stamps; the Japanese use of groups of nationals entailed their use of that nation's banking facilities, machinery, supplies, and so forth. Thus the major construction projects for railways, lighthouses, the Mint, and, shortly, naval and commercial shipping facilities were coups for British commerce. The many conflicts marking the British yatoi experience were partly the result of their numbers, partly of the often helpful but aggressive stance of Parkes, but more especially of the nature of administrative and financial arrangements using British yatoi and Britain's stand against treaty revision. Japan was primarily dependent on British help. Japanese officials kept arrangements to a minimum, dispensed with most of them in the first decade, and alternated with loans from other nationals, but the onus was real.

In addition to diplomatic pressure per se under the treaties and foreign representatives competing to press their nationals on the Japanese, consular protection for nationals was another facet of pressure. In the early years, assaults on foreigners drew serious threats of foreign intervention. Takahashi Korekiyo, later an outstanding statesman and himself a victim of assassination, recounted that as a young man it was with fear and trembling that he acted as interpreter in such attacks. To shake the entire bureaucracy, an incident did not have to involve an important or an innocent person, simply a foreigner. One recalls that in the 1870 Instructions, officials had been warned that foreigners had "much influence."

The case of a Niigata Prefecture employee involved hundreds of Japanese officials. An Englishman named King had been hired as a teacher and technician, but he was totally unqualified and unsavory in several respects. In 1871, badly slashed, he reported to officials that someone had broken into his quarters at night and attacked him. The incident raised a furor in Tokyo as well as in Niigata. A foreign doctor was despatched from Yokohama, with bearers on forced run. Niigata authorities called out extra police, halted all movement within the city for twenty-four hours, and rounded up and interrogated hundreds of possible suspects. Under steady pressure from Tokyo, the search continued, and the governor of Niigata called on troop reinforcements from neighbouring han, all to no avail.

The consternation, both cultural and political, of Tokyo officials is revealed in the orders relayed by the Foreign Ministry. Before the arrival of the foreign doctor, King's bedding was to be changed daily and the room and garden cleaned to prevent complaints because Western people thought health was harmed if things were not clean. The Foreign Ministry official pointed out that, in view of the attack, King was no longer an ordinary yatoi; the problem had become one of foreign relations, and the central government would assume all cost for his care.

Meanwhile King kept himself in a semi-drunken stupor, took a dislike to the foreign doctor when he arrived, and had the Japanese doctors recalled. Transcripts of King's remarks and accounts of his actions throughout this incident and his return to Yokohama reveal him as a rough and ignorant man. Foreign witnesses confirmed this impression, but Tokyo officials were dismayed that the attacker was not found, and a Council of State directive informed Niigata officials that it was clear that orders were not being carried out. The efforts to apprehend King's attacker were intensified. The Niigata assistant governor finally concluded that King's wounds must have been self-inflicted in order that he could claim compensation. Whether this was fact or not (and there were a number of such cases, especially in outlying regions), King was well compensated, and Tokyo officials were able to still complaints.[8]

Incidents involving foreign employees too often reflected the power complexes of their countries. Some, under consular protection, refused to be removed even for proven fault. Major A. G. Warfield, for instance, discharged firearms during drunken sprees, but he refused the back salary twice offered by the Japanese in their attempt to remove him. The case went before United States minister DeLong and was reported in despatches to the U.S. secretary of state. DeLong maintained that an American could not be discharged from Japanese government service without his being convicted of a serious offence in an American court. Again, the credibility of Japanese witnesses was eschewed. The charges, reluctantly tendered by Japanese officials, of Warfield discharging firearms in public places, shooting dogs, and firing on officials were not accepted as valid. As an American legation secretary reported in the same correspondence, Kuroda Kiyotaka tried to spare general feelings by not pressing for full examination. In the end, to rid itself of Warfield, the Japanese government paid him all his back salary from the time of his suspension, plus half salary from the date of his dismissal to the expiration of his contract, and $500 as transportation stipend to the United States, and withdrew the charges.[9] In the crucial early 1870's, Japanese officials were able to make little headway in their direct confrontation with foreign representatives.

A rallying point among Japanese officials became their opposition to the unequal treaty system. Although the Iwakura Mission had as part of its purpose to probe into revision possibilities and United States officials tried to move towards a bilateral arrangement, Americans were especially exercised over British monopoly of harbour master posts in Japanese ports. According to the bakumatsu commercial treaties, harbour regulations for the open ports were to be drawn up by foreign consuls and Japanese officials in mutual consultation. However, in Nagasaki, for example, British and American consuls, claiming they had the permission of the bakufu commissioner (*bugyō*), published a set of regulations. The Meiji government refused to recognize them. Meiji officials thought that by hiring foreign harbour masters to provide a liaison between foreign consuls and local Japanese officials, uniform regulations could eventually be drafted. The British were eager to fill these posts themselves. Because of British dominance of the Japanese trade, the appointment of British subjects seemed the most logical to the Japanese, but the reaction of other foreign powers was antagonistic, and the drafting of harbour regulations had not progressed by 1872.[10]

In Washington in 1872, Iwakura and other Japanese officials conferred with DeLong and Secretary of State Hamilton Fish, suggesting that the Japanese government resolve the matter alone. The Americans flatly rejected the suggestion and demanded a voice in the appointment of harbour masters. English harbour masters were characterized by the Americans as drunken incompetents guilty of preferential treatment towards British shipping.[11]

In a later conference, the Americans reiterated their rejection and made other complaints against the English habour masters in Hakodate and Hyogo.[12]

On their return to Japan, Japanese officials were confronted by German and Portuguese representatives who supported the American protests. The German minister proposed that the appointment of harbour masters come under international administration.[13] This type of extension of foreign prerogative was the most feared by Japanese, and so they refused the proposal. In Hakodate, Alexander P. Porter was relieved of his duties, and in Yokohama the English harbour master was not allowed to function formally until 1889, when long-term British employee Captain A. R. Brown served as adviser to Kanagawa Prefecture. Only in Hyogo was British monopoly so complete as to allow Britain to retain both John Marshall (1871–87) and John J. Mahlman (1870–1928).

Later incidents demonstrate the same Japanese fears and concerns. Many yatoi commented that with each setback in treaty revision, the Japanese became less co-operative. Dr. Erwin von Baelz recorded in his diary for April 22, 1879, that a major failure in treaty revision, the British rejection of the American revision, caused a sharp change in the government attitude towards foreigners in Japan and towards yatoi in particular. He mentioned the abrupt discharge of twenty-three British instructors in the Navy School as a direct result of that failure. Whereas earlier the government had been eager for yatoi, from the late 1870's the official position was that they were no longer necessary.

Between 1876 and 1878 the United States and Japan came to an agreement on a gradated equitable revision, beginning with tariff revision. This progress was a result of field diplomats, yatoi lawyers such as E. Peshine Smith and Eli Sheppard, and a State Department convinced of the necessity of revision to allow the Americans to compete better with British trade. The British, however, upheld the principle of the system; for revision by one nation to become effective the acquiescence of all treaty nations was required.

Besides lawyers, other yatoi, especially Americans in finance and postal revision such as George B. Williams and Samuel Bryan (1871–87), encouraged Japanese officials to assert jurisdiction where possible, especially in currency and postal areas. These early yatoi were criticized by other foreigners in Japan and by their own government representative, but their advice affected both Japanese and American government positions. The United States agreement to tariff revision caused the Japanese to give General Ulysses S. Grant's unofficial visit in 1879, coinciding with the ratification of the treaty, an unusually joyous welcome. Grant's frank statements about what he would do if similarly confronted with infringements of national sovereignty won him popularity for himself, the United States, and American yatoi.[14]

Parkes came under attack by his own countrymen as well. Interestingly, copies of two relevant letters are in the Ōkuma Shigenobu Collection. On June 24, 1879, J. P. Hennessy, governor of Hong Kong, wrote to British Foreign Secretary Lord Salisbury recommending removal of Parkes because "your representative has been here too long without going home." His relations with Japanese Foreign Minister Terajima were strained, whereas the United States, Russian, and Italian ministers received smooth, swift service from him. Hennessy continued that it was necessary to revise British policy regarding long-time experts on China and Japan. Their knowledge of the Chinese and Japanese languages had become of small importance in comparison with "the real and regular training of the Foreign Office. The expert appears to look at nothing beyond his own circle whereas the man of wider experience does not forget the difficulties the government may be involved in elsewhere and he has a larger appreciation of what British interests really are."[15]

On August 24, 1879, in a letter to former Prime Minister Gladstone, Hennessy wrote that the Japanese attitude towards England was one of suspicion because of Parkes's aggressive policy in support of British traders and that much of the Foreign Office management of China and Japan had drifted into the hands of the former attorney-general of Hong Kong, Sir Julian Pauncefote. Further, he noted:

Everything British is now flavoured in Japan by the somewhat acrid policy of our Minister here—the former consul Parkes of Canton . . . who for all his ability is more an exponent of the British trader abroad than of real English interests.

Over and over again Members of the Mikado's cabinet have said to me, how different would be the feeling of this country toward England if the generous policy that Mr. Gladstone has shown not only in Europe but in distant Borneo was adopted by the British Minister instead of the constant bullying we receive.

Whilst the bullying has not strengthened British influence in Japan, it has enabled the Russian and U.S. Ministers to gain a position in the Empire they are not—according to Board of Trade returns—entitled to hold.[16]

Hennessy's remarks reveal his own political alignments as well as political differences within the British home government, but they also reflect a body of opinion in Japan. The amicable position of Russia recalls that it was with Russia that Enomoto Takeaki had in 1875 discussed yatoi coming under Japanese jurisdiction. And of course the extended hostility between Parkes and Terajima was well known. Criticism of Parkes continued, and in 1881 the American, E. W. House, Ōkuma's roving adviser, reported that "to wish well to Japan has become identical with wishing destruction to Parkes" and admitted that in his travels in Europe and America he tried hard to discredit Parkes.[17]

These criticisms depict the milieu of treaty port politics. This kind of criticism mushroomed and brought a British replacement in 1883, but the British position was little altered. Commitment to the prime trading position was too pronounced. Treaty revision was not accomplished until the late 1890's, when the United States and other nations made inroads on that trade, when the United States had developed its own policy towards Pacific interests, and when the labours of yatoi advisers who firmly defended Japan's refusal to open the interior at last bore fruit.

Parkes was highhanded, but Ōkuma for one did not forget his genuine assistance.[18] Ōkuma was always the most flexible among Meiji leaders vis-à-vis the West, but the pervading climate of bureaucratic opinion was closer to that expressed by House. From the late 1870's, the trend away from hiring British and French employees towards hiring Americans and Germans was clearly connected with treaty revision problems. Reductions of British yatoi in the Navy, in Public Works, and in Education were accompanied by animosity on both sides.

In 1878, British yatoi in the Komaba Agricultural School were replaced by Germans.[19] In the 1880's, the release of more British in favour of German legal translators and advisers was directly related to the encouraging attitudes of Germany towards treaty revision as well as Japanese interest in German legal theory. The careful handling of German employees in the 1880's was intended to preserve this rapprochement. When architects were sought for the design and construction of state buildings in 1886, Inoue Kaoru initially thought to hire British, but changed abruptly and hired German architects instead. Previously most architects had been British; Josiah Conder responsible for many state buildings in Tokyo, was much respected. It was routine, therefore, for Inoue to wire the Japanese minister in London (January 5, 1886) to have him find a competent architect and to telegraph how soon he could come and how much salary would be desired. But on January 18, Inoue sent a brief message to London: "I cancel my telegram of 5 instant about architects"; he simultaneously began communications with Japanese officials in Germany.[20]

Baurath Boeckman, the chief architect being considered, had different ideas on construction from those of Japanese officials and his cost estimates were higher than anticipated. Inoue conferred with Itō Hirobumi and they decided to accept the German plans as much as possible despite the expense. They reasoned that in the problems connected with treaty revision the

German minister was showing himself to be kind and helpful. It was a "delicate relation."[21]

Failure to win British (and French) concurrence when other nations were moving towards revision set the tone of Japanese reaction in the 1880's and stoked the reaction against the westernization of Japanese society. The liberal Ozaki Yukio, for example, had strong words against the British. In 1889, for the British press, he wrote that Japanese reaction against the treaties had risen to fever pitch over the previous fifteen years. The Japanese were unable to alter tariffs, and the burden on agriculture was insupportable. There were eight thousand insulting foreigners in Japan, and Japan had no redress. "If you think you can spare such a little friend as Japan, it is a great mistake. An Empire of forty million inhabitants cannot be despised; especially when she is on the sure road to eventual wealth and prosperity, and to a civilization unparalleled, probably in the history of the world."[22]

Under onus of the treaties, Meiji officials were very much aware that Japan was on stage before a world audience. This consciousness, observable in so many ways, was reflected in imperial utterances (*chokugo*) honouring yatoi. Purportedly words of encouragement or gratitude from the emperor, they were prepared by Meiji bureaucrats. As public announcements they were advertisements to the diplomatic world. W. W. Cargill was encouraged to work hard for the railway project because the nation's future reputation depended on the success of new construction projects being undertaken. Thus, Verny, Brunton, Capron, Kinder, legal advisers, and scores of others were enjoined to work diligently for the nation's success.[23]

With the eyes of the world on the Meiji experiment, the silver yen was not honoured for a decade, the unfair tariff ceiling prevailed until 1911, and the question of alien land tenure was subject to constant foreign pressure. Eventually the foreign right to perpetual leases, including buying, selling, and trading rights, and to perpetual use of the land was obtained and successfully upheld by foreign powers even after treaty revision. This problem was taken by Denison to The Hague for arbitration after the turn of the century.

These actions—diplomatic rivalries of countries in hawking their nationals for Japanese government service; dubious transactions for machines, ships, and materials; narcotics smuggling; violations of international quarantines by ships carrying cholera and smallpox—were all evidence for Japanese officials of the economic rapacity of Westerners ensconced in their territory.

Japanese officials became more rigid and made every effort to hold foreigners to the letter of the treaties until inequities were resolved, treaties the government technically did not recognize as legal.[24] Tremendous tensions were produced. Officials could not fail to view yatoi as part of the unequal treaty syndrome. Too often the yatoi himself reinforced the ugly foreigner image—disorderly, money-grubbing, overbearing, conspiratorial. However well employees, in fact the majority, served the Meiji government, Japanese suspicions were too deeply reinforced by fact and experience to be disregarded. Foreign employees tied too closely to their foreign representatives or reflecting the aggressive tendencies of their nations furthered those suspicions. Even when it receded into the subconscious, the image of the foreign employee was the image of his nation in the official Japanese mind.

SYMBIOTIC TENSIONS

Even in the most favourable circumstances, human interchange is subject to strain. Because the use of foreign assistants was undertaken in a milieu of internal and external constraint, the normally anticipated tensions of aliens living and working together were compounded. Concomitant with foreign pressures were tensions among Japanese modernizers themselves. *Kyōhei* conservatives and *fukoku (kyōhei)* progressives differed radically; indeed, they were sometimes aliens to each other during the early years. The nature of the resulting tensions was part of the symbiotic experiment in foreign borrowing. Official attitudes towards the employment of foreigners ranged from disapproval to enthusiasm. Conservatives were always reluctant; progressives were committed to the necessity. Both attempted to be selective.

The enthusiasm of Ōkuma Shigenobu never seems to have flagged. As a thousand letters in his collected papers attest, during his long political life he personally attracted foreign advisers. His curiosity was unquenchable and his affability legend. Other leaders shared his vigour, if not always his multifaceted vision. Among other Japanese modernizers, those most involved in the engagement of yatoi were Inoue Kaoru, Itō Hirobumi, Kawamura Sumiyoshi, Ōkubo Toshimichi, Iwakura Tomomi, Yoshida Kiyonari, Yamao Yōzō, Mori Arinori, Enomoto Takeaki, Aoki Shuzō, Etō Shimpei, Tanaka Fujimarō, Kuroda Kiyotaka, and Yamagata Aritomo. They all insisted upon hiring practical instructors, rather than scholars, artists, or persons of high rank. They wanted, and by and large obtained, persons capable of doing the job required. Only employees amenable to direction were acceptable. Theirs was a hardheaded approach to nation-building and to the employment of foreign assistants. Yet leaders were obliged to be sensitive to possible reactions in foreign circles. So broad was the Meiji experiment in foreign borrowing that by the second decade there was an element of international rivalry for the prestige of employment, whereas in the first decade competition had been principally for political leverage and commercial gain.

Cable communications relating to the employment of legal translators in 1886 illustrate most of the tensions experienced by Meiji modernizers: the insistence on quality (specific delineation of the function expected of the foreign employee), sensitivity to foreign reaction, obstacles faced by major officials in using foreign diplomatic channels, and the obtuseness of some Japanese officials who lacked the grasp of the modernizers.

Iwakura Tomosada, adopted son of Iwakura Tomomi, was a frequently used messenger. In 1886 he was the Berlin go-between for a legal translator sought by Foreign Minister Inoue Kaoru. In the following series of cables sent via St. Petersburg to Berlin, the language used was English:

Inoue
No special guarantee from the Minister of Justice of Germany but choose [chose] after consultation with Stacke 3 judges out of 11 persons selected by Minister of Justice who seemed suitable telegraph amount of salary 400

Iwakura

[Received December 10, 1886]

Iwakura Petersburg
With regard to judicial translators at first you made the contract without waiting my sanction. In fact we do not want more than one translator. Choose the best one out of three and take from him guarantee that he can correctly translate French or German laws into technical English law terms. Cancel the other two even there may be some expenses incurred for so doing.

Inoue

[Despatched December 15, 1886. Above the word guarantee the word "personally" was entered and then scratched.]

Inouye Tokio
With regard to judicial translators I beg you please to consider the matter once more. The engagement indirectly having regard to our revision of treaty and future jurisdiction. I have applied to Gaimukyo [German Foreign Minister] and Shihosho [German Justice Ministry] to recommend some jurists and in this sense having taken pains with looking for suitable jurists, they recommended me jurists and I made contracts with them. Most disagreeable now for me to be obliged to cancel after contract signed a long time ago. . . consider once my disagreeable situa-

tion and please to telegraph me immediately because jurists will start very soon.

Iwakura

[Received December 18, 1886. Inoue added a note to this cable copy: "Prefer to cancel contracts of all 3"]

Iwakura Petersburg
At first you miscarried my instructions. We need absolutely only one judicial translator and you must cancel contracts of the other two even if paying some compensation. Remember that we want judicial translator, not judges, who can translate French or German laws into correct technical English law terms. As to guarantee it should be given to you from the person to be engaged.

Inoue

[Despatched December 18, 1886.]

Inoue Tokio
With regard to contract of translators, although I am willing to be reprimanded for not waiting sanction of the Gaimudaijin yet contracts having been already entered into, situation in which I am placed cannot allow them to be cancelled for these jurists have been chosen by Minister of Justice at my request and this being second time since affair of Mohl the matter will reflect greatly on the discredit of our government and will moreover enhance difficulty of establishing good relations in future towards German government. I beg you therefore to reconsider before pressing cancellation of their contracts and if it is hardly necessary to cancel other two contracts, can they not be transferred to other engagements? Jurists already have obtained leave of absence from Ministry of Justice and having already finished preparations they are very glad to start soon. Please use your influence with [as?] Gaimudaijin and answer immediately.

Iwakura

[Received December 20, 1886.]

Minister Inouye Tokio
Your last telegram received. I am able to be reprimanded for miscarry-

ing your instructions, but now it is not the question of my disobedience and my own disagreeableness, but cancelling contracts, Japanese government will run risk of losing confidence towards German government not here to say of the mischance of the two whose contracts will be cancelled for they lost . . . work for some years to come for that no compensation with money. But this engagement being here commonly known and for re-establishing their position they must publish that the cause of cancellation not their fault. I cannot tell you all in telegram. Consider the situation I beg you give them some one position in Japan and let them come. I beg you to do so. Answer immediately. Directly. The affair is urgent.

Sinagawa

[Received December 21, 1886. Shinagawa Yajiro was Japanese Ambassador in Berlin.]

Sinagawa Berlin
We want only one as translator, but considering your situation let other 2 give you guarantee that they can and willing to serve as professors in law school and mention fact in additional agreement. Under this condition they may come all 3.

Inouye.

[Despatched December 21, 1886.]

Inoue Tokio
Please answer me as to jurists as Professor of law school the following questions under which what employment; lecture in which language; what number of lectures daily.

Iwakura

[Received December 24, 1886. Inoue wrote the following notes to the left of the above telegram, indicating replies to questions: employment—"Uncertain whether Public or private school"; lecture in which language—"English and German"; number of daily lectures—"4 hours daily." These notes were despatched December 24, 1886.]

Inouye Tokio
Without answers to my questions I can do nothing with jurists. As

soon as you know answer me, term public or private very vague. Of course must be engaged as professors of law. Telegraph me clearly your intention as to their position.

Iwakura

[Received December 26, 1886.]

Iwakura
Term of years to be engaged already fixed as also the amount of salary. As to employment in public or private school it must be left to my convenience.

Inouye

[Despatched December 26, 1886.]

Inoue Tokio
Affairs of jurists almost finished I beg to answer by telegraph if I should give travelling expenses to the wife of Landrichter [magistrate] who had been engaged at first and who was left as translator.

Iwakura

[Received December 31, 1886.][25]

A reply has not been found, but perhaps this enquiry influenced Inoue's abrupt "No allowance for wife" answers to Iwakura's requests regarding more German architects early in 1887.[26] Ambassador Shinagawa was recalled on December 27, 1886, and Inoue Kasanosuke was appointed to Berlin. This experience, serious despite its touch of farce, led Inoue in future to instruct officials to make their initial application for foreign employees secretly and without recourse to foreign public officials.[27]

The Mohl affair alluded to by Iwakura was another example of injudicious discussion which in this case, led to the Japanese government's being obliged to hire Prussian court chamberlain Ottmar von Mohl for the Imperial Household Ministry as an adviser on court etiquette. Von Mohl was candidly dubbed a supernumerary by Japanese officials, but for diplomatic reasons the engagement had to be honoured.[28] Inoue's practical approach was reflected in the activities of many of the Meiji modernizers.

Officials in fact viewed ruefully the whole phenomenon of special treatment. In 1876, Home Minister Ōkubo Toshimichi wrote Foreign Minister

Terajima Munenori that in Japan there was no custom of giving honours to persons who had simply fulfilled their duties as there was in Western countries.[29] Pragmatically, Japanese officials hoped that their public relations efforts would assist their ends. As yatoi have observed, the purpose of the officials was to soothe and placate yatoi and their governments. Their efforts created surface harmony, but officials had to be careful not to provoke yatoi jealousies; however, their naive manipulation did not pass unnoticed and was often labelled as insincerity by yatoi.

Meiji leaders were well aware that differences in social etiquette could hinder their efforts. Western dress and other customs were introduced as a social bridge to foreigners. In the new Engineering School in Public Works, students were divided into two groups—those pursuing technology where social background was not a criterion and those forming an academic group drawn from the new nobility (*kizoku*). The latter were to be given special training in Western social amenities by yatoi. The underlying motivation in these arrangements by Itō Hirobumi was study of foreign conditions so as to prevent Japanese from being deceived by foreigners.[30] Pragmatism prevailed. Shibusawa Eiichi has commented that Itō was often criticized by his colleagues for his "high-collar" ideas, but the social dancing and banquet balls in the Rokumeikan which he and others promoted, along with beef-eating, wine connoisseurship, and the social display of wives of Japanese officials, were rooted in this pragmatism as well as in a flair for pageantry. It was also this basic pragmatism which led Inoue Kaoru in 1887 to argue in the Cabinet for the creation of a "European-style Empire on the Eastern Sea" in order to make headway in treaty revision.[31]

Sometimes naive from the yatoi's viewpoint, but more often shrewd, pragmatism was ever present. Japanese officials could indulge in clever opportunism just as Westerners did. The British journalist from Australia John Reddie Black was persuaded to relinquish his opposition newspaper (*Nisshin shinjishi*) to Japanese control by being offered a government position which would ostensibly allow him to revise and liberalize newspaper regulations. However, owing to the injunction against business activities by yatoi, he could not accept the position while he owned the paper. Believing the appointment would lead to much-desired journalistic freedom if he helped with the revision of regulations, he reluctantly turned his paper over to the Japanese in 1875. He then was shifted from bureau to bureau, each official in turn complaining there was no work for him in the Seiin. Meanwhile, new regulations were issued prohibiting foreign editors for Japanese-language newspapers. From both his own and the Japanese official correspondence, it is clear that the sole purpose of Black's employment was to ease him out of his position as editor of a Japanese-language newspaper. Because his reporting was irksome to his own and other foreign governments as well as to the Japanese and since he was not incumbent at the time the new regulations were issued, he received no satisfaction from his charges of discrimination in courts either in Japan or England.[32]

Not all Japanese officials were receptive to the Meiji experiment, but in the early years, educated, major, and responsible Japanese officials were sometimes harangued by foreign representatives and even by some of their own employees. Foreigners took advantage of official courtesy, special treatment, and social permissiveness while maintaining smugly superior attitudes. Personal animosity towards yatoi was also bound to arise. However, officials, over-sensitive to foreign manners and methods, often sought refuge in their dignity—a quality not unique to the Japanese—rejecting egalitarian give-and-take. Even the most conscientious employees on occasion deplored what they described as Japanese suspiciousness, officiousness, and tendency to practise situation ethics, illustrating that the foreigner also suffered cultural paroxysms. Even outstanding advisers did not establish rapport with officials at large, but only with those with whom they worked directly.

Long before the formal higher civil service examination system was inaugurated, achievement orientation had become a general criterion for bureaucratic appointments. Certainly the core of Meiji modernizers were outstanding, innovative people who attracted competent assistants. While their ability and esprit were also to be found among lower officials, it is unrealistic to assume that this was consistently the case. Core leadership provided the catalyst and the patriotic tinge intrinsic to Japanese nation-building gave cohesion to the Meiji experiment, but the whole bureaucracy, like the leadership, was flawed by paternalism and factionalism. Differences in outlook, method, and motivation of various officials often spelled the expansion or demise of particular projects. Yatoi worked in the midst of this bureaucratic friction and rivalry.

There were difficult yatoi, but there were also difficult Japanese officials. There was pride of class even *after* schools were officially open to commoners and samurai alike and after a conscript army had removed arms from upper class monopoly. There was class pride in the new status gained by commoners elevated through their inclusion in new educational programmes. And there was "native pride" exacerbated by misunderstandings with foreigners and distaste for foreign tutelage.

These attitudes and tensions have been pointed out by many yatoi, such as E. G. Holtham. His relations with his Japanese railway crew were good, and he admired their enthusiasm. He was, however, less impressed with his interpreters and therefore often disregarded them, preferring example, sign language, and broken Japanese. The class-consciousness of those interpreters made their lack of language even more ineffective. Holtham noted also that

Japanese foremen wore gloves when off-duty to distinguish themselves from lower workers. Officials on any level disdained manual labour and looked askance when Holtham gave practical demonstrations.[33] Likewise, Commander Archibald L. Douglas had found it difficult to convince naval cadets that as future officers they had to go through the basic training of seamen. In the bakumatsu era, Dutch naval instructors similarly commented that young samurai refused to swab decks and perform menial tasks in training.[34] Pompe de Meerdevoort had trouble with the inflexibility of interpreters and finally used younger untrained Japanese who could grasp the meaning of the new medical concepts he was explaining.[35] François Verny's experiences were similar, and he pleaded for persons of lower rank willing to accept instructions.[36] These problems carried over into the Meiji period; and progressives, in particular, experienced them in working with other Japanese.

Administrative co-ordination was always a problem. Like other yatoi and many Japanese, Holtham took a dim view of bureaucracy. The "can't-be-helped" way of looking at things was a usual attitude of lower officials. When Holtham was transferred to Tokyo as chief railway engineer, he was shocked both by the poor work which he declared was the norm in the capital and by the grandiose ideas of the Japanese. While working in the field, engineers had found themselves under the constant suspicion of local officials, but the situation in the capital was more difficult to deal with.[37] Bureaucratism stalked Japanese officials as well as yatoi responsible for specific projects. Both—like Verny, Cargill, Inoue Masaru, and others—had often to seek clarification from officials in "full authority."

At the same time, access to top leaders by yatoi, even those in minor positions, appears to have been the norm. Major leaders always found time for yatoi, and officials made time to handle their numerous petty complaints and grievances. This was surely evidence of their intention to get good work done as well as to fend off consular interference. Yet, as Holtham concluded, "everywhere was tension, fatigue, and the cry for relief."

The language medium of the Meiji experiment was principally English, and the Japanese suddenly found themselves having to use a foreign language in work and study. Language study received primary emphasis. Government translation activities became a principal means of the importation of Western knowledge. Some 3,300 areas of study may be distinguished among the myriad books translated in the Meiji period.[38] Each ministry had a translation bureau, most with yatoi and Japanese canvassing textbooks from other countries. All yatoi translators were multilingual; that many translated from other European languages into English points to how important English was as a vehicle for learning. Some yatoi were also competent in Japanese, and in the early years almost all the interpreters attached to foreign legations served as part-time or temporary employees. Despite the base laid in the pre-Meiji era, the scale of the Meiji endeavour meant that able translators and inter-preters among both yatoi and the Japanese were too few.

More than language, learning attitudes were crucial to an experiment of this kind. There was the naivete of the masses who obstructed railway tracks to "see the engine jump," who snipped humming telegraph lines from fear of the unknown, and whose other superstitious reactions would, with time, be overcome.[39] Yatoi impressions, like those of the early Christian fathers, reveal admiration for the ordinary Japanese, but ingrained habits were cou-pled with racial pride as well. Foreign employees were no more able to get Japanese to follow precise instructions in new farming methods than they were able to alter Japanese preference for a rice diet. At one point in his reports Horace Capron complained that he needed an ordinary American farmer or a Japanese who would follow directions. And in fact the Hokkaido Development Commission hired Chinese farmers to carry out specific ex-perimental farming projects.[40]

Officials who countermanded reasonable work orders and obstructed rou-tine procedure, Mint guards who smoked in areas in which dangerous gases were present and used cauldrons filled with molten metal for rifle practice, lighthouse watches who deserted the beacons and necessitated the use of Filipinos, workers and officials who absented themselves from their posts during work hours, officials who tampered with official accounts and reports and double-entry ledgers prepared by yatoi—the actions of all these workers reveal temperamental disharmonies, cultural conflicts, and the ingenue qual-ity of an emerging modern labour and bureaucratic force.

Japanese officials, of course, were obliged to exercise an inordinate amount of patience at times with difficult yatoi temperaments and with frauds. They suffered mediocrity and gross negligence on occasion in the early years, but their having to endure rudeness was the proverbial straw. Japanese officials were so sensitive to boorish behaviour that they could apparently charge an employee—with the same degree of gravity—for eating rice cakes in class, poking a hole in a school wall to install a heating device, going hunting on Sunday and missing Monday classes, and for ridiculing and punishing students.[41] Such were the tensions engendered by contacts with aliens.

By the end of the decade, a nationalist reaction was setting in. Excessive Europeanization (*Ōkashugi*) provided momentum for backlash, and the neutral middle ground was crossed over. After the completion of the Kyoto-Otsu railway line in 1879, which had serious tunnelling problems, officials remarked that such problems were better understood in Japan, and the as-sistance of foreign technicians was not acknowledged.[42] In later years, Inoue Masaru, Japanese commissioner of railways, wrote that foreigners were employed only as advisers for plans for tunnels and iron bridges; he claimed that they had not been allowed to interfere with the superintending of construction.[43]

In a similar vein in 1879, Dr. Erwin von Baelz related an incident in Tokyo University which moved him to complain formally to the German chargé d'affaires. The opening ceremony of the medical department had been postponed for two and a half years. When it was at last held, the emperor did not utter the customary words of gratitude to the foreign faculty. The tenor of the address implied that the Japanese alone were responsible for the progress of the university. According to Baelz, in the draft of the speech there had been words of thanks but the Education Ministry had deleted them. This demonstrated, he felt, not Japanese dissatisfaction with foreign faculty but anti-foreignism related to treaty revision failure.[44]

A desire to avoid crediting aid from foreign employees is evident in the essays by Meiji leaders in Ōkuma Shigenobu's *Fifty Years of the New Japan*. Tongue-in-cheek, Japanese officials called the foreigners they hired "yatoi." Yatoi themselves used the word with the same sense of irony. In August 1874, Thomas W. Kinder, Mint director in Osaka, wrote to the resigning Japanese acting head that:

Even the government regards me by the name of yatoi [both *kana* and *kanji* are entered], that this character in Japan is the word for lower level daily worker, I certainly have known . . . even the person who comes after you will be filled to the brim with the aforementioned enlightened opinion. [Here the Japanese translator noted for Endō Kinsuke that *bummei no iken* was sarcasm.][45]

According to newspaper reports, the Japanese maintained they had no more suitable word than yatoi. A defensive, emotional element was pervasive, but the utilitarian approach was dominant. Emphasis was on the *use* of these foreign employees.

In the bakumatsu era, a Japanese official who was purchasing machinery from abroad remarked: "What I am thinking of is not a dead machine but a live machine."[46] This epitomizes the Japanese view of yatoi. They were live machines for factories, farms, railways, mines, ships, arsenals, schools, and government offices. They were to be regulated by contracts and oiled with special treatment for maximum use. A personal adviser to Itō Hirobumi, Francis Piggott also emphasized the *use* of foreign advisers as living reference books. Piggott's son commented:

In after years he often referred to its [the Meiji Constitution] outstanding feature, namely that it was a purely Japanese document based on their own genius and history; and he likened his role and that of other foreign advisers to living books of reference. He had no hand in the preparation of the Constitution except in the elucidation of various points of law.[47]

This view of foreign employees as well-kept live machines and books meant in practice that obstreperous employees would be removed or their activities nullified and that employees amenable to direction and of continuing worth could attain lengthy tenure, barring political exigencies. It was this very outlook towards foreign employees which created friction and preconditioned official receptivity in the overall borrowing process. These live machines and books provided the manual tools and instruments of knowledge for the New Japan. The mass of informants served as a memory bank. The living reference books were file cabinets and computing machines. This official view of hired foreigners suggests the limitations placed on their performance and at the same time helps to explain the breadth of their activities.

THE NEW ENLIGHTENMENT

Anesaki Masaharu has commented that "there was never a period in Japanese history when foreign assistance was so welcomed and made use of as in the eighth decade of the nineteenth century," but "the memory of these foreign advisers has been much obliterated, partly wilfully, due to the conservative reaction of the nineties." He thought that the "new enlightenment" of the first half of the seventies was "advocated equally by Government and the people," but from the later 1870's certain aspects of that enlightenment had become disagreeable to authorities.[48]

The new enlightenment was not uniformly sponsored by government officials even in the early years, and serious study is required to determine how much that new enlightenment penetrated Meiji society. Certainly, "the basic economic occupations and mode of life of the common people remained substantially unchanged through the first twenty-five years of the Meiji era."[49] There are scholars, as there were yatoi, with great attachment to the Imperial Charter Oath. Many yatoi considered themselves to have been called out under the fifth injunction, and there was an amazing openness in some quarters to the importation of Western learning. The Five Articles Oath (April 1868) called for the formation of deliberative assemblies and the making of decisions by public discussion, the unification of all classes in carrying out the administration of the nation's affairs; for common people as well as officials to pursue their own calling; the abolition of evil customs, and the pledge that "knowledge shall be sought throughout the world so as to strengthen the foundations of imperial rule."[50]

Articles 1, 3, and 4 were especially promising for political and social development. But the day after the Five Articles Oath was announced, a Council of State decree was issued prohibiting both public meetings and the open discussion of opinions. The decree called for preservation of the virtues of one's class and position. Japanese sociologist Tsurumi Kazuko cites these pronouncements as illustrative of Meiji methodology. The first was for foreign and the second for domestic consumption. A different ideology was expressed for a different purpose.[51] It was with this bifurcation of policy and a progressive-conservative dichotomy that the Meiji experiment was undertaken.

Yet progressive modernizers in particular did not allow their awareness that economic strength was an element of military power to dominate their approach to industrial power.[52] It has been astutely observed that this distinction, "ostensibly a quibble over means, actually involved for some . . . a reorientation so drastic as to remind one that, beyond a certain point, means tend to define, or re-define, their own ends."[53] This subtle redefinition of ends, by conservative as well as progressive modernizers, probably best explains the massive use of foreign assistants in all aspects of government, technology, and education. Essentially it was the determination of Meiji leaders to acquire modern technology which gave such broad dimensions to the borrowing process, and it was their determination to control the process which gave to their nation-building and to the yatoi experience their symbiotic character.

During the Meiji period and since, some writers have focussed on the deficiencies in Japan's nation-building efforts. Bureaucrats who prepared the Public Works Ministry history blamed the postponement of Japan's industrial revolution not only on its lack of capital but on its technological power being in the hands of foreigners. They contended that not only in industry but also in law, economics, fine arts, and other fields, the real power was in the hands of foreigners in the formative years of the Meiji era.[54] As the Meiji centennial approached, a critic has cited a number of cases of technological failure in Meiji industry caused by bureaucratic mismanagement and the failure of leadership by foreign technicians. The thesis deals with Japanese technological and industrial failure as a whole, but some remarks pertinent to foreign employees in the government reflect a certain school of thought. The selection of poor machines, by which apparently is meant machines unsuited to Japanese conditions and needs, and the use of incompetent foreigners explain Japan's failure to establish even an "initial footing in technology"—a disadvantage which had yet in 1960 to be offset. Paul Brunat, Tomioka model spinning factory adviser, Curt Netto, mining engineer and professor, and Gottfried Wagner, chemist and pioneer in manufacturing techniques and vocational education, were competent; the others were so hampered by their experience and training that they were incapable of adapting to Japanese conditions and needs. Bureaucratic management respected and copied foreign technicians, to its detriment. While capital accumulation was slight, which was therefore a serious problem, much of the capital that was accumulated was wasted. By the middle of the Meiji period, Japanese technicians had become competent but their numbers were few and their abilities were expended on "cleaning up the mess" created by foreign technicians and the Japanese bureaucracy.[55]

Implicit in these criticisms is the premise that the metamorphosis of Japan into a modern industrial state should have been instantaneous. Opprobrium therefore falls first on the out-group (*yoso*) presence and then on the in-group (*uchi* but really *yoso*) élite. Thanks largely to postwar scholarship, it is clear that Meiji bureaucratic management was not monolithic in ideology or methodology. Foreign instruction was under that varied bureaucratic management.

In the late nineteenth century, Japan attempted to achieve in a decade or two or three what had taken Europe a century and more to evolve; and not all Western nations reached the same level of development. Later, the Japanese affinity with Germany may well have arisen from the fact that both were emerging technologically. The Japanese necessarily suffered strain caused by modernization. A host of several thousand teachers from more than two dozen nations were selected, usually because they had the experience and knowledge required, but sometimes for political expedience. There was confusion caused by machines and methodology. For the Japanese, their training with yatoi in the military services, the schools, and workshops and their selecting of foreign models meant literal westernization in diet, clothing, living quarters, social manners, and so on. The army was on the metric system and the navy used English measurements. Machine and material standards for industry were not uniform through the Taishō period (1912–26). One can point to important examples today of the continued use of old Japanese measures. Not only did a German-oriented army and a British-oriented navy develop, but schools with different orientations emerged in diplomacy, education, and other fields.

The foreign-language work and study milieu caused not only tension among participants but also social strains. It was not until 1884, when Kanda Kōhei criticized Tokyo University as a foreign-language university that there was a serious call for education in the Japanese language in government institutions. Use of the Japanese language progressed first in private law schools. In fact, private schools, influenced by private foreign employees and returning overseas students, conceived of their role as critics of government educational policy. By making Japanese legal and other studies indigenous, they attempted to counter the prevailing idea that only government schools were good. Other aspects of the strain associated with modernization were the inevitable gaps in industrial development, society, and government, inherent in growth. From the original decision to choose yatoi from particular nations came many conflicting and contradictory influences.[56] Therefore, criticisms about lack of co-ordination in the Meiji experiment have some validity.

Pronounced deficiencies were the result of limitations of timing, scope, and organizational management. Bureaucratic management and organizational management were not the same thing. Modern industrial and organizational techniques were insufficiently pursued by the government fostering the infant modern technology.[57] And organizational innovation, the essence of nineteenth-century modern Western—especially Anglo-Saxon—techniques, was slow to develop in Japan perhaps because not only the machines but also the machine value-system were required.[58] Social scientists could pursue profitably this aspect of the Meiji experiment.

As a result of real and imagined fears about foreign incursions, officials forbade yatoi assumption of more than minimal direction. By the time of the Sino-Japanese War of 1894–95, Japanese technicians had, in a practical sense, replaced foreign employees, but the pattern of government protection and business ties with government had become habitual and inhibiting. Ronald Dore comments that: "The samurai traditions which elevated government and warfare above the baser pursuits of industry and trade could be carried over into the Meiji period because the political revolution preceded the industrial revolution and businessmen remained clients of the statesmen rather than vice versa."[59] Facts to date point to the yatoi role as symbiotic, not parasitic. Foreign technicians did not provide overt leadership, but rather worked under Japanese leadership as trainers. Allusion to bureaucratic managerial respect for foreign technicians borders on myth. In the context of this study of the motivation for, and milieu of, the experiment; of foreign pressure, internal instability, and factionalism; of the abnormal atmosphere of urgency; of symbiotic tensions inherent in cultural interchange; of the self-defence mechanisms erected for bureaucratic survival; and the administrative policy towards foreign employees, the question arises whether foreign technicians or other foreign advisers had a leadership role.

Under Japanese bureaucratic management, the degree and area of assistance were delineated. Foreign leadership was rejected. Even so, yatoi had a decision-conditioning role, some to such an extent that they also had sub-leadership roles. Reports and proposals by yatoi did not receive wide dissemination even among officials. Influence was usually limited to particular officials with whom yatoi were in direct contact. That some could fill a subleadership role speaks to the ability of those yatoi and the quality of those Japanese leaders.

Too much was attempted and expected in too short a time because of the "council of gods" aspect of the experiment. Japanese students of yatoi nevertheless put up a virile defence against foreign encroachment, erected a formidable bureaucratic state and assured its endurance by overseeing the education of the next generation of bureaucrats. The aim of the Meiji experiment became in essence to establish a modern state rather than to build a nation. This aim was achieved. The good of the people was rationalized as a future thing, but this too was a modern outlook. Leaders judged it politically defensible to channel yatoi activities. As modernization fatigue taxed energies and as international frustrations continued, motivations for, and application of, foreign borrowing were channelled more and more to the service of the state. It seems that in translating the knowledge of the modern West into Japanese, foreigners were employed in technology and in institutional architecture principally to elucidate obscurities in the text.[60] Nevertheless, and notwithstanding deliberate attempts to diminish the evidence, Meiji Japan's "live machines" left marks that are impossible to obliterate.

6

The Yatoi Legacy

British journalist and sometime yatoi John R. Black observed: "The Japanese only look upon foreigners as schoolmasters. As long as they cannot help themselves, they make use of them; and then they send them about their business."[1] Yet foreign employees gave some 10,000 man-years of service to Meiji Japan. Those day labourers, salarymen, tutors, and consultants tilled the ground and shared the burden of the day's heat in building the New Japan. Essentially, they were teachers, and it is to their students that one must look to assess their historical importance. Japanese receptivity is at issue.

The impact of the expanding modern West thrust Japanese intelligentsia, in and out of government, into future shock and began Japan's race with time a century ago. The initial Japanese response was cohesive with respect to its ends of self-defence and preservation. Because ends covertly define means, the prime end of political independence necessarily coloured the experiment in foreign borrowing. Yet, just as ends may define means, means also shape ends. Early on, different means were advocated by conservative and progressive modernizers. Both their world views were expanding. From recognition of sovereignty and acquisition of a new technology for purposes of competing with foreign powers, the Japanese moved to aspirations of security and equality.

Professional yatoi, by their warnings and their encouragement of Japanese political independence, in concrete and specific ways influenced the Japanese official world view. Legalist and opportunist yatoi, solicited for advice or not, urged that Japan assert itself. Education in the Western manner familiarized Japanese with Western international pragmatism and techniques. If the seesaw of conciliation and firmness, the soft line and the hard line, which was apparent in Japanese politics from the end of the last through the first half of the present century was residual from the bifurcation of progressive and conservative early Meiji managers, the hard line was bolstered by yatoi advisers, theorists of the balance of power, working within a Japanese framework. But surely the soft line, a professional, flexible diplomatic approach, stemmed from the early progressives and the total yatoi borrowing experience. By and large, yatoi were information brokers, and dedicated yatoi tutors and co-workers helped Meiji leaders to redefine national interests.

Education in all forms was the experimental vehicle. Since the bakumatsu era, foreign employees had encouraged sending Japanese overseas for study, but that programme was inconsistently applied in the first decade and a half of the Meiji period. Yet, by the end of the 1880's yatoi education had borne fruit in Japan and among students returning from abroad, as evidenced by the increased competence of students entering leadership positions in the fields of government, education, finance, and technology. While yatoi, by serving in local areas, initiated by their encouragement the despatch of students from areas such as the east and north, which previously had been untapped, in the first decade at least 90 per cent of the students were of samurai origin, and the later selection of students was still limited to the social élite. An élitist trend was also evident in the students selected for academic work with yatoi professors in colleges under government sponsorship. Even though modernizers argued that talent was the criterion for professional leadership, talent was not drawn from a broad base in the first two decades.

Robert M. Spaulding points out that government colleges in the 1870's were

> designed chiefly to give future bureaucrats a more specialized and systematic education in some useful branch of Western learning, such as bookkeeping, banking, economics, agriculture, construction, telegraphy, mechanics, science, mining, law, or languages.
>
> Though most of these schools—and their private imitators—were hastily improvised and inadequately staffed, they supplied the civil service in the 1880s with a growing number of reasonably well-trained specialists. By 1887, the government felt able for the first time to define educational qualifications for office, and to divide the civil service into specialized career fields. The principal innovation was establishment of a new managerial élite, a career administrative corps open only to men trained in law.[2]

Education became the prime qualification for office. This concept was created by the Japanese leaders whom Sakata Yoshio has defined as "restoration new bureaucrats"—*kyōhei* and *fukoku* advocates. It was certainly influenced and accelerated by their yatoi tutors. Both the restoration new bureaucrats and the yatoi quasi-bureaucrats promoted high standards. The development of Tokyo Imperial University, especially the law school, which was a legacy of yatoi lawyers and jurists, provided incentive for formalization of recruitment by merit. The "new bureaucrats" of the 1890's, products of the upper civil service examination system, were predominantly Tokyo Imperial University law graduates.[3] A new educational élite was substituted for the former social élite and in turn formed a new social and political élite. However, family status based on origins or wealth was still dominant in the third decade.[4] The evolution of merit criteria for the Japanese bureaucracy coincided with the application of merit in the administrative policy for yatoi. The former was the initiative of restoration new bureaucrats, but yatoi, by applying merit criteria to themselves, provided a tangible example for Japanese leaders.

However, as Ronald Dore has commented:

The Meiji Restoration, and the drive to "civilization and enlightenment" which followed it, probably left the majority of Japanese little affected, hoping for and expecting out of life not much more than their fathers had had. . . . The new ethic [educational ambition] was gradually diffused beyond the circle of the ex-samurai élite, by example, by the gradual removal of all legal status distinctions, and more particularly by the schools. . . . By the time these attitudes and beliefs spread to the mass of Japanese people the change in the mechanisms of mobility noted earlier [group patronage and school competition as a preliminary filter] was already well under way.[5]

In their drive for "civilization and enlightenment" (*bummei kaika*), the Japanese directly entered the specialist stream in nineteenth-century Western civilization. Their cultural-educational childhood was skipped. As Maruyama Masao has described, in the nineteenth century when Japan took on European learning, that learning had just evolved into specialization and individualization of study. In Europe, there had been a long evolution in learning, and the emerging individual science shared a common root, like a bamboo with a flanged tip or a hand with fingers (*sasaragata* is Maruyama's term). In the ideological dichotomy of the early Meiji period between Eastern spirit and Western science, and with the strain of modernizing, the mutual root of Western civilization was literally cut off and discarded at the time of its importation to Japan. Only the individualized, specialized tips were taken. Japanese scholars fell into a technological learning frame rather than an intellectual and cultural learning frame. This early entry into the specialist frame led to closed divisions in academic learning, but which extended throughout society. Maruyama concludes that in the absence of a mutual root, each science or field is a separate octopus-pot (*tako tsubo*), and that Japanese learning has that characteristic of form (*tako tsubogata*)—a fragmented group society, each group in its own pot.[6] There is a similarity between Maruyama's octopus-pots and Nakane Chie's analysis of singular-group or single-cell society within a vertically organized society.[7] Maruyama, however, points out that while the groups are closed to each other within society, the country as a whole is open to the world. In the limited open country era of the late nineteenth century, the Japanese élite thronged the high road to the outside world in a breathless race to borrow from the West.

One recalls Captain Huyssen Van Kattendyke's observation. In his report on the second Dutch naval mission in the bakumatsu era, he wrote that the Japanese wanted everything they saw, but as soon as they had something, they were finished with it, and wanted something else. Like the French, they were "happy types lacking patience."[8] But one also recalls French minister Léon Roches's remark that it would be a mistake to confuse the Japanese with other Asians.[9] Many foreigners continue to be impressed with Japanese energy and that which must have motivated it—curiosity.[10]

Tsurumi Kazuko has probed the sociological phenomenon of Japanese curiosity and the effect it had upon Japan's foreign borrowing. Japanese curiosity is directed towards material society, person/thing rather than thought/philosophy oriented, especially unusual concrete things from outside. This curiosity makes for receptivity, and nothing previously borrowed is discarded. Tsurumi suggests that Japanese society as a multilevel structure is highly compartmentalized and based on a principle of cutting off and separating (*kirihanashi*) so that every experience can be subsumed without confrontation or interaction. Thus, all past experience is alive and at work in society. This compartmentalization allows behaviour and policy to accommodate themselves to the convenience of the immediate situation (*tsukaewake*) and obviates the necessity to address contradictions.[11]

The concepts of these social scientists help explain the gaps between political, industrial, and social development in Japan.[12] Tsurumi's sociological thesis in particular helps to explain the megalomania which was a characteristic of the Japanese in their borrowing in the Meiji era. The sweep of yatoi activities, like all foreign borrowing in that era, is easily observable; the depth is more difficult to calculate. Strong teacher-student ties developed, but some yatoi also questioned the quality of educational reception. On his silver anniversary in Tokyo Imperial University, von Baelz observed that on occasion Japanese misunderstood Western learning. He declared that the Western academic world was an organic body, not a machine, and that the

Japanese tended to think of learning as a machine. The Japanese wanted to carry their study everywhere to everything. Whereas deep study needed a lifetime of effort to acquire, the Japanese were content to live on only the interest on their spiritual capital.[13]

What may appear to be a contradiction between Maruyama's and Baelz's assessment of Japanese receptivity is rather differing sides of a single issue. The Japanese possessed an inveterate and impatient curiosity; without acquiring a painstaking general background, they entered and gulped down the specialist stream. This observation, it seems, may be applied without overextension to Japan's total modernizing effort. By the nature of this receptivity, Japan made a rapid physical transformation to a modern state, which precluded its reduction to colonial status, but there was a gap between extrinsic and intrinsic change. The metamorphosis was swift, the metanoia slow. Meiji Japan set out in pursuit of Western science, but never basically doubted the superiority of Eastern spirit. The attitude towards yatoi and modern Western learning techniques as machines was reflected in the Japanese view of themselves as machines.

In considering the Meiji experiment, it is easy to observe political promptings and establishment élitism, but these neither explain the variegated pattern nor the contradictions in that experiment. Rather it is in Japanese views of modernization that some answers are suggested. Critic Iizuka Kōji comments that technology was easiest to acquire, human consciousness and growth far more difficult. The material civilization of the West was praised, but the mentality and consciousness of the Western process was not probed and not understood. This, he concludes, resulted in a Japanese-Western compromise (*WaYō setchū*). The "mental climate" was retained and used by those promoting reform from above.[14] One cannot help but recall Itō Hirobumi's urging political reorganization while the feudal "afterglow" lingered among the masses. Iizuka also writes of the persistence of the lord-vassal, master-servant relationship (*kunshin no gi*) and the Meiji government utilization of this relationship for state-building and industrialization. What occurred was a delay between material and spiritual modernization.[15]

A number of Japanese writers contend that in emphasizing the practical, material aspects and practical, material application of the modern West, the Meiji government committed a basic error; Western civilization was mistaken for modernization. In their early equation of westernization, especially Western technology, with modernization, Japanese leaders in and out of government limited the meaning of modernization. Ishizuki Minoru, however, argues that before the octopus-pots took shape, the Western rational and scientific spirit predominated in students returning from abroad in the second decade. From the bakumatsu era through the early 1870's, students had a superficial formal Western posture, but national consciousness provided the second wave of students from the mid-1870's to the mid-1880's with a check and balance for objective evaluation. Those students strove to avoid equating modernization with westernization. Although groupism coloured the effort, the early broad sampling of different countries by students created a multivision, and they were able to put Japanese culture in a universal dimension. Overseas students were a cornerstone in Japan's modernization, but government attitudes and policy, which favoured the use of students for the state, engulfed student efforts. The Meiji government policy of "formal modernization" was too strong for them, and they succumbed to the establishment.[16]

Nevertheless, as Kano Masanao observes, by the early equation of westernization and modernization, the Japanese intelligentsia precluded the possibility or opportunity of seeking modernization outside westernization.[17] Kano also observes that the limited, formal definition of modernization led to a confrontation between national welfare and the people's welfare. Therein is the locus of the scholastic division between modernizationists and other schools and positions. This debate about modernization is the core of the yatoi legacy.

Utilizing historical determinants and preoccupied with imperialism and stage revolution, postwar Japanese Marxists, freed from political restraints, stimulated the renascence of Japanese history studies by renewing their earlier attacks on the emperor system and by focussing on the 1868 Meiji restoration in that context. At the same time, as before the war, there were solid non-Marxist studies and criticisms. As the centennial of the Meiji Restoration approached, however, the early postwar debate produced so much scholarship that in the 1950's and 1960's the field of Japanese history studies became an arena for thrashing out the failure/success hypotheses vis-à-vis Japan's modernization.

Scholarly debate is said to have been polarized between Marxist and modernizationist factions. Neither is monolithic and there has been much ebb and flow. Some argued that the Meiji restoration was a bourgeois revolution, others that it was a bourgeois revolution that lacked a transition of power to a bourgeoisie. Yet others write in terms of renovation/restoration, sense of nation, and national revolution. Tōyama Shigeki has pointed out that Marxism has been unable to explain the people's consciousness, or unconsciousness, and Maruyama Masao has offered a fresh approach in an internal analysis of the emperor system. Maruyama perceived a basic historical thread woven through the emperor system ideology; the system remained the same but the role was altered by environmental change. The spiritual structure, the people's ethos, remained constant. He did not carry his findings to problem resolution as other scholars have felt the need to do.

In particular, Japanese scholars of European history applied their research

to the Japanese scene. Using the problem-solving technique, and being in-
debted to both Marx and Weber, Ōtsuka Hisao in prolific writings on modernization carried his argument to the equation of modernization with
democratization. Japan, with its "artificial capitalism" (to the Second World
War) and its "institutional democracy," fell short because it failed to absorb
the ethos of modernization. Ōtsuka exercised considerable influence on all
streams of Japanese historiography.

While the re-evaluation of the Meiji restoration was initiated by Marxists,
the debate has come to include a re-evaluation of Marxist views, especially
of those on Japanese imperialism. In this process some writers tie the Meiji
restoration with the present. For example, Umezawa Tadao, engaged in
comparative studies, has emphasized the similarities of Japan with Europe
and the differences between Japan and developing nations. Perhaps Kuwabara Takeo best sets out the full-blown success hypothesis with his comparison of the Meiji restoration with the present—Japan excelling all other
nations. His argument focusses on Japan's quantitative gains, with no address to the qualitative aspects of these gains: the Meiji restoration was a
bourgeois revolution, according to Kuwabara, there is no other way to account for Japan's present prosperity (*fukoku*).

It has been necessary for academic positivists to respond seriously to
Marxist assumptions, but they also eschew problem consciousness. As
Tōyama points out, problem consciousness as a technique is almost non-
existent among positivist academics, who tend to reject it as amateur. Yet
he argues that the positing of questions and/or extrapolation of models and
their steady reworking and revision in the course of research is a way of
integrating isolated historical phenomena.[18] Actually, Western academic
modernizationists have given considerable effort to positivist conceptual
frameworks, and Japanese academics are influenced by the presentist orientation of Japanese society. Some seem obliged—even the innovative Sakata
Yoshio—to insert sentences or phrases defending facts of Meiji modernization, though some of those facts seem to argue against a democratizing process.

In particular, the academic modernizationist school, Western and Japanese, has laboured to define a value-free approach. In this effort scholars
are dealing effectively with the two extremes in views towards Meiji modernization, the failure/success hypotheses. The Princeton University series, Studies
in the Modernization of Japan, reflecting the variegated nature of this major
modernizationist school, has provided testimony to Meiji receptivity, conditioned as it was by dilemmas of growth and ingrained socio-political ideological motivation.

The postwar renascence in Japanese studies in the West has been largely
a positivist response to the early stimulus of Canadian E. H. Norman's pro-

vocative study and his particular debt to Japanese socialist thought and scholarship. It is perhaps the propensity of social science to be almost clinically occupied with structure and function that has resulted in so much serious scholarship being addressed to continuity and congruity. Perhaps discontinuities and incongruities are ever fated to be unresolved though they are not extraneous to the subject.

It took little over a decade to dismantle Norman's theory that the coalition of lower samurai and merchants provided the fulcrum for restoration. But his modernization refrain—"It was only through an absolutist state that the tremendous task of modernization could be accomplished without the risk of social upheaval"—is yet to be sufficiently analysed.[19] To some scholars it appears to be an acceptable premise and to have been the perception of the event by some restoration new bureaucrats, but that perception is not apparent among other new bureaucrats. However integral the perception of the event is to the event itself, the two remain distinct. Bernard Silberman has written:

By 1880 it is clearly evident that internal development rather than external expansion was the primary goal. More specifically, internal development was embodied in the following preferences: industrial development as opposed to agricultural development, political centralization as opposed to political particularism, military development as opposed to military adventurism, and the achievement of equality in international relations through elimination of the "unequal" treaties. It is important to note that all of these goals involved use of Western institutional models and the utilization of Western systems and categories of causation or knowledge since no other meaningful alternative models of development then existed. Against the background of the emergence of these preferences evolved the problem of making day-to-day and long range decisions consonant with these preferences.[20]

Japan's attainment of unanimity in these goal preferences was evolutionary; the dynamics of this evolution are as yet an unexplored link, the discussion of which may include but extends beyond structural-functional examination into the limbo of attitude and value-conditioning. Norman comments that the apparent result of such conditioning has been that "in Japan there has been a time-lag between the adoption of a new mode of life and the full maturing of its cultural and psychological expression." However acceptable Norman's conclusion that Japan's "modernization" was far from being catholic, it is neither inevitable nor logical from his absolutist premise precisely because Meiji goals were evolutionary.

Rather, incongruities and discontinuities are pertinent. These are largely grist for the Japanese scholars who feel their history, and we know little of emotional motivations, of the relation of the knower to his data, other than that they are significant to behavioural and institutional history. In this vein, Tsurumi Kazuko, in analysing Japan's receptivity within a multistructured society, suggests that greedy curiosity attracts the alien and that nothing drawn in by the Japanese is destroyed. Rather, there is a piling up and a random selection from an endless stockpile. The best studies in Japanese technological history have been produced by Saigusa Hiroto and his colleagues. In their approach, based on solid, empirical reporting, one cannot avoid their implication that the Westernization of Japanese technology did not mean rapid modern industrialization. From Saigusa and many scholars to a new breed of social scientists, including Maruyama Masao and, more recently, Nakane Chie and Tsurumi Kazuko, there is a continuity in an empirical but negativist view of Japanese receptivity. Actually, because the Japanese are totally unable to imitate, the question of adoption does not apply. But adaptation or assimilation is called to question.

However modernization is defined, it is growth and process and has been sought, fought, and pined for as nothing has been since the Holy Grail. In the long history of modernization strain, in the West and Japan, it has often been assumed that if government and other power complexes pursued state and economic development with abandon, progress would be inevitable and benefits would accrue to all society. The late nineteenth century, the era of the impact of the modern West on Japan, was the heyday of this view, but time has surely revealed that modernization requires judicious courting. Students of modernization theories thus are rightly concerned to gather empirical views of this phenomenon, that is, the observable facts, events, and circumstances.

The major Western academic school of modernizationists and its more moderate Japanese counterpart, based in positivism, not only counters more dogmatic ideologies but balances Japanese negativists. Logical positivism does not always come to terms with its own theoretical assumptions, however. Empirical objectivity of evidence is often too readily assumed. The subjectivity of the "knower" is ignored, and correlations are rarely drawn between the observer and his data. The striving for a value-free approach reflects an image preference, and in that there is inherent the danger of positing an artificial value judgment.

Modernizationist scholars, however, do distinguish correctly between westernization and modernization. John W. Hall summarizes a major approach when he states that "westernization" indicates "too great a cultural passivity," whereas, "to say that Japan 'became modern' after 1853 puts the emphasis on a more universal process, one in which the Japanese themselves served as active and creative participants." He thus argues that, for Japan, "Westernization . . . phased into modernization."[21] The distinction is essential because even though "the modern condition [was] historically the result of the evolution of Western society," modernization emerging first from the cauldron of change in Europe, has revealed itself a complex series of growth processes subject to environmental conditioning.[22] Abstractly, modernization is the substance of this dynamic and westernization one accident or particular of it. The Princeton series has brought attention to this fact. One may suggest that Japanization, sanskritization, and so forth, are other accidents or particulars.

As modern industrial nations enter the post-industrial era, when some old conflicts have been resolved, but new relationships have engendered different conflicts and nowhere has socio-industrial growth become balanced, the question being asked with more insistence is not merely how phenomena of history and society operate but to what end. The question is neither epistemological nor a search for noumena. "What is modernization" and "what does it mean to be modernized" are pragmatic questions, but because modernization strain is yet to be brought within manageable proportions, the question of meaning is not post- but preter-modern.

As the academic empiricist searches for what really happened, the pretermodern empiricist (both work from observable phenomena) contends that integral to what really happened is what did not happen. This gap is perhaps like the pause in music or the unbrushed portion of a Zen painting. To ignore what did not happen approaches a value judgment. Chronicling what did not happen is no less true for being less positivist or for being less analytically and theoretically developed. Nor is this approach a rejection of phenomenology per se. Empirical knowledge is limited to the observable and demonstrable. What has occurred and what has not occurred are thus both observable. It is thus possible to demonstrate that certain procedures bring about certain non-results as well as certain results. Pieces of the puzzle of knowledge are often apt to be missing because of human limitations. James Morely has suggested, in the last volume of the Princeton series, that their study could be enhanced if a pathology of growth were available. The suggestion ought not be ignored. But surely, along with ascertaining functional and structural changes caused by disease or malfunction in society, it would be useful to probe the ontology of healthy growth, and it would not be remiss to remember that life itself is highest in the order of being and reality.

The Western cauldron of change which first gave birth to the modernizing dynamic produced several new alloys; one was the antimony created by the joining of empiricism and unification of the sciences, or logical positivism. Modernizationist schools thus share a positivist image preference, whereas a good many contemporary Japanese empiricists tend to retain a phenomenological negativist image preference. It seems that Ronald Dore has come closest to striking a balance between the two. Japanese preter-modern, problem-consciousness but hardly amateur, scholarship is tending towards the supra-historical in search of a total view, of an ontology of growth.

Reflecting a democratic commitment in their problem consciousness, these writers assert that Meiji statism was not inevitable but that it found fertile soil in the Meiji/Modern West frame of references. According to Kano, for example, the Japanese assumption of a limited view of modernization stifled the "people's modernization," which was burgeoning throughout the nineteenth century. The limited perception of the intelligentsia in effect denied the background of change perceptible in the people as a whole. Thus, early nineteenth-century agrarian unrest, agrarian religious revival, and an emerging "people's culture" are viewed as portents of a rice-roots modernization which did not reach fruition. A modernizationist viewing the same phenomena sees "end-of-the-regime overtones" in the utopianist religious revival and concludes that "for all the evidence of economic distress and dissatisfaction, one is struck by a lack of overt and effective protest . . . voices of alarm were raised in the main by isolated individuals. None developed a following dedicated to revolutionary action or created a lasting political organization. . . . Discontent was strong but it did not feed political or social theories calling for action against the regime."[23] Negativists thus appear to focus on the thwarted undercurrents in human history and positivists on the successful mainstream. Perhaps what is required are further attempts to reconstruct the value views of the era under study, a greater effort to see with the eyes high and low of the time in question. Within this context, from the 1960's, though the base was laid earlier, a trend in Japanese scholarship is clearly towards what did not happen in the Meiji experiment.

Both Tōyama Shigeki and E. H. Norman made genuine contributions when they refused to equate modernization take-off with the Meiji restoration. More recently, Shinohara Hajime of Tokyo University has written that Meiji Japan suffered a paroxysm in its sudden and severe impact with the modern West, but did not experience a social breakdown. Traditional Japanese style was maintained, absorbed the impact, and accomplished a conditional adjustment. The experiment did not bring a "people's revolution," that phrase is non-ideological. The state assumed a modern form, but the individual remained pre-restoration.[24] A number of these writers hold that Meiji modernization earns a plus for rapidity and a minus for superficiality. Tsurumi points out that emotional motivation only changed slowly, despite the rapid change in ideology. She suggests there was no limit to receptivity in the sense of syncretism, but the implication is that the result of foreign borrowing was a piling up, not an assimilation of materials and ideas.[25] Unfortunately, the question of the West's assimilation of the modernizing dynamic is not raised.

Yet, unbidden, some machine values came with machines. Restoration new bureaucrats, in transcending regional consciousness, were modern. The transition in thought from cannon (kyōhei) to machines of all types (fukoku) was modern.[26] But the idea that farmer-soldiers (tondenhei) were to be used for reclamation of underdeveloped areas from Hokkaido to Taiwan to Manchuria was in accordance with the entrepreneurial pioneer, modern (kyōhei) spirit, and the concepts of cordons of sovereignty and cordons of advantage were modern (kyōhei) and in line with balance of power, buffer zones, satellite states, and the domino theory. Nationalism created by politicians to enhance the state was modern, as was unbridled competition vis-à-vis other nations. (In the words of one of Ōkuma's foreign merchant advisers: "the True Spirit of competition, that great civilizer and lever of modern progress."[27]) A century later, on a worldwide scale, nationalism and international rivalry are yet to be transcended. Thus, Meiji leaders pursued modernization in the official Western manner. Yatoi were their tutors and assistants.

A disparity between extrinsic and intrinsic change remained. Iizuka Kōji reminds us that even before E. H. Norman propounded his thesis, Thorstein Veblen pointed out that there is an interval between material and spiritual modernization and that Japan could safely use that delay for a little while. But, as Iizuka has put it, one must examine both the visible and invisible aspects of modernization. Japan's modernization was visible, without the underpinnings of citizen consciousness. As citizen consciousness develops, Japan's modernization will enter a crisis stage.[28]

Yet the yatoi experience and the borrowing phenomenon made extrinsic change rapid and planted seeds for intrinsic change as well. With the impact of the modern West there was also a meeting with Japan. Pots of humanistic, social, and democratic ideas were formed. Foreign academic continuity survives, stemming from Kaempfer, Thunberg, and Siebold, who are in a sense proto-yatoi, through the scholarly amateurs Chamberlain and Aston et al., to today's academic professionals in Europe and America who had early ties with Japan. This continuity is part of the yatoi legacy.

The yatoi were also one medium for the transmission of Western spirit in its multiplicity. Early missionaries ruefully remarked that the Japanese wanted everything except opium and Christianity.[29] The Japanese prevented ingress of the former, but the latter filtered through yatoi carriers of their own culture and other foreigners and provided the motivation for social protest in the Meiji and Taishō periods in particular and in a more subtle but wider form today.[30]

Had a technological base not been laid and a spirit of constitutionalism engendered in the Meiji period, the post-Second World War American occupation's laboratory experiment in legislated social change could hardly have had the social and intellectual effects it has had.[31] The present technological explosion and postwar commitment to the new constitution, whatever the varied and changing motivations, have their origins not in the ashes of defeat but in the Meiji experiment.

A similar bifurcation of policy perceived in the Meiji government persists, as it does in the West. Metamorphosis still takes priority over metonoia in politics and society, the Meiji view of a limited élitest modernization and a limited open country. However, compartmentalization and situation ethics are being decried by professional scholars and citizen amateurs who demand that modernization fulfil its delayed promise of balanced growth and enhancement of human life.

Shinohara suggests that social democracy has come to the fore in the citizens' movement from the 1960's. He describes the phenomenon as an empirical, individual, and amateur political movement in confrontation with statism *and* nationalism, independent of parties but bound together by the commitment to democracy.[32] Other observers contend that mutual group dependence militates against development of anything more than a temporary localized phenomenon based in group self-interest. Some contemporary commentators argue that since Japanese social organization has always been imposed by a group from above and change has always come from a series of groups displacing each other from above, local movements are ephemeral.[33] These academic observations are not as significant as the fact that open debate on the present course of society is in progress and that the Meiji experiment is the historical reservoir being plumbed for insight. And the "live machines" are an important part of that reservoir.

Japanese intellectuals are still in fragmented groups. Increasingly, some are making their way out of their octopus-pots, singular social cells, and isolated compartments to provide interpretive leadership. Unlike Meiji intellectuals who, Kano writes, were never associated with the distortions and contradictions of Japanese society and who therefore were blind to the aspirations of the "foolish" masses, some of today's intellectuals are investigating "another modernization"—not that of the Meiji government but that desired by ordinary people.[34] Even among advocates of Nihonism (Japanism), there is a hopeful sign in the sense that the sentiment of nation is replacing that of state. Their dated position, a reaction to modernization strain, was summarized by yatoi sculptor Vincenzo Ragusa in 1912 when reapplying for government employment. He wrote: "Japan still has a muse which smiles and enlivens the sentiment of the nation's heritage."[35] Both these intellectual streams stem from the Meiji experiment and yatoi tutors.

Even pessimists, in viewing today's social unrest and disavowing a viable citizen consciousness, define the citizens' movement (*shimin undō*) and even the residents' movement (*jūmin undō*), a segment of the former, as a citizen-consciousness education movement. The people, largely "ab-used" in the Meiji experiment, appear to be moving under the positive aspects of the legacy of that experiment in pursuit of a redefined modern muse. The nature of experiment remains, however. Some scholars solemnly date the end of European civilization in the decade of the 1960's. The world has shrunk, and the implication is that there is no future source abroad for Japanese curiosity to tap for another run at "civilization and enlightenment." A further implication is that Japan must build on the positive aspects of the legacy of its late nineteenth-century encounter. The search for universal modernization is underway. The negativist position stems perhaps from the negative ideal in the Japanese ethos, but affirmation is subsumed in the logic of negation. Thus, the "mud-swamp" of Catholic novelist Endō Shūsaku, which sucks in the alien, is ideal for a new floral bloom, a species perhaps heretofore unknown. Thus, even as the Meiji government is being faulted today for overlearning the Western pattern of modernization, those "live machines" and "living reference books" echo in the streets.

Table 1

Meiji Government Foreign Employees: Areas of Service by Nationality (1868–1900)[a]

Ministry (other)	Britain*	France	U.S.A.	Germany	China	Manila	Holland	Italy	Russia	Canada	Austria*	Switzerland	Denmark	Portugal*	Belgium	Malaya	Sweden	Korea	Spain	Norway	Finland	Mongolia	Other*	Total
Public Works	553	90	13	24	46	69	1	10			1	1	8	1		1	2			1	1	1	2	825
Education	86	39	105	93	7		12	2	8	3	2	1	1		3			2	1					367
Prefectures	119	27	94	38	17			2			1	3				4							1	315
Navy	118	69	12	8	1	4	21					3		2										215
Home	26	2	15	43	5		5	1	1		1	1	1	1	2		1							117
Army	2	75		16	13		3	7		7	1													108
Hokkaido Development	4	1	56	5	1				5		1													88
Finance	38	20	13	6	1		2	2	1		3			2										88
Council of State	11	59	8	3				1			1													83
Government Shipping	29	1	15	1	3	3	5	1																54
Justice	6	14	2	5	1		1	1																30
Agric. & Commerce	4	1	8	15			1																	28
Foreign	4	1	6	12			1	2	1			1												27
Cabinet	19	1	1	5																				26
Communications	14		1	3																				21
Imperial Household	1	2	2	2						1														8
Total	1034	401	351	279	95	76	51	27	16	11	11	10	10	6	5	5	3	2	1	1	1	1	3	2400

aCompiled from Foreign Ministry, Navy, Prefecture records, the Cabinet, Ōkuma, and Griffis Collections.
*Britain (Ei): includes Australia, New Zealand. Austria: Hungary. Portugal: Goa, Macao. Other: Indies. Council of State and Cabinet numbers reflect administrative changes.

Table 2

Meiji Government Foreign Employees: Man Years by Area of Government (1868–1900)[a]

Year	Council of State (Dajōkan)	Cabinet (Naikaku)	Imperial Household (Kunaishō)	Foreign Ministry (Gaimushō)	Justice (Shihōshō)	Finance (Ōkurashō)	Home (Naimushō)	Public Works (Kōbushō)	Communications (Teishinshō)	Agric. & Commerce (Nōshōmushō)	Hokkaido Development (Kaitakushi)	Government Shipping (Kaisō Toriatsukaijo)	Navy (Kaigunshō)	Army (Rikugunshō)	Education (Mombushō)	Prefectures (Fuken)	Total
1868	[60]			1		(4)		(7)							(1)	19	92
1869	[60]		1			(5)		(34)						(4)	6	23	133
1870	1		1	1		15	1	135					(7)	(9)	21	84	275
1871	1		1	3	1	29	4	209			10	19	(3)	(13)	40	128	461
1872	1		1	5	4	50	7	281			25	25	53	33	68	121	674
1873	2		1	6	5	45	15	310			30	2	72	42	90	82	702
1874	15		1	4	3	51	35	392			26	3	96	46	107	79	858
1875	16		1	4	3	48	48	397			21	16	66	53	75	66	814
1876	3		1	4	11	27	49	325			26	1	85	37	88	63	720
1877	2		1	4	11	17	51	259			22	1	69	29	56	49	571
1878	2		2	6	9	15	47	204			24	1	61	16	59	33	479
1879	1		3	6	9	12	47	184			18	1	51	14	58	40	444
1880	2		3	6	9	10	33	143			21		28	13	65	35	368
1881	3		3	6	5	8	24	108		7	18		25	6	52	24	289
1882	3		3	6	3	6	13	86		12			15	5	44	26	222
1883	4		3	7	4	4	13	64		12			13	6	42	24	196
1884	7		3	6	5	5	12	46		14			21	12	36	26	193
1885	8		3	8	5	4	13	36	13	15			24	12	35	25	201

Table 2 (cont.)

Year																	Total
1886		[25]	3	12	5	4	15		14	14			27	13	50	22	204
1887		[13]	4	10	6	4	21		9	9			8	15	56	17	172
1888		[12]	4	6	6	4	24		8	10			9	20	57	22	182
1889		[10]	4	5	6	2	14		8	10			9	12	55	28	163
1890		[10]	3	3	5	2	15		8	8			14	8	47	41	164
1891		5	4	2	7	2	11		8	7			15	8	49	63	181
1892		3	4	2	6	1	7		9	5			7	8	46	46	144
1893		3	3	2	6	1	2		9	4			6	7	42	15	100
1894		2	3	2	5		2		7	3			6	7	33	7	77
1895		1	3	2	5		2		8	2			5	5	34	7	74
1896			3	2	4		2		7	2			6	5	31	5	67
1897			3	2	4		1		6	2			6	4	44	4	76
1898			3	2	4		1		5	2			9	3	44	4	77
1899			3	2	4		4		5	2			6		45	4	75
1900			3	2	1		4		3	4			3		34	4	58
Total	191	84	81	140	161	375	537	3220	127	144	241	69	825	465	1610	1236	9506

[a] [ ] Council of State and Cabinet numbers reflect administrative changes. Office unclear (1871, 1881); nationality unclear (1882).

Table 3
Meiji Government Foreign Employees: Man Years by Nationality (1868–1900)[a]

	Britain	France	Germany	U.S.A.	Holland	China	Manila	Italy	Austria	Russia	Denmark	Portugal	Canada	Belgium	Switzerland	Malaya	Sweden	Finland	Korea	Spain	Norway	Mongolia	Other	Total
1868	20	58	1	7	4	1									1									92
1869	43	67	3	9	7	4																		133
1870	111	90	16	22	18	7	3	2							2	4								275
1871	223	111	25	51	27	16	8	2	2	1				1		4								471
1872	292	174	43	93	36	15	8	2	2	4	1	1		2				1			1			674
1873	354	142	51	85	33	13	3	2	5	3	3	2	1	2			2	1			1			702
1874	433	145	62	94	34	17	46	2	5	1	6	3	2	1		1	2	1				1	2	858
1875	386	139	53	86	35	36	54	4	2	3	5	3	1	1	1		2	1					2	814
1876	362	113	57	76	34	40	15	8	1	4	3	4					1						2	720
1877	286	90	44	65	28	28	12	7	3	4	4						1						1	571
1878	255	63	38	61	20	18	5	5	3	4	3	3			1									479
1879	232	50	46	64	19	10	5	6	2	2	2	2	1	1	1								1	444
1880	168	43	47	63	17	8	4	8	2	1	1	2	1	1	1				1					368
1881	135	22	50	53	9	4	3	6	2	1	1	1	1		1				1					290
1882	103	18	41	32	7	6	3	4	1	1	1	1	1		1				1					221
1883	92	17	34	28	8	5	1	2			1	1	1	1	2				2				1	196
1884	86	18	40	24	7	6	1	7					1		2				1					193
1885	89	18	45	25	7	7	1	4		1		1	1	1					1					201

Table 3 (cont.)

Year																							Total
1886	84	21	59	22	3	4	5		1	1	1	3											204
1887	59	21	60	19	4	1	5		1	1	1												172
1888	54	22	65	27	3		6			1			3				1						182
1889	56	18	51	26	3		4			1			3									1	163
1890	62	13	49	32	1		2			1			3									1	164
1891	71	17	42	36	1		2		1	1			7		1	2							181
1892	67	12	26	28	1		2		1				4		1	2							144
1893	40	11	32	11	1		3		1					1									100
1894	30	11	23	8	1		2		1					1									77
1895	29	12	17	12	1		2							1									74
1896	30	9	14	10	2		1							1									67
1897	28	10	22	12	2		1							1									76
1898	29	9	22	12	2		1							1	1								77
1899	27	8	25	10	1		1							1	1					1			75
1900	17	6	20	10	1		1							1	1					1			58
Total	4353	1578	1223	1213	377	246	172	109	36	35	31	30	28	19	18	13	9	5	5	2	1	11	9516

[a]Cf. note Table 2.

Table 4

Meiji Government Foreign Employees: Areas of Service (Man Years by Nationality)

Ministry of Public Works (Kōbushō)	Britain	France	Manila	China	Germany	U.S.A.	Italy	Denmark	Sweden	Portugal	Finland	Switzerland	Austria	Norway	Holland	Malaya	Mongolia	Other	Total
Main Office	41																		41
Mine Bureau	133	136			52	7									1	1			330
Railway Bureau	1070	9		2	15	26	6	10	6	5	5			2					1156
Communications Bureau	301				4	2		9											316
Workshop Bureau	171	165			9	4						3							352
Building & Repairs Bureau	21	22			1		2												46
Education Bureau	201	3					24												228
Lighthouse Bureau	439		169	122		6	3						2				1	9	751
Bureau Office	*263*			*11*		*6*													*280*
Tōmyō maru	*14*																		*14*
Thabor maru	*80*		*44*	*54*															*178*
Meiji maru	*82*		*125*	*57*			*3*						*2*				*1*	*9*	*279*
Total	2377	335	169	124	81	45	35	19	6	5	5	3	2	2	1	1	1	9	3220

Note: Figures in italics are sub-totals.

Table 5

Meiji Government Foreign Employees: Periods of Service (Man Years by Nationality)

Ministry of Public Works (Kōbushō)	Britain	France	Manila	China	Germany	U.S.A.	Italy	Denmark	Sweden	Portugal	Finland	Switzerland	Austria	Norway	Holland	Malaya	Mongolia	Other	Total
1868	6	1																	7
1869	28	4				1													34
1870	68	60	3	1	1													1	135
1871	136	55	5	3	1	2								1				1	209
1872	192	62	8	9	4	2	1				1	1		1				1	282
1873	251	23	3	9	8	7	1	2	2	1	1	1						2	311
1874	283	22	46	10	9	8	1	5	2	1	1	1	1		1	1		2	393
1875	265	20	54	10	10	9	2	4	2	1	1		1		1		1	1	397
1876	247	22	15	25	8	5	5	2		1	1							1	325
1877	198	19	12	17	5	4	5	3		1									258
1878	164	18	5	10	2	4	4	2											204
1879	144	15	5	4	5	3	5	1											183
1880	109	11	4	5	6		6												142
1881	87	3	3	6	10		2												108
1882	69		3	3	9		2												86
1883	56		1	3	3		1												64
1884	42		1	3															46
1885	32		1	3															36
Total	2377	335	169	124	81	45	35	19	6	5	5	3	2	2	2	1	1	9	3220

The Ministry of Public Works was established in 1870. Employees listed before that date were largely Civil Affairs Ministry employees.

Table 6

Monthly Salaries of Foreign Employees in the Meiji Government (Dollars) (1868–1900)[a]

Ministry (other)	Under $50	50	100	200	300	400	500	600	700	800	900	1000	1200	1300	1800	2000	Total
Council of State	3		32	5	5	5	3	9				1					63
Cabinet				12		4	1	6	2		1			1			27
Imperial Household				6	1			1									8
Foreign			5	5	2	5	2					2	1				22
Justice		1	3	4	5	3	3	3				1	1				24
Finance	5	10	11	21	10	4	8	2			1	1					73
Home		8	12	9	20	13	5	2	1	5							75
Public Works	132	113	352	96	61	35	13	10	2	5	1	3	1			1	825
Communications	3	1	1	4	4	2	1	1									17
Agric. & Commerce		1	1	3	4	3		1									12
Hokkaido Development	12	8	25	22	8	3	2	1		3							84
Government Shipping		5	13	28	2	3											51
Navy	3	27	90	29	12	8	4	1		1					1		176
Army	4	3	32	26	23	7	3	5									103
Education	3	12	64	103	74	21	5	6	1								289
Prefectural Government	31	34	46	44	27	13	3	2	1								201
Total	196	223	687	417	258	127	53	50	8	14	3	8	3	1	1	1	2050
		(74%)				(19%)						(7%)					(100%)

[a]Major employer selected.

Table 7
Ministry Expenditures for Overseas Students (Yen)

1876–1877		1877–1878	
Finance	1,350.——	Finance	None
Army	21,401.155	Army	11,400.——
Navy	42,133.774	Navy	34,928.344
Education	31,939.627	Education	21,855.367
Justice	12,273.210	(Supervisors	6,454.201)
Hokkaido Development	4,578.940	Justice	10,738.304
Public Works	None	Hokkaido Development	2,000.——
(Engineering School			
Students:	19,839.612)	Public Works	None

1878–1879		1879–1880	
Home	2,266.667	Home	3,200.——
Army	24,840.873	Army	29,819.716
Navy	28,274.588	Navy	28,778.307
Education	22,369.672	Education	32,428.452
(Supervisors	6,686.781)	(Supervisors	3,279.585)
Justice	12,366.140	Justice	17,873.555
Hokkaido Development	4,222.554	Hokkaido Development	6,615.564
Public Works	593.027	Public Works	4,986.844

1880–1881		1881–1882	
Home	4,541.911	Home	None
Army	59,587.843	Foreign	541.065
Navy	38,216.284	Army	30,302.203
Education	44,550.——	Navy	8,470.505
(Supervisors	3,349.750)	Education	33,874.861
Justice	6,426.521	Justice	11,185.981
Hokkaido Development	7,736.806	Hokkaido Development	3,605.180
Public Works	None	Public Works	12,963.827

1882–1883		1883–1884	
Foreign	None	Home	243.123
Army	22,543.436	Army	20,518.623
Navy	4,984.124	Navy	3,455.660
Education	22,543.436	Education	16,153.691
Justice	2,158.539	Justice	1,368.594
Hokkaido Development	Abolished	Public Works	1,941.227
Public Works	13,317.149		

Table 7 (cont.)

1884–1885		1885–1886	
Home	366.082	Home	None
Army	20,154.146	Army	15,270.114
Navy	5,851.280	Navy	8,717.989
Education	23,711.033	Education	23,942.900
Public Works	None	Public Works	405.—
Justice	1,315.417	Justice	None

[a]Compiled from *Sainyūshutsu kessan hōkokusho*, MZZKSS, 4, 5, 6.

Appendix 1

Instructions for Hiring Foreigners, 1870

(Gaikokujin yatoiirekata kokoroe no jōjō, Meiji 3/2, Foreign Ministry Records Bureau, Tokyo)

There are at the present time foreigners engaged for various work. Regarding this, formerly, after complying with the procedure of an Imperial directive, the employment of foreigners was permitted. However, due to ignorance of employment methods inadequate contracts were made or the manner of selection in regard to the character of those employed was not sufficiently detailed. Gradually because of this, unfortunate aspects of these things have come to light. Therefore a summary of instructions is issued in separate enclosure. In general, these instructions are to be the standard. In each case when application is made, care should be exercised so as not to neglect these stipulations. Thus this directive is issued as above.

FOREIGN MINISTRY, MARCH 1870 (MEIJI 3/2)

Article 1: In contact with foreigners trust is the first consideration. It should be uppermost in our minds not to lose the honor of the Empire. In reference to employment, consultation should be approached only after full knowledge of the candidate's depth of learning and propriety of character, for deceitful and frivolous persons are not excluded from among the foreigners who come to oriental countries.

In many cases their selection is imprudent; irresponsible rumors, etc., are believed, or trusting their empty boasts, there are instances in which the foreigners are unsuitable for the situation for which they are hired. Thus it has come to notice that salaries are spent uselessly. Therefore it is decreed that employment should take place after repeated close investigation.

Article 2: When employing foreigners application must be made; and since it is necessary that the Foreign Ministry or officials of the open ports, according to the status of the employee, report to the officials of the country of the foreign employee, the fact of dismissal also must be communicated.

Article 3: In the matter of employment in various fields, the employee should be used only in his own area. Among these foreigners even if desirous of their own profit they wish to engage in business, etc. with Japanese in addition to their special occupation, permission may not be granted. Furthermore in the event of exercising his influence in the channels of foreign trade or of appearing to engage secretly in trade, the foreign employee naturally, but also the person responsible for hiring him should be punished. This injunction [against business] must be agreed upon from the outset.

Article 4: Regarding employment, various accounting methods, term of employment, salary and manner of payment, whether in advance or later, and preparation money, etc. should be arranged clearly so as not to raise argument afterwards.

Article 5: It seems that by foreign custom when a contract is broken before expiration, in most cases the full term of salary must be handed over; therefore, keeping this in mind, as much as possible contracts should not be made for long periods.

After his service if an employee has worked very diligently and proven efficient in his work, then, at that time upon consultation, his service may be continued.

Addendum. In case of an employee who is to be dismissed, he should be informed of this intention about six months or a year in advance.

Article 6: At the time of employment the difference between the expenditures to be borne by the employer and the items to be incurred from the employee's monthly salary—not only the employee's rent, food, furniture, office supplies, etc., but also incidental expenses and servants—should be arranged clearly beforehand and then the contract is to be signed. Otherwise it should be evident that from the employer's side, in addition to salary, excessive expenditures will be involved.

Article 7: At the time of payment of the monthly salary and other expenses, without fail a receipt in Western language is to be received and kept; and, in fact, a check made that there is no error in the Western language translation. This is an essential matter to have ready for future reference.

Article 8: During the term of employment if the employee asks to be discharged at his own convenience, since the contract is altered by the employee, after inquiring well into the facts regarding termination, suitable disposition should be made concerning the method of salary reduction, etc.

Article 9: It is proper to dismiss for neglect of duties over a five or six day period and to dismiss, even during the term of agreement, for immoral behavior such as indulging in wine or women, when it impedes the functions for which employed. However, if fault cannot be proven, there are no grounds for reproof. Therefore, the foregoing points should be written into the contract from the outset; and also after evidence is obtained, reproof should follow. Addendum. Work hours or leave regulations and methods of dealing with those sick for long periods should be written into the contract.

Article 10: Upon dismissal, regarding the manner of transfer [for release], attention should be given to the process of returning the employee to the locale of engagement, i.e., to each open port area, etc. It should be written into the contract that travel expenses to the employee's home country will not be given.

Article 11: According to the foreigner's status, there should be differences in treatment. However, since there is a tendency for social relations to deteriorate in consequence of the manner of direction by supervisers, it should be agreed upon from the outset by whose directions the employee should work.

Article 12: In the writing of dates, the Japanese calendar should be used throughout. In the case of inconvenience to the employee, it is permissible to use the Western calendar date after the Japanese calendar date. The same should apply to the foreigner's period of employment, etc.

Article 13: Even if a house for residence is sold, the land may not be. Prior suitable measures must be taken in order to avoid future argument at the time of dismissal.

Article 14: Foreigners in case of death due to illness during employment must be given suitable funeral services. If no relative is present, according to the gravity of the illness, he is to be made to prepare a will if possible. Moreover, his personal effects from clothes and personal property to trivial items should be listed, and conference undertaken with the employee's sponsor. Moreover a report is also to be made to the Foreign Ministry; and directions will be given according to the circumstances.

Article 15: In matters relating to development by the civil administration, after application to the Civil Affairs Ministry, work may commence. For weapons, drill, and other military related matters, after application to the Military Affairs Ministry work may be undertaken. Even though permission may be granted to hire foreigners; depending on the work to be undertaken, it is difficult to foresee what may be convenient for the government. Therefore, prior attention should be given this matter.

Article 16: In the event of achievement as evidenced by the use of inventions of foreigners employed, the matter should be written in detail and reported to the ministry office related to this work.

Article 17: A foreigner who is employed will not easily be permitted to go out from the place of employment. However, if it cannot be avoided, he is to be allowed to travel. In the event of passing through an area under another's supervision, guards are to be despatched and negotiations made with those quarters.

Article 18: Individual services of foreign religious denominations will be free, but proselytizing of Japanese will not be done. These religious denominations are never to argue among themselves.

Attention is to be given to the foregoing, and remaining matters should be inferred from these points.

March 1870 (Meiji 3/2)

Appendix 2

Regulations for the Employment of Foreign Teachers and Others and Their Expenses While in Japan

(Gaikoku kyōshi nado yatoiirekata oyobi zairyūchū shohi kisokusho, September 28, 1873, Foreign Ministry Records Bureau, Tokyo: Gaikokujin yatoiire toriatsukai sankōsho, fol 1)

General Instructions [brackets are inserted for notes; parentheses are in original]:

Article 1: In each ministry and urban and rural prefecture when hiring from foreign countries teachers, for language, the military, science and learning, arts and crafts, and various workers, do so after first reporting the intention and receiving permission.

Article 2: After receiving permission to hire foreigners already resident in Japan, the contract should be signed with the name of the head of each ministry or prefecture or the names of their assistants (*yū, jō, kashira, sei, jikan*) acting for the government.

Article 3: Also when employing a person presently in his own country, Article 2 applies; if the engagement is entrusted to a minister or official stationed abroad, that person's name should be used.

Article 4: When entrusting to a foreign representative in Japan and to a teacher or other presently employed the employment of a person from his own country, without fail a written request should be sent under the official's name, showing beforehand the contract draft (attached at the end) and requesting his good offices so that the contract may be signed according to the intent of the draft. Moreover, some amount of travel money for passage to Japan (written in the table on the last page) is entrusted to him to be sent to the prospective employee. But according to the occasion, travel money to Japan may be paid after arrival.

Article 5: The term for a person hired in his own country is a two or three year period. When hiring a person living in Japan the first term is six months; and then, after observing whether the person is suitable for the work, a contract may be made which continues the term.

Article 6: In order to bring his family or to support his family, etc., in circumstances beyond control, action may be taken according to the situation when a person requests to borrow some money within a year's salary.

Article 7: When it is written into the contract (Art. 2) to provide a house, one Western style house is to be given. All furnishings except interior decoration and floor covering basically belongs to the employee's expense. But it is difficult to give everyone a Western style house immediately; Japanese houses can be used. Besides if a person wants to build his own house, he may do so.

Article 8: If a house cannot be supplied for some time or if some circumstances prevent it, lodging money (written in the table on the last page) may be given according to the number of days while the employee stays with relatives, friends, or in a hotel.

Article 9: Although salary depends on the degree of learning and skills, it is difficult to fix a single standard for the amount. In general the salary scale (written in the table on the last page) should be standard.

Article 10: Although in cases of persons of especially wide and deep learning and notable achievement the amount naturally cannot be fixed without breaking the standard, as these cases are very few, suitable arrangements may be made upon consultation at the time.

Article 11: In case the head teacher or director requests increase or decrease of salary because of diligence or negligence (fix the degree by referring to Article 10 of the contract), the chief official checking in detail may fix the amount. In a place having no head teacher or director [foreign], the chief official [Japanese] there is always to check prudently and then may increase or decrease the amount. But in that case a very reasonable action is necessary.

Article 12: Travel pay to and from the employee's home country, at the time of engagement and termination, is to be given on the level of travel pay for that country (written in the table on the last page).

Article 13: After arrival at the port, for travel pay, etc. to the post of duty, refer to Articles 14 and 17–20.

Article 14: For round trip travel for regular [*zaikin*] or temporary [*shutchō*] work in each area (*zaikin* means to engage in regular duties in that area and *shutchō* means to engage in temporary work in that area) and for itinerant travel [*junkai*], regardless of distance near or far, each day's travel allowance (written in the table on the last page) should be given. (This travel is limited to 10 *ri* [24.4 miles] a day.) However, the employee and his servant will pay for their own lodging and rest stops.

Article 15: Upon arrival in all areas for regular work or where employed by prefectures or temporary government offices, that place becomes the main residence and from the next day travel allowance (written in the table on the last page) will not be paid. If a house is not ready, refer to Article 8 and give lodging allowance per day.

Article 16: During temporary duty half of itinerant travel per diem (written in the table on the last page) is to be given. During temporary duty if the employee stays in one place more than two months, lodging per diem is to be given, referring to Article 15, on the level of that for regular work.

Article 17: Although all baggage transport both by ship or horse will be paid for entirely by government funds, limitation is according to the weight allowance for regular and itinerant duty (written in the table on the last page). However, any excess should be paid by the employee.

Article 18: For ship travel in Japan government ships will be furnished at government expense, and both passage and board on mail ships will be borne by the government. Class will be according to carriage and ship class regulations (written in the table on the last page). Both will be 2/3 of travel per diem (written in the table on the last page).

Article 19: For journeys over both water and land, refer for shipboard to Article 18, for land to Article 14.

Article 20: When debarking prior to land travel and when embarking after land travel, for the arrangement of baggage and waiting for transportation, etc., considering the situation, half of itinerant duty travel per diem (written in the table on the last page) is to be given if the period is within half a month, if longer lodging per diem (written in the table on the last page) will be given. However, for postponement due to illness or at the employee's convenience, nothing will be given.

Article 21: For travel to Yokohama, half of travel per diem (written in the table on the last page) will be given. During the stay, half of the itinerant duty travel allowance (written in the table on the last page) will be given, and when making the trip within a day the round trip travel allowance to Yokohama (written in the table on the last page) will be given. However, when a person is provided with train tickets, during temporary duty, half of the itinerant duty travel allowance will be given but round trip per diem will not be given.

Article 22: From main residences in each urban and rural prefecture, on inspection tours for bureaus and for construction, etc., tickets will be provided where the round trip may be made by train. Where there is no railway, 75 sen will be given for jinriksha up to 5 *ri* [12.2 miles] round trip. Beyond that 2/3 of itinerant duty travel per diem (written in the table on the last page) will be given.

Article 23: A person of special merit or distinguished achievement during employment should be given praise and awards on completing his term of employment or taking a leave of absence. However, in cases of ordinary good work, it is naturally a matter of duty therefore neither of the above is necessary.

Article 24: In case of death due to illness or accident during employment, report to the nearest legation of the employee and arrange the procedure for burial and for turning over personal effects. Moreover, put in writing an agreement that employment ceases from that date, that it is recognized that salary will not be given, and that there is no intention to complain later on behalf of the deceased. When there is a head teacher or director consult with him on everything. And handle this matter so as not to lose the intent of this written statement.

Contract Model [brackets, parentheses, and asterisks (*maru*) are in original]:

This text is a model for hiring foreigners living in Japan. When hiring foreigners abroad, because it is substantially the same and in order to save trouble, a mark [ ] is put on phrases requiring change and indicates what should be replaced by additional annotational phrases marked.* The contract which [a certain chief official of a certain ministry, prefecture, etc.]

On occasion the name of assistants (*yū, jō, kashira, sei*, or *jikan, gakuchō*) is used.

*name of minister on official tour or resident official

makes on behalf of the Japanese Government with Nationality, Name the following:

Article 1: Nationality, Name is employed for Japan as instructor, principal, for what ministry, school, subjects, prefecture, location, work, director, duties [from what day, month, year for how many months]

*for how many years from date of arrival at what place (within Japan)

Article 2: During employment, Mr. Name will be loaned without cost one house for residence. In the event of damage the government will carry out repairs.

However, food, furniture, servants, etc. will be entirely at the expense of Mr. Name.

Article 3: Mr. Name's salary [from the date of arrival at what place]

If the place of the contract and the place of the work is the same the bracketed phrase should be deleted.

*from the date of arrival in what place in Japan

is fixed at what amount Japanese gold yen for one month and will be paid at the end of the month.

However according to the occasion when other kinds of currency are paid accounting will be based on gold coin.

Article 4: Mr. Name [as travel pay before departure from what place within Japan—Refer to Regulations, Article 13.]

*travel pay before embarking—Refer to Regulations, Articles 12 and 13.

will be paid what amount gold yen and when he leaves employment on expiration of the contract term [as return travel within Japan,]
    *as return ship's passage
moreover, what amount gold yen will be paid.

Article 5: The right of fixing various regulations for education, technology, other work, length of time of instruction, engagement and the order of work, etc. rests with the chief official, school head, and the length of time is fixed at what number of hours.

Article 6: On the matter of proposals by Mr. Name, in everything he is to converse with certain persons—officials (*kashira, sei*) or school head and if there is a principal or director their names are to be used also, and the decision rests with the authority of the chief official.

Article 7: During employment he will not have any connection with business.

Article 8: When Mr. Name interrupts his work at his own convenience on occasions other than on rest days fixed by the government or specially announced holidays, salary for those days will be deducted.

Article 9: Moreover, if employment is to be continued after expiration of the term of employment, this must be indicated before the end of the term.

Article 10: If during the term of employment he is dismissed in unavoidable circumstances by the Japanese government, he will be paid from the following day the amount of three months salary and [return]
    *return ship's passage
travel pay.

However, if within three months of the term of employment, he will be paid salary to the expiration date and [return]
    *return ship's passage
travel.

Article 11: In case Mr. Name is unable to perform his work or negligent or at fault, even within the fixed term he will be dismissed from employment and salary from the following day and [return]
    *return ship's passage
travel will not be paid.

Article 12: During the fixed term, if he is sick more than [ten days]
    *twenty days
Mr. Name must get a replacement at his own expense. If he is still sick after [two months]
    *three months
he will be dismissed from employment and from the following day salary will not be paid. [Return travel]
    *Return ships's passage

will be given.

However in case of death by illness or accident he will be handed over immediately to his own country's nearest resident minister. From that day his employment ceases and salary will not be paid.

Day, Month, Year (Meiji)
[Name of Chief Official]
    *Name of minister or resident official
Name of Principal
Name of Director
Name of Instructor
Name of Worker

Appendix 2 (Cont.)

Table for Expenditures for Foreign Employees[a]

Monthly Salary (yen)	1000 and Over	900 — 999	800 — 899	700 — 799	600 — 699	500 — 599	400 — 499	300 — 399	250 — 299	200 — 249	150 — 199	100 — 149	0 — 99
Salary Bases	Principals, Directors					Specialists		Technology / Humanities			Elementary School Workers		
Lodging per day	3.	2.25	2.25	2.	1.75	1.75	1.25	1.25	1.	1.	.75	.75	.50
One Way Transportation (from home country)	First Class						Second Class						Third
Travel per diem (to post within Japan)	9.	8.	8.	7.	6.	6.	5.50	5.	4.50	4.	3.50	3.	2.
Itinerant Duty Travel per diem (within Japan)	6.	5.25	5.25	4.75	4.	4.	3.75	3.25	3.	2.75	2.25	2.	1.25
Carriage and Ship Class	First Class						Second Class						Third
Baggage Weight (to post within Japan)	140	140	126	126	112	112	98	84	70	56	42	35	28
Baggage Weight on Itinerant Duty	70	70	56	56	49	49	42	42	35	35	28	28	21
Round Trip Travel to Yokohama within a day	2/3 of travel per diem						3/4 of travel per diem						2

One Way Travel from Abroad
1st Class / 2nd Class / 3rd Class — England, France, Austria, U.S.

Consultation with Foreign Ministry — England, U.S.; France; Austria; Prussia

Percentage of Baggage Weights

England, U.S. × kan ÷ 120 =
France × kan ÷ 267 =
Austria × kan ÷ 150 =
Prussia × kan ÷ 126 =
Kan = 3.75 kilo = 8.72 lbs.

[a] Appended to Gaikoku kyōshi nado yatoiirekata oyobi zairyūchū shohi kisokusho ("Regulations for the Employment of Foreign Teachers and Others and Their Expenditures While in Japan"), Sept. 28, 1873, Gaikokujin yatoiire toriatsukai sankōsho, Gaimushō kiroku: fol. 1.

Appendix 3

Yatoi Licence for William Elliot Griffis

(Foreign Ministry Records Bureau, Tokyo: Gaikokujin yatoimenjō hikae and for explanation of the last sentence: Gaikokujin yatoiire kagami)

Record No. 38
Science and Chemistry Instructor
American, William E. Griffis
27 years of age
Salary: 300 *gen* per month
Employment Term: Meiji 3/12/6 to Meiji 5/12/5, three-year period.
Place of Employment: Yokohama
This person hired by request of Fukui han.
Meiji 3/12, Ministry for Foreign Affairs
This foreigner during employment, etc.

This last sentence is a standard abbreviation for the following:

This foreigner during employment is to be treated the same as a Japanese and may travel in the interior without hindrance. Moreover both the foreign employee and Japanese are to honor strictly the articles of contract and when the employee is released, this licence is to be returned.

(This licence for Griffis also had a marginal notation: "On Meiji 5/1/10, licence returned, Ministry of Education employment." It had been recalled for reissue because it was worn.)

Notes

NOTES TO INTRODUCTION

1. E. O. Reischauer, "The Hour of the Ox," in *Horizon* 11:1 (1969): 12–25.
2. Cf. William W. Lockwood, ed., *The State and Economic Enterprise in Japan* (Princeton: Princeton University Press, 1965), intro., p. 4.
3. William Elliot Griffis Collection, Box 8–8. Throughout this study dates cited after employee names are taken from primary sources and may not reflect the full term of employment.
4. In *Brinkley's Japanese-English Dictionary* (originally published in 1896), 2:1621: "Yatoi . . . a government employé (not a regular official); lowest grade of officials . . . Yatoi ni deru . . . to become a government employé." Captain Frank Brinkley was himself a yatoi; cf. *Japan Weekly*

Mail August 30, September 6, November 22, 1890 and July 30, December 17, 1892.
5. Anesaki Masaharu, *History of Japanese Religion* (Tokyo: Tuttle, 1963), p. 350.
6. Studies are currently being undertaken by Steven J. Ericson (Harvard) and Deborah Church (Hawaii). From Japanese scholars, the Oyatoi gaikokujin series (17 vols. from Kashima shobō) provides a helpful introduction. The 1975 *Shiryō oyatoi gaikokujin* volume edited by UNESCO Higashi Ajia bunka kenkyū sentā is an invaluable introduction to documents and their location, reviewed by this writer in *Monumenta Nipponica* 30:4 (1975): 465–68.

NOTES TO CHAPTER ONE

1. H. J. Jones, "Bakumatsu Foreign Employees," *Monumenta Nipponiac* [MN] 29:3 (1974): 305–27.
2. GHS: Keiō 2–3, Eikoku yori kaigun kyōshi yatoiire ikken.
3. Brooks and Fleury Herard in Paris served the bakufu in this unique capacity; in the Meiji era, Brooks and others served as "hired consuls" (*yatoi ryōji*).
4. Cf. Dutch contracts from 1854. GHS: Dutch folios.
5. GHS: Bunkyū 1–3, Yezo chihō kōzan tanken no tame Beikoku kōshi yatoiire ikken.
6. Ibid.
7. Ibid.
8. Umetani Noboru, *Oyatoi gaikokujin: Meiji Nihon no wakiyakutachi* (Tokyo:

Nihon keizai shimbunsha, 1965), p. 59.
9. Ibid., p. 57.
10. *Nihon teikoku tōkei nenkan* (Tokyo, 1882–1940), esp. 1–19. See charts entitled "Kyoryū gaikokujin" and "Hompō kyoryū gaikokujin."
11. Ibid., charts entitled "Kanyatoi gaikokujin," vols. 1–18, and "Kanyatoi gaikokujin gekkyū betsu," vols. 4–18.
12. Ogata Hiroyasu, *Seiyō kyōiku inyū no hōto* (Tokyo: Kōdansha, 1961); Saigusa Hiroto, *Gijutsushi*, Gendai Nihon bummeishi, 14 (Tokyo: Tōyō keizai shimpōsha, 1940), and *Nihon kindai seitetsu gijutsu hattatsushi* (Tokyo: Tōyō keizai shimpōsha, 1957); and Saigusa et al., *Kindai*

Nihon sangyō gijutsu no seiōka (Tokyo: Tōyō keizai shimpōsha, 1960).

13. Shigehisa Tokutarō, "Meiji jidai ni okeru seiyōjin no bunka jiygō," *Dōshisha kōshō ronsō* 20:10 (1939): 134–48; Shigehisa and Amano Keitarō, "Meiji bunka kankei ŌBei jimmeiroku," *Toshokan kenkyū* 10:4 (1937): 347–72.

14. Anesaki Masaharu, *History of Japanese Religion* (Tokyo: Tuttle, 1963), p. 350.

15. Australians make up a large portion of the "British" category. H. S. Williams has commented that it is improbable that journalist John Reddie Black considered himself an Australian, and most yatoi were content to be listed as British. But some, such as D. W. A. Jones, identified themselves as Australians. Some Canadians are also included in the British category, but at least eleven identified themselves as Canadians (Confederation occurred in 1867).

16. Cf. Toyohara Jirō, "Kōbushō to oyatoi gaikokujin ni tsuite: Meiji sangyō kindaika no issetsu," *Shōdai ronshū* 60:1 (1964): 36–56.

17. Ogata, *Seiyō kyōiku inyū no hōto*, pp. 72–152, especially p. 102.

18. Cf. GHS: Keiō 1–3, Hompō rikugun kyōshi ni Futsukoku shikan yōhei ikken.

19. GK: Gaikokujin yatoiire toriatsukai sankōsho.

20. Honjō Eijirō, ed. *DaiNippon kaheishi* (Tokyo: Naikaku insatsukyoku, 1936–37), 1:512; Okada Shumpei, *Meiji zenki no seika seisaku* (Tokyo: Tōyō keizai shimpōsha, 1958), pp. 53–80.

21. KS: Kōbun ruisan, 1872–81, T8. Correspondence between Sanjō Sanetomi (Council of State) and Kawamura Sumiyoshi (Navy); cf. Shimomura Fujio, *Meiji ishin no gaikō* (Tokyo: Ōyasu, 1948), pp. 96–107; Tsuchiya Takao, "ŌBeijin no Nihon shihonshugi seiritsu ni hatashita yakuwari," *Keizai shutaisei kōza 6 rekishi 1*, edited by Arisawa Hiromi (Tokyo: Chūō kōronsha, 1960): 265–305; GK: Gaikokujin yatoiire toriatsukai sankōsho; Tsuchiya Takao, "Ōkubo naikyō jidai ni shokusan kōgyō seisaku," *Keizai-*

gaku ronshū 4:9 (1934): 106–7.

22. Cf. SY figures (1872–98): for employees with monthly salaries below 200 yen: 69 per cent; from 200 to 500: 22 per cent; and 500 and above: 9 per cent.

23. "Kantō oyobi gekkyū hyō," in *Kaninroku*, printed for government use (Tokyo, 1874).

24. Ship architect Louis E. Bertin (1885–98) at $22,000 annually, over $1,800 a month, and Railway Director William W. Cargill (1872–77) at $2,000 a month.

25. "Kantō oyobi gekkyū hyō," in *Kaninroku*, 1874 and 1877. See 1880, 1881 for changes.

26. Shibusawa Keizō, ed., *Japanese Life and Culture in the Meiji Era*, trans. Charles S. Terry (Tokyo: Ōbunsha, 1958) p. 309.

27. *Kōbushō enkaku hōkoku*, MZKS 17: 19–20.

28. Lafcadio Hearn (1884–1903), for example, received 100 yen from Matsue middle school; the principal received 55 yen and the vice-principal 45 yen. Negishi Iwai, *Izumo ni okeru Koizumi Yakumo* (Matsue: Yakumokai, 1931), p. 109. Hearn's later salaries were 200 yen in high school and 400 yen in the university.

29. Nakamura Yoshimi, "Meiji shonen oyatoi gaijin no sararii," *Nihon rekishi* 80:1 (1955): 43–45. A foreign engineer in the Railway Bureau has remarked that Japanese salaries were a sixth of those for foreign employees. Edmund G. Holtham, *Eight Years in Japan, 1873–1881* (London: Kegan Paul and Trench, 1883), p. 254.

30. Cf. case studies of two types of Japanese labourers in Shibusawa Keizō, *Japanese Life and Culture*, pp. 321–22.

31. Ōuchi Hyōe and Tsuchiya Takao, eds., *Sainyūshutsu kessan hōkokusho*, MZKS (1931–36), vols. 4, 5, 6, especially 4:224–58. In this collection some separate listings of expenditures for foreign employees are given: December 1867–December 1868: 70,904 yen (of total government expenditures of 30.5 million yen); January 1869–September 1869: 125,596 yen (of 20.7 million yen); October 1869–Septem-

ber 1870: 285,494 yen (of 20.1 million
yen); October 1870–September 1871:
145,873 yen (of 19.2 million yen). The
next separate listing is July 1876–June
1877:1,395,227 (of 59.3 million yen).in
the Cabinet Records Bureau Classified
Collection of Laws (from 1890), the
same 1876–77 report is given in HBT:
1, *Zaiseimon, kessan* 3: 261–89. In
HBT: 1, *Zaiseimon, kessan* 4: 469–
980, the entire fiscal report for July
1880-June 1881 is printed as an example of one of the most detailed
accounts of the Meiji government.
The report lists separate columns for
yatoi expenses in each ministry and
includes extensive breakdown of salaries and other expenditures, including expenses for foreigners employed
in legations abroad (especially pp.
487–903). The total expenditure listed
for foreign employees (excluding those
employed abroad) is 801,533 yen
(1880–81) of total expenditures listed
at 63.1 million yen.

32. *Ōkuma monjo* (Tokyo: Waseda dai-
    gaku shakai kagaku kenkyūjo, 1962),
    5:62 (A3024); ŌM:A2985 (2 fols.)
    Yokosuka seitetsujo yatoi Futsujin
    kyūryō chōsho and A2986 Yokosuka
    seitetsujo yatoi Futsujin meibo; GK:
    Kaku shōchō fuken gaikokujin kan-
    yatoi ikken, 3 fols.; *Yokosuka zōsen-
    shi* (Tokyo: Yokosuka chinjufu en-
    kakushi hensan iin, 1880), pp. 75–78,
    96–99.

33. Osatake Takeki, "Oyatoi gaikokujin
    ichiran kaidai," *Meiji bunka zenshū*
    [MBZ] (1928), 16:20–1, 349–62.

34. HBT: 1, *Heiseimon 1, heiseisō, riku-
    kaigun kansei, rikugun* 1:78.

35. Osatake, "Oyatoi gaikokujin," MBZ,
    20–1; Nakamura Yoshimi, "Meiji
    shonen oyatoi," *Nihon rekishi* 80:1
    (1955): 43–45.

36. ŌM: A4219 Ryūgakusei o kaigai e
    haken suru no riyū narabi ni kakkoku
    taihi ryūgakusei meibo, July 1879.

37. *Nihon kagaku gijutsushi taikei 8,
    kyōiku 1* (Tokyo: Nihon kagakushi
    gakkai, 1964), p. 339; *Kyū-Kōbu
    daigakkō shiryō* (Tokyo: Kyū-Kōbu
    daigakkō shiryō* hensankai, 1931):
    353–56; Toyohara Jirō, "Kōbushō to
    oyatoi gaikokujin ni tsuite Meiji

sangyō kindaika no issetsu," *Shōdai
ronshū*, 60:1 (1964): 36–56 provides
a good summary.

38. *Kido Kōin monjo*, vol. 4 (Tokyo: Ni-
    hon shiseki kyōkai, 1932), entry for
    Meiji 4/5/11.

39. Shibusawa Eiichi, *Jijoden* (Tokyo:
    Ijin resshi den hensanjo, 1937), p. 255.

40. Ibid., p. 797.

41. Georges Bousquet, *Le Japon de nos
    jours et les échelles de l'extrême Orient*,
    vol. 1 (Paris: Librairie Hachette,
    1877), preface.

42. Ibid., 1:353; 2:203–4, 211.

43. Cf. KS: T3 for angry exchanges be-
    tween officials in competing min-
    istries, especially the Navy, Public
    Works, and Education ministries.

44. HBT: I, *Gaikōmon* 4: 633.

45. Ibid., p. 634.

46. Nishikawa Midori, "Meiji shoki ni
    okeru Kōbushō setchi no igi," *Shiron*
    10 (1962): 733 for a detailed compara-
    tive table of expenditures for the
    Public Works Ministry and for samu-
    rai stipends.

47. See James H. Buck, "The Satsuma
    Rebellion of 1877," MN 28:4 (1973):
    427–46.

48. Holtham, *Eight Years in Japan,* p.
    117.

49. Ibid., pp. 216, 271, 312–13; several
    instances are reported by yatoi in the
    Griffis Collection.

50. Cf. *Hokkaidōshi* (Sapporo: Hokkaidō-
    chō, 1937).

51. Merritt Starr, "General Horace Cap-
    ron, 1804–1885," *Journal of the Illi-
    nois State Historical Society* 18 (1925):
    259–349.

52. John R. Black, *Young Japan: Yoko-
    hama and Yedo* (London: Trubner,
    1880), 2: 329–30; William Elliot
    Griffis, *Mikado's Empire* (New York:
    Harper Brothers, 1877), p. 607; David
    F. Anthony, "The Administration of
    Hokkaido under Kuroda Kiyotaka,
    1870–1882" (Ph. D. dissertation, Yale
    University, 1951), p. 145.

53. Anthony, "Administration of Hok-
    kaido," pp. 31–38, 51; *Hokkaidōshi*
    3: 231–33; Satō Shōsuke, "Hokkaido
    and Its Progress in Fifty Years" in
    Fifty Years of New Japan, edited by
    Ōkuma Shigenobu, (New York: E. P.

Dutton, 1909), 2: 517; Robert S. Schwantes, *Japanese and Americans: A Century of Cultural Relations* (New York: Harper Brothers, 1955), p. 53; John A. Harrison, *Japan's Northern Frontier* (Gainesville: University of Florida Press, 1953), p. 56.

54. Kamata Hisaaki, "Kuruto Netto no Nihon kōzangyō shinkōsaku," *Keizaishi kenkyū* 29:3 (1933): 42–59.

55. For example, in 1894 N.Y.K. had 540 Japanese employees and 210 foreign captains, engineers, and pursers. By the First World War Japanese tonnage had reached sixth in the world, and N.Y.K. still employed 30 foreigners.

56. Holtham, *Eight Years in Japan*, pp. 101–8, 198–99, 207–8, 314.

57. Erwin von Baelz, *Baelz no nikki*, trans. Suganuma Ryūtarō (Tokyo: Iwanami, 1964), April 22 and May 6, 1879.

58. *Kōbushō enkaku hōkoku*, pp. 5, 547.

59. Telegraphy is a clear example of a field which advanced rapidly. British yatoi were the first to erect a hundred-mile surface wire. Begun in 1871 with Danish yatoi, the undersea cable was laid simultaneously in six sections from Nagasaki to Yokohama. Completed in 1873, trunk lines were extended to Tokyo and Aomori. In less than five years, telegraphic communication from Hokkaido to Kyushu was established, and Japanese operators were steadily trained under British yatoi.

60. Thomas C. Smith, *Political Change and Industrial Development in Japan, 1868–1880* (Palo Alto, CA: Stanford University Press, 1955), p. 103.

61. Maruyama Masao, *Nihon no shisō* (1936, reprint Tokyo: Iwanami shoten, 1973), p. 131.

62. George C. Allen, *A Short Economic History of Modern Japan 1867–1937*, rev. ed. (London: Unwin University Books, 1972), especially pp. 2–12, 42, 95; George C. Allen and Audrey C. Donnithorne, *Western Enterprise in Far Eastern Economic Development: China and Japan* (London: Allen and Unwin, 1954), pp. 197–98; William W. Lockwood, James I. Nakamura,

and Thomas C. Smith on agricultural revenue.

63. Thomas C. Smith, *Political Change and Industrial Development in Japan, 1868–1880*, pp. 86–100, 103; W. W. Lockwood, *The Economic Development of Japan: Growth and Structural Change 1868–1938* (Princeton: Princeton University Press, 1954), p. 507.

64. Thomas C. Smith, *The Agrarian Origins of Modern Japan* (Palo Alto, CA: Stanford University Press, 1959), pp. 108–23, 201–13, especially p. 212.

65. Paul Akamatsu, *Meiji 1868: Revolution and Counter-Revolution* (London: Allen and Unwin, 1972), p. 250.

66. Solomon Levine in Lockman, ed., *The State and Economic Enterprise in Japan*, especially pp. 641–45.

67. Allen, *Short Economic History of Modern Japan* p. 9 and chap. 5; see Levine on wage scales and dualism.

68. Cf. Murakami Nobuhiko, *Meiji joseishi* (Tokyo: Rironsha, 1969–72), vol. 3; Ōhama Tetsuya, "Ito o tsumugu onnatachi," *Kindai no josei gunzō, Nihon joseishi* 7, edited by Kasahara Ichio (Tokyo: Hyōronsha, 1973): 23–28, 131–88.

69. Akamatsu, *Meiji 1868: Revolution and Counter-Revolution*, p. 280.

70. Ibid., p. 250.

71. Allen, *Short Economic History of Modern Japan*, pp. 38–39, 65ff., and 165; cf. Lockwood, *Economic Development of Japan*, pp. 3–37, especially 16–17.

72. ŌM: A4251, section entitled Ken'ō gakuto senkyo. One sees in the list of subjects to be pursued in a given country an early Meiji view of the advancements of other nations: England: mechanics, commercial law, geology, iron manufacturing, construction, ship-building, stock-raising, social work; France: criminal, customary, and civil law, international relations, transportation, manufacturing, coin and paper currency, census, astronomy, mathematics, chemistry, construction; Prussia; politics, economics, astronomy, geology, chemistry, botany, zoology, medicine, pharmacology, schools systems; Holland: hydraulics, construction, ship-build-

ing, government, economics, social work; U.S.A.: postal services, industrial arts, agriculture, stock farming, commercial law, mining.

73. Inoue Kaoru Kō denki hensankai, *Segai Inoue Kō den* (Tokyo: Naigai shoseki, 1933–34), 2:320.

74. ŌM: A2 Kōbuin kenchi no gi, 1870 and A3875 Kōburyūgakusei haken, 1871.

75. ŌM: A4191 Ryūgakusei haken narabi ni gaijin yatoiire ni kanshi Ōkurashō ukagai ni taisuru Seiin shirei, 1871.

76. Cf. Ivan P. Hall, *Mori Arinori* (Cambridge, MA: Harvard University Press, 1973), chaps. 2 and 3; Ishizuki Minoru, *Kindai Nihon kaigai ryūgakusei* (Kyoto: Minerva shobō, 1972), early chapters.

77. Ogata, *Seiyō kyōiku inyū no hōto*, pp. 15–71, and "Meiji shoki no kaigai ryūgakusei seiritsu katei," *Shakai kagaku tōkyū* 2:3 (1960): 1–31.

78. ŌM: A4219 and A4217 Mombushō taihi ryūgakusei sembatsu ni kansuru jōshinsho, April 16, 1879.

79. ŌM: A2996 Yokosuka zōsenjo keikyō hōkokusho.

80. Ishizuki, *Kindai Nihon kaigai ryūgakusei* chaps. 8 and 9, especially pp. 169–71, 189, 230–31; Watanabe Minoru, "Japanese Students Abroad and the Acquisition of Scientific and Technical Knowledge," *Journal*

of World History [JWH] 9:1 (1966): 254–93 and "Meiji seifu no Ōka seisaku to gaijin kyōshi," *Nihon rekishi* 38:7 (1951): 16–21 and 39:8 (1951): 22–25.

81. Ibid., especially *JWH*: 276; see Ishizuki, *Kindai Nihon kaigai ryūgakusei*, pp. 301–29 for name list.

82. Watanabe in *JWH* 9:1 (1966): 282–83, 287; Ishizuki, *Kindai Nihon kaigai ryūgakusei*, chap. 10. From 1875 to 1894, two and one half times as many Japanese studied in Germany as in any other country (in order the next three were England, the U.S.A., and France). From 1895 to 1912 three and one half times as many studied in Germany as in all other countries combined. Watanabe Minoru concludes that "modern science and technology of the entire Meiji era was imported from Germany." Next in order were England and the United States; other nations contributed little. The conclusion enjoys some vogue in certain academic circles. However, the early Anglo-American base continued to be valued in higher education, and Anglo-American yatoi continued into the twentieth century.

83. Nakamura Takeshi, "The Contribution of Foreigners," *JWH* 9 (1966): 294–319, especially p. 297.

NOTES TO CHAPTER TWO

1. Ōyama Azusa, *Kaishi kaikō no kenkyū* (Tokyo: Ōtori shobō, 1967) is an important study.

2. NGB: 1:1: 37–38, 42–43.

3. Sakata Yoshio, *Meiji zenhanki no nashonarizumu* (Tokyo: Miraisha, 1958), pp. 9–12; Sakata Yoshio, *Meiji ishinshi* (Tokyo: Miraisha, 1960), pp. 214–15.

4. Sakata, *Meiji ishinshi*, pp. 205–29.

5. Cf. Bernard S. Silberman, *Ministers of Modernization* (Tucson: University of Arizona Press, 1964) and "The Bureaucracy and Economic Development in Japan," *Asian Survey* 11

(1965): 529–37, especially 533; Johannes Hirschmeier, *The Origins of Entrepreneurship in Meiji Japan* (Cambridge, MA: Harvard University Press, 1964).

6. Sakata, *Meiji zenhanki no nashonarizumu*, pp. 12–14.

7. Ibid.

8. ŌM: A2816 Tetsudō shisetsu nado ni kansuru naigaijin ikensho. Cf. Tanaka Tokihiko, *Meiji ishin no seikyoku to tetsudō kensetsu* (Tokyo: Yoshikawa kōbunkan, 1963), pp. 305–15; Sakata, *Meiji ishinshi*, pp. 241–42.

9. Sakata, *Meiji ishinshi*, p. 232.

10. Ogata Hiroyasu, "Ōkuma Shigenobu to Furubekki," *Waseda daigakushi kiyō,* 1 (1965): 115–17.
11. Sakata, *Meiji ishinshi,* pp. 229–63.
12. Tsuchiya Takao, "Keizai seisakuka to shite no Ōkubo Toshimichi," *Chūō kōron* 50:4 (1935): especially 98–99; Sakata Yoshio, "Meiji ishinshi no mondaiten," *Meiji ishinshi no mondaiten,* edited by Sakata Yoshio (Tokyo: Miraisha, 1962), p. 30.
13. ŌM: A925 Jōyaku kaisei ni tsuki zenken shisetsu saken riyūsho.
14. FS: Nagasaki ken and Kanagawa ken.
15. Correspondence in Saigusa Hiroto, *Gijutsushi* (Tokyo: Tōyō keizai shimpōsha, 1940), pp. 181–82.
16. *Ōkuma monjo* 5: 65–67 (A3024).
17. ŌM: A3027 Yokosuka seitetsujo kensetsu ni kansuru jōyaku narabi ni kankeisho, especially pt. 10.
18. Ōtsuka Takematsu, ed., *Iwakura Tomomi kankei monjo* (Tokyo: Nihon shiseki kyōkai, 1927), 2: 450–53. The Yokosuka and Yokohama enterprises were brought under the foreign affairs section of the Council of State, but from the bakufu period technical administration was by the Kanagawa saibansho.
19. Jean Raoulx, *Yokosuka kaigun kōshō no sōsetsu to Furansujin no mitaru reimeiki no Nihon,* trans. Kuranaga Shōzō (Yokosuka: Yokosuka shi kyōiku kenkyūjo, 1952), pp. 10–11.
20. Ibid., p. 13.
21. *Ōkuma monjo* 5: 68–70 (A3024).
22. Cf. *Yokosuka zōsenshi* (Tokyo: Yokosuka chinjufu enkakushi hensan iin, 1880), pp. 125–29; ŌM: A3027, pts. 5 and 16; KS: T1–18.
23. Sawa Kannojō, *Kaigun nanajūnenshidan* (Tokyo: Bunsei dōshisa, 1943), pp. 223–26.
24. ŌM: A3026 Yokosuka seitetsujo kisoku tsuika no gi.
25. Ibid.; A2991 Yokosuka seitetsujo kisoku kaisei sōan. The extended contracts included an average of 50 per cent increase in salary.
26. The school closed in 1868 was reopened temporarily in 1870 but again shut down because of political exigencies. According to the 1870 regulations, the school was to be open to samurai and commoners, 13 to 20 years of age (*Ōkuma monjo,* 5: 81–82, A3024).
27. ŌM: A2996.
28. KS: T1–18.
29. Cf. GHS: Keiō 1–3, Hompō rikugun kyōshi ni Futsukoku shikan yōhei ikken and Keiō 2–3, Eikoku yori kaigun kyōshi yatoiire ikken.
30. Ōtsuka Takematsu, *Bakumatsu gaikōshi no kenkyū* (Tokyo: Hōbunkan, 1952), pp. 357–58.
31. *Ishinshi* (Tokyo: Ishin shiryō hensan jimukyoku, 1939–41), 5: 619.
32. Nakamura Kōya, *Shishaku Nakamuta Kuranosuke den* (Tokyo: Kyōrinsha, 1919), pp. 483–86; Tamura Eitarō, *Kawamura Sumiyoshi-Nakamuta Kuranosuke den* (Tokyo: Nihon gunji tosho, 1944), p. 296ff.
33. Sawa, *Kaigun nanajūnenshidan,* p. 230.
34. Nakamura Kōya, *Shishaku Nakamuta,* pp. 486–88, 577–79; Henri Chevalier, "Old World Chit-chat," William Elliot Griffis Collection, Box 8, Rutgers State University Library, New Brunswick, N.J.
35. KS: T6.
36. *Ishinshi,* 5: 611.
37. "Ōmura Masujirō," *Nihon kindaishi jiten* (Kyoto: Kyoto University Press, 1958), p. 57.
38. *Ishinshi* 5: 613.
39. Ibid., pp. 517–19; cf. Ōtsuka Takematsu, "Fukkoku kōshi Reon Rosshu no seisaku kōdō ni tsuite," *Shigaku zasshi* 46:7 (1935): 809–50 and 46:8 (1935): 982–1001 for a good summary of French contributions in the bakumatsu era.
40. *Ishinshi* 5: 613–15.
41. Ibid., p. 616.
42. Tokutomi Iichirō, *Kōshaku Yamagata Aritomo den* (Tokyo: Yamagata Aritomo Kō kinen jigyōkai, 1933), 2:42, 185. Conscription was not introduced in France until 1872.
    Ibid., pp. 618–19. Yamagata and Saigō were aware of German training in Wakayama han. Sergeant Karl Köppen, a gunsmith, came in 1869 to teach use of rifles purchased from a German firm. He was hired at $200

a month to train troops for six months. He drilled them without respect to rank or status; his contract was renewed in 1870 and 1871 to teach manufacture of gunpowder, and he was joined by a few other Germans. Their contracts were cancelled with the political change to the prefecture system. Two of these men (Lubowsky and Heidkaempfer) remained to initiate boot manufacturing. Maxim von Brandt, *Reimei no Nihon* (Tokyo: Kokusai bunka shinkōkai, 1942), p. 369; Shigehisa Tokutarō, "Wakayama bunka hattatsu ni kōken seru Doitsujin," *Eiryō*, 17 (1936): 1–7 and "Wakayama han ni okeru Doitsujin," *Kyōto Rangaku kenkyū hōkoku* 166 (1965): 1–8.

43. NGB: 3: 327–28.
44. See Du Bousquet's advice in ŌM: A4352 Seiyō bankoku rikugun kenchi no gensoku oyobi Futsukoku rikugun kenchi narabi ni hensei; and see Umetani Noboru, "Meiji shinsei guntai no kensetsu tōsho ni okeru Furansushugi no saiyō to Ju Busuke no kōken," *Ōsaka daigaku bungakubu sōritsu jisshūnen kinen ronsō* (Osaka: Osaka University Press, 1959), pp. 97–120, especially pp. 103, 107–8.
45. Cf. NGB: 4:2: 333.
46. Ernst Presseisen, *Before Aggression: Europeans Train the Japanese Army* (Tucson: University of Arizona Press, 1965), pp. 35–37, 41. Actually, by 1871 eight of the original French military mission were again in Japanese employ. Cf. Ōtsuka, *Bakumatsu gaikōshi no kenkyū*, chart following p. 272; *Rikugunshō nempō* (1875), 1: 177–79.
47. Georges Le Bon, "Au Japon il y a quarante ans; Lettres de M. le Général G. Le Bon," *Bulletin de la Société Franco-Japonaise de Paris* 21 (1911): 113–18; Ōi Narimoto, *Mekkeru shōgun no omoide* (Tokyo: Gunjishi gakkai, 1939), pp. 5–11, quoting Ōyama Iwao correspondence; Watanabe Shūjirō, "Meiji nenkan rikugun kaku hōmen koyō no gaikokujin," *Meiji bunka kenkyū* 4:10 (1929): 56–62.
48. Paul Akamatsu, *Meiji 1868: Revolution and Counter-Revolution* (London:

Allen and Unwin, 1972), p. 242; George C. Allen, *A Short Economic History of Modern Japan 1867–1937*, rev. ed. (London: Unwin University Books, 1972), p. 39.
49. ŌM: A1691 Gaisai oyobi akukinginka shori no kansuru gaikokukan ukagaisho, 1869; Gaikoku kōsai no gi ni tsuki mondai yonjō, *Nakamikado ke monjo* (Tokyo: Waseda daigaku shakai kagaku kenkyūjo, 1965), 2: 270–71.
50. Shimomura Fujio, *Meiji ishin no gaikō* (Tokyo: Ōyasu, 1948), pp. 128–33.
51. Hattori Kazuma, "Kaikō to Nihon shihonshugi," *Nihon keizaishi taikei*, 5 *kindai 1*, edited by Osanishi Mitsuhaya (Tokyo: Tokyo University Press, 1965), pp. 3–32.
52. Egashira Tsuneharu, "Takashima tankō ni okeru kyūhan makki no Nichi-Ei kyōdō kigyō," *Keizaishi kenkyū* 13:2 (1935): 1–25; cf. ŌM: C30 Bauduin to Ōkuma (October 20, 1875) and C67–C70.
53. HBT: 1, *Gaikōmon* 4: 697; ŌM: A4033 Kōzan kankei gaijin gishi yatoiire ni tsuki fuken tasshian ni kansuru todokesho, 1876. Permission to operate private mines was withdrawn if Japanese capital was insufficient, and private as well as government foreign employees in the mines were supervised by the Public Works Ministry.
54. Tanaka, *Meiji ishin no seikyoku to tetsudō kensetsu*, pp. 184–85 and notes 4–5, 7–8; see Alt, Batchelder, Bauduin, and other foreign firm iistings in ŌM, especially C650.
55. Tanaka, *Meiji ishin no seikyoku to tetsudō kensetsu*, pp. 2–11, 110–48, 155ff.
56. ŌM: especially C162–63 (1871) and C644 (1873), Cargill-related correspondence.
57. HBT: 1 *Seitaimon, seido zakkan 3, kahei*, 1: 15–28.
58. Inoue Kaoru kō denki hensankai, *Segai Inoue Kō den* (Tokyo: Naigai shoseki, 1933–34), 2: 329–49.
59. ŌM: A2187 Zōheiryō kaikaku ni kansuru Ōkuma-Yoshida ōfuku shokan oyobi dempō, July–August 1874;

A2304 Zōheiryō yatoi gaijin ni kanshi Nihon seifu narabi ni Tōyō ginkō jōyaku ni taisuru ikensho.
60. ŌM: C144 Brunton contract and C145 Brunton to Parkes. In fact, the Meiji government was soon obliged to raise Brunton's monthly salary (from $450 to $600) to bring it in line with the higher pay received by other foreign employees in administrative positions.
61. Tanaka, *Meiji ishin no seikyoku to tetsudō kensetsu*, p. 279; cf. ŌM: A2 Kōbuin kenchi no gi, 1870 and A457 Kōbushō shokyoku shogakari ni kansuru ikensho, 1871.
62. *Kyū-Kōbu daigakkō shiryō*, (Tokyo: Kyū-Kōbu daigakkō shiryō hensankai, 1937), pp. 4–5.
63. Allen, Lockwood, Saigusa, and Smith still provide the best coverage. See bibliography.
64. *Kyū-Kōbu daigakkō shiryō*, pp. 49–50, 73–79, 102–4.
65. Ishii Kendō, "Meiji no genkun wa kokumin shūshin no kyōiku o wasuretari," and Fujita Tōichirō, "Daigaku Nankō no ichi kenkyū," *Meiji no shinkenkyū*, edited by Osatake Takeki (Tokyo: Ajia shobō, 1944), pp. 233–54 and pp. 201–32; Irisawa Tatsukichi, "Reeoporudo Myurureru," *Chūō kōron* 48:9, pp. 291–301.
66. Ōtsuka, ed., *Iwakura Tomomi kankei monjo*, 1:452, 455.
67. Ibid., 1:456.
68. HBT: 1, *Gaikōmon* 4: 634.
69. Ibid., 635–37; GK: Gaikokujin yatoi-ire toriatsukai sankōsho, fol. 4.
70. GK: Gaikokujin Nihon seifu e yatoi-ire seigan ikken.

71. Hanabusa Nagamichi, *Meiji gaikōshi* (Tokyo: Shibundō, 1960), p. 74; and see especially JKK 3jo for comments on treaty revision by Denison and Roesler and 2:35 (Denison).
72. Cf. *Segai Inoue Kō den* 3:882–97; Hanabusa, *Meiji gaikōshi*, pp. 70–74.
73. *Segai Inoue Kō den* 3:886.
74. Ōyama Azusa, "Jōyaku kaisei to gaijin hōkan," *Kokusaihō gaikō zasshi* 59:4 (1960): 1–29.
75. ŌM: A951 Jōyaku kaisei nisshi, 1888–89.
76. Hanabusa, *Meiji gaikōshi*, p. 77; Fukufuji Hiroji, "Teikoku kempō no yōgo—Meiji nijūninen no jōyaku kaisei o megutte," *Nihon rekishi*, 53:10 (1952): 40–48. The angry nature of these Cabinet discussions was such that the question of unilateral denunciation of treaties was raised. Yatoi advisers agreed that the Japanese had the right to do so, although exercise of the right would be impolitic. Richard T. Chang, "The Question of Unilateral Denunciation in Meiji Japan" (Research report before the Tōhō gakkai, Tokyo, May 24, 1974).
77. Cf. Robert M. Spaulding, Jr., *Imperial Japan's Higher Civil Service Examinations* (Princeton: Princeton University Press, 1967).
78. ŌM: C943. In this draft, foreign jurists were to "make submission to the jurisdiction of the Imperial Japanese Courts of Justice." The draft condoned consular court jurisdiction in foreign settlements until 1897, after which time all jurisdiction would revert to Japan.

NOTES TO CHAPTER THREE

1. HBT: 1, *Gaikōmon* 4: 608; GK: Gaikokujin yatoiire toriatsukai sankōsho, fol. 1.
2. HBT: 1, *Gaikōmon* 4: 611.
3. Ibid.
4. Ibid., p. 626.
5. The only concrete report included in files was the scale for teachers in the

San Francisco elementary school system supplied by yatoi consul Charles Wolcott Brooks, ibid., pp. 647–48. The following guidelines were suggested: "European primary school teachers, 150–200 yen a month; humanities teachers, 200–50; technology teachers, 250–300; specialists (as in medicine, mechanics, astronomy), 300–400; head teachers (as [Guido F.] Verbeck [in the arts school] Nankō and [Leopold] Müller and [Theodor E.] Hoffman [in the medical school] Tōkō) 500–600." Ibid., p. 655.

6. Ibid., pp. 649–51.
7. Ibid., pp. 649–57.
8. Ibid., p. 682.
9. Ibid., pp. 694–95.
10. Ibid., pp. 639–47. Whereas the Education Ministry allowed 30 days grace before mandatory discharge for illness if hired in Japan and 50 days grace for those hired abroad, Navy regulations provided that in cases of illness lasting more than 15 days the employee would be put on half salary and dismissed if indisposition continued after 90 days. Lay-offs due to work-related injuries incurred no loss of salary and every possible treatment, including services of foreign physicians, was assured. Additional shipboard increments, if such duty were not normal, were provided. A special stipulation was included that the contract would not be altered even if the employee were promoted in rank in his home country during the term of contract. Bakumatsu era foreign employees had claimed this privilege.
    Actually these regulations, including the above stipulation, were virtually the same as those revised by Japanese officials and Director François Verny for French employees in the Yokosuka dockyards before they came under Navy administration (see ŌM: A2991).
11. GK: Gaikokujin yatoiire toriatsukai sankōsho, fol. 1.
12. Ibid.
13. Ibid.; HBT: 1, *Gaikōmon* 4: 700.
14. GK: Gaikokujin yatoiire toriatsukai sankōsho, fol. 1.
15. ŌM: A2193 Yatoi gaijin gekkyū hankanen torishirabekata ni kansuru Ōkurashō ukagai ni tsuki shireian, 1874.
16. HBT: 1, *Gaikōmon* 4: 629.
17. Ibid., pp. 627, 631; GK: Gaikokujin yatoiire toriatsukai sankōsho, fol. 3.
18. HBT: 1, *Seitaimon* 4, *Fukokushiki*: 60 and *Gaikōmon* 4: 634.

19. GK: Gaikokujin yatoiire toriatsukai sankōsho, fol. 4.
20. Cf. HBT: 2, *Gaikōmon* 9.
21. Robert K. Reischauer, *Alien Land Tenure in Japan*, Transactions of the Asiatic Society of Japan, 2d ser., 13 (Tokyo, 1936), p. 20. In the open ports of Niigata and Hakodate, the number of foreigners was never large enough for the complicated *kyoryūchi* machinery to operate, although it was attempted in Hakodate.
22. Georges Bousquet, *Le Japon de nos jours et les échelles de l'extrême Orient* (Paris: Librairie Hachette, 1877), 2: 224.
23. Interesting coverage may be found in John R. Black, *Young Japan: Yokohama and Yedo*, 2 vols. (London: Trubner, 1880–81).
24. Sakata Yoshio, *Meiji ishinshi* (Tokyo: Miraisha, 1960), pp. 217–18.
25. *Tsukiji kyoryūchi*, Tōkyō-to toshi kiyō (Tokyo: Shinyōdō, 1968), pp. 272–74 and chart p. 288.
26. HBT: 1, *Gaikōmon* 1: 3; HBT: 1, *Shajimon* 1: 13.
27. *Shichū torishimari enkaku*, Tōkyō-to toshi kiyō (Tokyo: Shinyōdō, 1953–). pp. 183–87.
28. HBT: 1, *Keihōmon* 1: 535.
29. HBT: 1, *Keisatsumon* 1: 1.
30. *Ōkubo Toshimichi nikki* (Tokyo: Nihon shiseki kyōkai, 1927), 2: 141, 159–60.
31. HBT: 1, *Keisatsumon* 1: 236–38. Kanagawa Prefecture had hired foreigners as police very early, Tokyo and Kobe at least from 1873, and Nagasaki from 1875.
32. Reischauer, *Alien Land Tenure in Japan*, pp. 25–29; Ōyama Azusa, "Ansei jōyaku to gaikokujin kyoryūchi," *Nihon gaikōshi kenkyū: Bakumatsu jidai* (1960), p. 117; FS: Kanagawa ken, reel 84.
33. Ibid., and the U.S. minister in Japan, John Bingham, could boast that he upheld the Japanese decision over the protests of other powers (Despatches of U.S. Ministers to Japan to the Department of State [U.S. National Archives], no 555, May 7, 1877).
34. R. K. Reischauer, *Alien Land Tenure in Japan*, pp. 23, 40; Ōyama, *Nihon*

gaikōshi kenkyū, p. 115; HBT: 4, *Keisatsumon* 1: 236–38.

35. *Tsukiji kyoryūchi*, pp. 70, 130, 149, 246, 384.

36. HBT: 1, *Gaikōmon* 4, see Nagasaki, Yokohama, Osaka and Hyogo, and Tokyo Land Regulations and various arrangements relative to the foreign settlement at each of the above (Documents in English language); cf. Reischauer, *Alien Land Tenure in Japan*, pp. 30–31, 41–42.

37. GK: Gaikokujin yatoiire toriatsukai sankōsho, fol. 1; FS: Hyōgo ken, reel 230, for Hyōgo ken-Ōkurashō correspondence, July–November 1873.

38. FS: Hyōgo ken, reel 230 Kanda-Terajima correspondence, 1873.

39. Cf. Kurt Meissner, *Deutsche in Japan 1639–1960* (Tokyo: Deutsche Gesellschaft für Natur und Volkerkunde Ostasiens, 1961) and Meissner, "Die Deutsche in Yokohama," and Otto Refardt, "Die Deutsche in Kobe," *Deutsche Gesellschaft für Natur und Volkerkunde Ostasiens* (Tokyo: Deutsche Gesellschaft, 1956). Early Meiji newspapers and British consular reports make even more interesting reading. For serious assault, including manslaughter, on Japanese, the maximum punishment administered to a British subject was expulsion from Japan, but no notice was taken of return in three months.

40. GK: Kaku shōchō fuken gaikokujin kanyatoi ikken, fols. 1–3.

41. Cf. ŌM: A1223, Shinkokujin yatoiire ni kansuru Shihōshō ukagai ni tsuki shireian; GK: Kaitakushi mukigen yatoi kōchō Eikokujin Horutoru kaiko ni tsuki kujō ikken.

42. *Tsukiji kyoryūchi*, pp. 143, 145.

43. See GK: Gaikokujin yatoimenjō hikae and Gaikokujin yatoiire kagami.

44. GK: Gaikokujin yatoiire toriatsukai sankōsho, fol. 1.

45. Ibid., fol. 4.

46. Ibid., fols. 1–4.

47. Ibid., fol. 3.

48. Ōyama Azusa, "Jōyaku kaisei to gaikokujin kyoryūchi," *Rekishi kyōiku* 9:1 (1961): 60–69 and cf. Ōyama,

Nihon gaikōshi kenkyū (1960): 111–23; *Tsukiji kyoryūchi*, pp. 143–45.

49. Ishii Kendō, "Meiji no genkun wa kokumin shūshin no kyōiku o wasuretari," *Meiji bunka no shinkenkyū*, edited by Osatake Takeki (Tokyo: Ajia shobō, 1944), p. 235.

50. Despatches of U.S. Ministers to Japan, No. 20 (February 24, 1870 d. February 10); no. 41 (May 21, 1870, d. April 12).

51. William E. Griffis, *Verbeck of Japan* New York: Fleming H. Revell, 1900), pp. 269–71, 277–83. In December 1872, the Japanese changed to the Gregorian calendar and Sunday was an official holiday for foreigners. But in 1874 the one-in-six (*ichiroku*) native holiday system was revived. Under the *ichiroku* system one in six days of the lunar calendar was a holiday, actually the first, sixth, eleventh, sixteenth, and twenty-sixth days. This system allowed more days off for some yatoi, but protests were numerous. Respected foreign employees never had difficulty in getting the Sunday holiday written into their contracts. In the end, foreign teachers had their way (Sunday remained a school holiday), but some later contracts into the 1880's continued to specify the Sunday holiday as a precaution.

52. Despatches of U.S. Ministers to Japan, no. 390, April 29, 1873.

53. ŌM: C781 Smith to Terajima, May 22, 1874; also C441–45, C452 and LeGendre's April correspondence.

54. HBT: 1, *Seitaimon, seido zakkan* 3, *kahei* 1: 63–64.

55. GK: Kaitakushi mukigen yatoi kōchō Eikokujin Horutoru kaiko ni tsuki kujō ikken. Also several individual employees, owing to the nature of their work, exempted themselves from extraterritorial privileges. The Australian pioneer in Japanese sheep-raising, D. W. A. Jones (1873–83), a Home Ministry yatoi, did so to circumvent the injunction against commercial enterprise in the interior. Jones received monthly $500 plus one-third of increase in stock thus

sharing in the profits of the enterprise (GK: Gaikokujin yatoiire toriatsukai sankōsho, fol. 2; Tsuchiya Takao, "Ōkubo naimukyō jidai no shokusan kogyō seisaku," *Keizaigaku ronshū* 4:10 [1934]: 37–41; Nakamura Yoshimi, "Wagakuni bokuyo jigyō no senkusha Jyōnzu no jiseki," *Nihon rekishi* 52:9 [1952]: 14–18). Despite injunctions to the contrary, some mining engineers exempted themselves to share in the mine output. Saga han employee Samuel Morris (1858–88) received, at least between 1870 and 1876, three-quarters of the mine output; earlier he had received one-tenth. The account suggests that it was a small experimental station. (GK: Gaikokujin yatoiire kagami and Gaikokujin yatoimenjō hikae.) It was in these little ways that precedents were built up.

56. Hora Tomio, "Bakumatsu ishin ni okeru EiFutsu guntai no Yokohama chūton," *Meiji seiken no kakuritsu katei* (Tokyo: Meiji shiryō kenkyū renrakukai, 1957), pp. 166–269.
57. Cf. NGB: vols. 2, 3, 4, 8.
58. Ibid., 2:3: 560.
59. Ibid., 3: 323, 331–32.
60. Ibid., 3: 331.
61. Ibid., 4:1: 318.
62. Ibid., 8: 221. "The presence of this force has prevented serious embarrassment which must have ensued if foreign life and property had been attacked before the restored Government had succeeded in tranquilizing the country and in consolidating their authority. . . the resolution of our Governments to withdraw the remainder of that force has been taken on the termination of those difficulties which threatened, until towards close of last year, to disturb the peace of Japan."
63. GK: Gaikokujin yatoiire toriatsukai sankōsho, fol. 1, including correspondence in French confirming the conversations.
64. HBT: 1, *Gaikōmon* 4: 702; cf. S. Yajima, "Lettres d'un ingénieur français en Japon de 1877 à 1881," *Japanese Studies in the History of*

Science 10 (1971): 27–57. Thanks to Frank Schulman for calling attention to the Yajima article.
65. ŌM: A3990 Futsujin Kowanii yatoiire yakujōsho, 1868; *Ōkurashō enkakushi*, MZKS 3: 364–66. In the employ of Satsuma han at the time of the restoration, Coignet was initially engaged by the finance office (*kaikeikan*) in the Council of State.
66. GK: Gaikokujin yatoimenjō hikae.
67. Officials were ranked *chokujukan, sōjukan,* and *hanjukan.* The titles were soon changed to *chokuninkan* (appointments by imperial decree), *sōninkan* (appointments with imperial approval upon ministerial recommendation), and *hanninkan* (appointment by seal, that is, by decision of chief ministerial and prefectural officials). In 1869 *shinnin* (direct imperial appointments) were also authorized, supra-*chokunin,* but are not pertinent here (*Nihon kindaishi jiten* [Kyoto: Kyoto University Press, 1958], pp. 176, 293, 389).
68. *Ōkurashō enkakushi* MZKS 3: 133–34; HBT: 1, *Kanshokumon* 11, *kansei, Ōkurashō* 2:474–75.
69. GK: Kanyatoi gaikokujin mibun toriatsukaikata ikken. William Gowland (1872–88), chemist and metallurgist (rank 6), and Robert Maclagen (1872–89), machine technician (rank 7), were given *sōnin* status in 1886.
70. GK: Gaikokujin yatoiire toriatsukai sankōsho, fol. 1.
71. Ibid.
72. Ibid.
73. Ibid.
74. HBT: 1, *Gaikōmon* 4: 701.
75. Ibid., p. 702.
76. HBT: 1, *Saibansho* 1: 715.
77. GK: Kanyatoi gaikokujin mibun toriatsukaikata ikken. Henry W. Denison (salary $500), Durham W. Stevens ($450), Otto Rudorf ($200), François Sarazin ($150), and L. V. Janson von der Osten ($125) were all formally acknowledged for *sōnin* treatment.
78. Cf. *Nihon kindaishi jiten,* p. 293.
79. Francis S. G. Piggott, *Broken Thread: An Autobiography* (Aldershot, Eng.:

Gale and Polden, 1950), pp. 6–7.
80. GK: Kanyatoi gaikokujin mibun toriatsukaikata ikken.
81. Ibid.
82. Cf. *Nihon kindaishi jiten,* p. 143.
83. GK: Denison shi kankei.
84. This kind of information on yatoi is to be found in almost all Foreign Ministry folios. For a published chart on education yatoi, see Ogata Hiroyasu, *Seiyō kyōiku inyū no hōto* (Tokyo: Kōdansha, 1961), pp. 75–100.
85. Erwin O. von Baelz, *Baelz no nikki,* trans. Suganuma Ryūtarō (Tokyo: Iwanami, 1964), entries for December 26, 1879 and October 22, 1890 in particular.
86. Cf. KS: T3.
87. HBT: 1, *Gaikōmon* 3: 107–8. Actually, the first and last really grand display in traditional court costume was held in 1872. General Horace Capron was present and described it: Merritt Starr, "General Horace Capron, 1804–1885," *Journal of Illinois State Historical Society* 18 (1925): 259–349. Thereafter Western formal dress was

assumed for receptions.
88. Those who served more than thirty years include the lawyers H. W. Denison (thirty-four years) and H. T. Terry (thirty-six years) and possibly the Frenchman François Sarazin (1868–1906), translator and language teacher with the Foreign Ministry. Although records indicate his service was interrupted between 1875 and 1878, he may have served more than thirty years at least in a part-time capacity. William Henry Stone (1872–1917), a British engineer with the Public Works and Communications ministries, served forty years. William Douglas Cox (1874–1922), a British subject, served forty-eight years as an English-language teacher for the Education and Home ministries, especially in Komaba Agricultural College and Tokyo University preparatory high school. But the longest continuous term of any employee must be that of Kobe harbour master John Mahlman (1870–1928), a British subject, fifty-eight years.

NOTES TO CHAPTER FOUR

1. B. H. Chamberlain, *Things Japanese* (London: Kegan Paul and Trench, 1890), pp. 184–85.
2. Georges Bousquet, *Le Japon de nos jours et les échelles de l'extrême Orient* (Paris: Librairie Hachette, 1877), 1: 305.
3. Harold S. Williams, *Foreigners in Mikadoland* (Tokyo: Tuttle, 1972), pp. 79–84.
4. Umetani Noboru, *Oyatoi gaikokujin: Meiji Nihon no wakiyakutachi* (Tokyo: Nihon keizai shimbunsha, 1965), p. 167.
5. GK: Kokkai gijidō kenchiku no tame Doitsukoku kenchikugikan Piyoku-man yōhei kankei zassan.
6. GK: Kaitakushi mukigen yatoi kōchō Eikokujin Horutoru kaiko ni tsuki kujō ikken.
7. Cf. Yagisawa Zenji, "P. Mayeto no

Nihon ni okeru jiseki," *Keizaishi kenkyū* 12 (1934): 1: 1–16; 2: 27–44; 3: 25–33; Katō Fusazō, *Hakushaku Hirata Tōsuke den* (Tokyo: Hirata Haku denki hensan jimusho, 1927), pp. 38–40, 368–70. 1876–80, Education Ministry (Tokyo medical school language teacher, monthly salary $250); 1879–82, Finance Ministry (finance and auditing adviser, monthly $600); 1880–81, Council of State (accounting adviser, additional $1,000 annual stipend); 1883–86, Home Ministry (agricultural finance and research adviser, monthly $400); 1884–87, Education Ministry (German language teacher, Tokyo Foreign Language School, monthly $200); 1884–86, Agriculture and Commerce Ministry (research adviser on agricultural problems, monthly $100);

1885–87, Communications Ministry (adviser on rural communications, monthly stipend from $110 to $200); 1888–91, Agriculture and Commerce Ministry (research on agricultural problems, monthly $400). The overlapping dates and salaries taken from Foreign Ministry records illustrate simultaneous and multiple employment. In 1886, for example, he was formally employed in four offices for an aggregate monthly income of $900).

8. Brinkley worked for Fukui han (1867–71) and the Navy (1871–77) as gunnery instructor. From 1874 to 1877, as foreign head of the Navy School, he taught English. For Public Works (1878–80) he was mathematics instructor in the Engineering College. Skilled in the Japanese language, he also produced a large Japanese-English dictionary still valuable for Meiji vocabulary (recently republished by the University of Michigan Press).

9. ŌM: C431, 434, 438, 667, 670 in particular; C48 (code list), C20 (Anmen, U.S. Navy).

10. ŌM: C263, G. Galy to S. Ōkuma, May 31, 1875 (French).

11. Cf. ŌM: C329–48.

12. KS: T3–4 (Elgar); *Ōkubo Toshimichi nikki*, 2 vols. (Tokyo: Nihon shiseki kyōkai, 1927), October 11, 1874 (Pitman); cf. ŌM: C45–53 (Batchelder) and C219–25 (Iwakura-Dunn).

13. KS: T3.

14. Despatches of U.S. Ministers to Japan, no. 390, April 29, 1873.

15. GK: Kaku shōchō fuken gaikokujin kanyatoi ikken; Takahashi Korekiyo, *Jiden* (Tokyo: Chikura shobō, 1946), pp. 88–94; *Ōkubo Toshimichi nikki*, 2: 141, 159–60. (If this case refers to Ring, he died of his wounds.)

16. HBT: 1, *Gaikōmon* 4: 699; GK: Gaikokujin yatoiire toriatsukai sankōsho, fol. 1.

17. HBT: *Seitaimon* 3 *shochokushiki*, pp. 60–61; Ōtsuka Takematsu, ed., *Iwakura Tomomi kankei monjo* (Tokyo: Nihon shiseki kyōkai, 1927), pp. 150–61 (Ōhara Shigezane report,

1872); Inō Tentarō, "Meiji nananen ni okeru Mori Arinori no jōyaku shian to gaikō iken," *Kokugakuin zasshi* 63: 10–11 (1962): 130–39; Williams, *Foreigners in Mikadoland*, pp. 153–59, 270.

18. ŌM: C674.

19. For example, NGB: 24: nos. 152, 154.

20. Erwin von Baelz, *Baelz no nikki*, trans. Suganuma Ryūtarō (Tokyo: Iwanami, 1964), June 9, 1876, and preface, pp. 101–2.

21. Kawakita Rinmei, "Bijutsu to Meiji shoki no gaijin kyōshi," *Nihon rekishi* 26: 7 (1950): 16–21; Van Wyck Brooks, *Fenollosa and His Circle* (New York: E. P. Dutton, 1962), pp. 16–68.

22. Chamberlain, *Things Japanese*, p. 182.

23. Rupert Wilkinson, *The Prefects: British Leadership and the Public School Tradition* (London and New York: Oxford University Press, 1964), especially pp. 29–37, 100–9. The American title is *Gentlemanly Power*.

24. Ibid., pp. 30–31.

25. Ibid., pp. 102–4.

26. ŌM: A2970 Yokosuka seitetsujo kensetsu ni kansuru shoyakujōsho.

27. GHS: Keiō 2, Yokosuka zōsenjo narabi ni Yokohama seitetsujo yatoi Futsujin Uerunii shi ni taishi fusōtō no shochi arishi mune dōkoku kōshi yori kujō moshiide ikken.

28. Ibid. (French language), November 19 and December 3, 1866.

29. Cf. ŌM: A937 Meiji yonnendo tōdai jigyō shishutsu gaiyōsho.

30. R. Henry Brunton, "Pioneer Engineering in Japan: A Record of Work in Helping to Re-Lay the Foundations of the Japanese Empire (1868–1879)," booklength manuscript in Griffis Collection, The Rutgers State University Library, New Brunswick, N.J. (Box 9–1), pp. 92–93; cf. also Kieran M. Rohan, "Lighthouses and the Yatoi Experiences of R. H. Brunton," MN 20: 1 (1965): 64–80.

31. Captain A. R. Brown to William E. Griffis, November 19, 1906, Griffis Collection, Box 8.

32. Brunton, "Pioneer Engineering in Japan," p. 85; cf. ŌM: C719 for Ernest Satow's translation of Brun-

ton's proposals for operation and administration of the Lighthouse Bureau.

33. Cf. ŌM: A2304, A2187.
34. Nakamura Kōya, *Shishaku Nakamuta Kuranosuke den* (Tokyo: Kyōrinsha, 1919), pp. 486-87; Henri Chevalier, "Old World Chit-Chat," Griffis Collection, Box 8.
35. Horace Capron, *Reports and Official Letters to the Kaitakushi* (Tokei: Kaitakushi, 1875), especially pp. 71, 75, 84, 89–92, 265–67; David F. Anthony, "The Administration of Hokkaido under Kuroda Kiyotaka, 1870–1882" (Ph. D. dissertation, Yale University, 1951), pp. 51, 80–81.
36. Kojima Chōsui, "Chishitsu gakusha Nauman to Mori Ōgai no ronsō," *Shomotsu tembō* 7:9, pp. 162–69.
37. ŌM: C164 Tetsudō gashira jishoku o iken tosu.
38. ŌM: C163 Cargill to Ōkuma, April 20, 1871; cf. C162.
39. ŌM: C644, June and July correspondence, 1873.
40. Ibid.
41. Ibid.
42. Brunton, "Pioneer Engineering in Japan," p. 35.
43. Edmund G. Holtham, *Eight Years in Japan, 1873-1881* (London: Kegan Paul and Trench, 1883), especially pp. 216, 271, 312–13.
44. Cf. ŌM: C889–921. (Also of interest, Williams's nephew, a teacher in the Tokyo preparatory school for Hokkaido development, is credited with introducing baseball to Japan.)
45. Shigehisa Tokutarō, "Meiji jidai ni okeru seiyōjin no bunka jigyō," *Dōshisha kōshō ronsō* 20 (1939): 134–48.
46. Tsuchiya Takao, "Eijin Arekisandaa Shando no gyōseki," *Kin'yū jānaru* 4: 1–12 (1963); cf. ŌM: C726.
47. Griffis had studied at Rutgers College, which is now Rutgers the State University, New Brunswick, New Jersey. In 1967, Rutgers celebrated the bicentenary of its founding and the centenary of the Japanese-American cultural exchange. It is one of the institutions which received overseas Japanese students and provided yatoi from its

staff, such as David Murray (1873–79) as Commissioner of Education (in Japanese, *gakkō tokumu*, schools' supervisor) for revision of the Japanese school system.
48. Edward R. Beauchamp, *An American Teacher in Early Meiji Japan* (Honolulu: The University Press of Hawaii, 1976).
49. William E. Griffis, *Mikado's Empire* (New York: Harper Brothers, 1877), p. 578.
50. In a letter from Griffis in the Ithaca, New York, newspaper *Star*, July 24, 1919, Griffis Collection.
51. Manuscript (probably 1919), Griffis Collection.
52. Griffis, *Verbeck of Japan* (New York: Fleming H. Revell, 1900), p. 282.
53. Ogata Hiroyasu, "Kindai Nihon kensetsu chichi Furubekki hakase," *Shakai kagaku tōkyū* 18 (1961): 1–40.
54. HBT: 1, *Seitaimon* 3, *shochokushiki*, pp. 60–61.
55. Ogata Hiroyasu, "Ōkuma Shigenobu to Furubekki," *Waseda daigakushi kiyō* 1 (1965): 115–17.
56. Griffis discusses this in both *Verbeck of Japan* and *Mikado's Empire*, but Umetani Noboru has put it in the Japanese context of the argument between Ōkubo favouring a samurai base (sōheishugi) and Yamagata the conscription of commoners (*chōheishugi*), (*Oyatoi gaikokujin: Meiji Nihon no wakiyakutachi* [Tokyo: Nihon keizai shimbunsha, 1965], pp. 70–77; and cf. Umetani Noboru, *Meiji zenki seijishi no kenkyū* [Tokyo: Miraisha, 1963]).
57. Cf. Yasuoka Akio, "Iwakura shisetsu no haken to sono seika," *Rekishi kyōiku* 40: 1 (1966): 32–38.
58. Cf. Takahashi, *Jiden*, p. 170.
59. ŌM: A4352; Umetani Noboru, "Meiji shinsei no guntai no kensetsu tōsho ni okeru Furansushugi no saiyō to Ju Busuke no kōken," *Ōsaka daigaku bungakubu sōritsu jisshūnen kinen ronsō* (Osaka: Osaka University Press, 1959), pp. 97–120.
60. HBT: 1, *Gaikōmon* 4: 624.
61. KS: T3. In correspondence with the Council of State, Navy officials were informed that disposition of yatoi

funding required decision by Du Bousquet in the Sain.

62. Tetsuka Yutaka, "Meiji hōseishijō ni okeru Ju Busuke to Busuke," *Meiji bunka* 15: 12 (1942): 1–19.

63. Ōyama Azusa, "Jōyaku kaisei to gaijin hōkan," *Kokusaihō gaikō zasshi*, 59: 4 (1960) 1–29: Umetani Noboru, "Shoki jōyaku kaiseishijō ni okeru Ju Busuke no kiyō" in *Uozumi sensei koki kinen kokushigaku ronsō* (Osaka: Kansai University, 1959), pp. 103–18.

64. HBT: 1, *Gaikōmon* 4: 624 (contract).

65. NB: Seiin honyakukyoku oyatoi gaikokujin kankei shorui: Fu-Bu-Shi-Ga.

66. Ibid. for all correspondence.

67. Ibid., and HBT: 1, *Gaikōmon* 4: 616 (contract); cf. ŌM: A4208.

68. Ogata, *Shakai kagaku tōkyū* 18 (1961): 1–40; and see OM: A4665.

69. Irisawa Tatsukichi, "Reeoporudo Myurureru," *Chūō kōron*, 48: 9, pp. 291–301.

70 Cf. Griffis, *Verbeck of Japan*, pp. 269–71.

71. Ōyama Azusa, Inō Tentarō, and others hold that factional jealousies lay behind Boissonade's outbursts. The 1887 clash was a climax. Cf. JKK: *Tsuiho* 8: no. 48, p. 127.

72. Despatches of U.S. Ministers to Japan, no. 262 September 8, 1875, also other entries for 1874–75.

73. Ibid., no. 865, September 17, 1878.

74. F. Cunliffe-Owen, "Men Who Win Good Will for America in Foreign Lands," *The Sun* (New York), July 12, 1914, in Griffis Collection.

75. GK: Denison shi kankei; JKK, especially 3; TJK: 1–3; Shidehara Kijūrō, *Gaikō gojūnen* (Tokyo: Yomiuri shimbunsha, 1951).

76. GK: Denison shi kankei.

77. Ibid.

78. In Griffis Collection.

79. Ibid.

80. Martin Egan, "Henry Willard Denison—Statesman," *Journal of the American Asiatic Association* 14: 7 (1914), pp. 197–98 in Griffis Collection.

81. Cf. Imai Shōji, "Dension no hansei," "*Nihon rekishi* 80: 1 (1955): 24–25; Ōno Katsumi, "Meiji gaikō to Deni-

son komon no kenshin," *Bungei shunjū* 11: 11 (1966): 180–88.

82. Shidehara, *Gaikō gojūnen*, pp. 239–46.

83. Cf. for example, ŌM: A947 and A954 and JKK, especially 3.

84. Johannes Siemes, "Heruman Roesurā to Nihon ni okeru Doitsukokuhō no saiyō," *Sophia* 10: 1 (1961): 1–24 and *Hermann Roesler and the Making of the Meiji State* (Tokyo: Sophia University Press, Tuttle, 1968), pp. 3–46.

85. Letter of Itō Hirobumi to Inoue Kaoru (1881) quoted in Ike Nobutaka, *Beginning of Political Democracy in Japan* (Baltimore: Johns Hopkins University Press, 1950), p. 172.

86. Johannes Siemes, "Roesler und die Rezeption des deutschen Staatrechts in Japan," *Japanica* 1 (1961): 1–7 and "Meiji seifu shunōtachi to shakaiteki rikken shisō," *Kokka gakkai zasshi* 75: 7–8 (1962): 418–24.

87. Johannes Siemes, "H. Roesurā no kempō riron ni okeru shakai hatten to rikkenshugi no kankei," *Kokka gakkai zasshi* 75: 1–6 (1962): 1–41, 181–202, 307–30.

88. See Siemes, *Hermann Roesler and the Making of the Meiji State* for the text of the constitution and Roesler's commentary; quotation, pp. 12 and 14.

89. Kaide Sumiko, "Mori Arinori 'Saishōron' no rekishiteki shisōteki haikei: *Saishōron* to minpōten hensan," *Nihon rekishi* 302: 7 (1973): 83–101; Ōyama, *Kokusaihō gaikō zasshi* 59: 4 (1960): 1–29.

90. GK: Kaku shōchō fuken gaikokujin kanyatoi ikken, fol. 1 (German contract); HBT: 1, *Gaikōmon* 4: 616–17 (Japanese contract).

91. J. Milne to W. E. Griffis, November 3, 1906, Griffis Collection, Box 8. Dr. J. L. Hepburn, an American medical missionary, was deviser of the *heibon* system of romanization of Japanese still in use today despite government advocation of the national system as linguistically more accurate. Hepburn's grammar and dictionary were in wide use by foreigners in the Meiji era.

NOTES TO CHAPTER FIVE

1. Ōyama Azusa, "Jōyaku kaisei to gai-jin," *Kokusaihō gaikō zasshi* 59: 4 (1960): 1–29.
2. Ernest Satow, *A Diplomat in Japan* (London: Seeley Service, 1921), p. 44.
3. Ibid., p. 143.
4. GHS: Keiō 3, Doitsugogaku kyōshi yatoiire ikken.
5. Despatches of U.S. Ministers to Japan, no. 307, November 21, 1872.
6. Ibid., no. 102, July 17, 1874.
7. *U.S. Congressional Record*, 42d Cong. 2d sess., 1874, nos. 3629, 4876, 5210, May 6, June 11, June 19.
8. FS: Niigata ken: Niigata kenshi zenki seiji sōjō jiken, 1:65: Kingu, reel 96; Cf. *Niigata shishi* (Niigata: Niigata shiyakusho, 1934), 2: 423 and Ichijima Kenkichi, "Meiji bunka hasshō no kaiko," *Meiji bunka hasshō kinenshi*, Bummei taikan (Tokyo: DaiNihon bummei kyōkai, 1924), 6: 3–19.
9. Despatches of U.S. Ministers to Japan, no. 390, April 29, 1873.
10. GK: Jōyaku kaisei ni kansuru zasshorui: Jōyaku kaisei kyokuin and Hakodate kōnai torishimari.
11. JKK: 1:80, pp. 109–10.
12. Ibid., p. 122.
13. Shimomura Fujio, *Meiji shonen jōyaku kaiseishi no kenkyū* (Tokyo: Yoshikawa kōbunkan, 1962), p. 112.
14. *Tokio Times*, December 20, 1879; KS: T10 for Japanese Navy officials' attitudes.
15. ŌM: C300.
16. Ibid., C301.
17. Ibid., C333, E. W. House to S. Ōkuma, September 2, 1881. Later, House took credit for being instrumental in Parkes's removal, C336, October 7, 1887.
18. NGB: 22: 5–6, January 7, 1889. As Foreign Minister again in 1889, Ōkuma wrote that it was a pity that the Japanese always tended to heap blame upon the English and former Minister Parkes in particular. Parkes's contributions were quickly forgotten, and Japanese never have affection for the English in the way they have for Americans. Basically, Ōkuma thought that the Japanese attitude created obstacles to British agreement.
19. GK: Gaikokujin yatoiire toriatsukai sankōsho, fol. 3. See the Sekizawa Akekio-James Begbie correspondence. Begbie was dismissed "because he insisted on his own biased opinion," but the situation at Komaba (the principal agricultural experimental college) is clearly in the context of mounting hostility towards the British. After the end of British contracts in 1878, only Germans were hired. However, William Douglas Cox (1874–1922), a British subject, continued as language instructor.
20. GK: Kokkai gijidō kenchiku no tame Doitsukoku kenchikugikan Piyokuman yōhei kankei zassan.
21. Inoue Kaoru Kō denki hensankai, *Segai Inoue Kō den* (Tokyo: Naigai shoseki, 1933–34), 3: 661; cf. NGB: 3: 327–28.
22. ŌM: C970 Ozaki Yukio, *Western Times* (Exeter), June 13, 1889.
23. See HBT: 1, *Seitaimon* 3, *shochokushiki*, pp. 60–61 for examples.
24. Cf. Ōyama Azusa, "Ansei jōyaku to gaikokujin kyoryūchi," *Nihon gaikōshi kenkyū: Bakumatsu jidai* (1960), pp. 111–23.
25. GK: Gaimushō gaikokujin yatoiire ikken, fol. 2.
26. GK: Kokkai gijidō kenchiku no tame Doitsukoku kenchikugikan Piyokuman yōhei kankei zassan.
27. GK: Gaimushō gaikokujin yatoiire ikken, fol. 2. Letter from K. Tsudzuki (by order of Count Inouye) to Baron Kawase Masataka, Ambassador to London, August 7, 1887.
28. GK: Kaku shōchō fuken gaikokujin kanyatoi ikken, fol. 2, and Kanyatoi gaikokujin mibun toriatsukaikata ikken.
29. GK: Gaikokujin yatoiire toriatsukai sankōsho, fol. 1.
30. ŌM: A2.
31. Quoted in Donald H. Shively, "The Japanization of Middle Meiji," *Tradition and Modernization in Japanese Culture*, edited by Donald Shively

(Princeton: Princeton University Press, 1971), p. 91.

32. NB: Seiin honyakukyoku oyatoi gaikokujin kankei shorui: Fu-Bu-Shi-Ga and ŌM: C84–7; cf. Kanai Madoka, "Eijin Burakku to Nihon," *Kokusai bunka shinkōkai*, nos. 156–62 (1967).

33. Edmund G. Holtham, *Eight Years in Japan, 1873–1881* (London: Kegan Paul and Trench, 1883), pp. 43, 244.

34. Mizuta Nobutoshi, *Reimeiki no waga kaigun to Oranda* (Tokyo: Yūfūkan shobō, 1940), especially pp. 138–39, 157–61 for the Kattendyke Report.

35. Numata Jirō, "Bakumatsu ni okeru Ranjin kyōshi Pompe no jiseki," *Shigaku zasshi* 56: 8 (1946): 803–55.

36. GHS: Keiō 2, Yokosuka zōsenjo narabi ni Yokohama seitetsujo yatoi Futsujin Uerunii shi ni taishi fusōtō no shochi arishi mune dōkoku kōshi yori kujō moshiide ikken.

37. Holtham, *Eight Years in Japan*, pp. 55–56, 61–63, 94–97, 123, 202–3, 209–11, 288.

38. Cf. Ogata Hiroyasu, "Meiji no honyaku shakai kagakusho," *Shakai kagaku tōkyū* 3 (1960): 213–59; Ogata Hiroyasu, *Seiyō kyōiku inyū no hōto* (Tokyo: Kōdansha, 1961), pp. 153–240 for lists and figures. Sir George B. Sansom, *The Western World and Japan* (New York: Knopf, 1950), p. 362, comments as follows: "A study of what we call literary influences, though tempting to the historian, may be misleading, for often they do not penetrate beyond intellectual circles and find little response in practical life. It is probable that, despite the great number of Western books circulated in Japan during the first twenty years of Meiji, their effect was not so great as the aggregate influence of individuals consulted by Japanese on their journeys abroad and of foreign advisers employed in Japan, who were in close touch with officials, and students destined later to hold important posts."

39. See Holtham, *Eight Years in Japan*.

40. Horace Capron, *Reports and Official Letters to the Kaitakushi* (Tokei: Kaitakushi, 1875), pp. 71–75, 84–92, 265–67.

41. Cf. FS: Nagasaki ken, reel 346.

42. Holtham, *Eight Years in Japan*, p. 288.

43. Inoue Masaru, "Japanese Communications: Railroads," *Fifty Years of New Japan* edited by Ōkuma Shigenobu (New York: E. P. Dutton, 1909), pp. 424–46, especially p. 436.

44. Erwin von Baelz, *Baelz no nikki*, trans. Suganuma Ryūtarō (Tokyo: Iwanami, 1964), April 22 and May 6, 1879.

45. ŌM: A2186, Zōheiryō shuchō Kinshi to no ōfuku shokan. Ellipse indicates illegible character due to deterioration. Kana is the Japanese syllabary and *kanji* are Chinese characters.

46. Nakahara Kunihei, *Itō Kō jitsuroku* (Tokyo: Keibunsha 1909), pp. 185–86. This reference was provided by Professor Umetani Noboru.

47. Francis S. G. Piggott, *Broken Thread: An Autobiography* (Aldershot, Eng.: Gale and Polden, 1950), p. 7.

48. Anesaki Masaharu, *History of Japanese Religion* (Tokyo: Tuttle, 1963), p. 350.

49. William W. Lockwood, *The Economic Development of Japan: Growth and Structural Change 1868–1938* (Princeton: Princeton University Press, 1954) p. 17.

50. Cf. Tsunoda Ryusaku, W. T. de Bary, and Donald Keene, *Sources of the Japanese Tradition* (New York: Columbia University Press, 1958), p. 644.

51. Tsurumi Kazuko, *Kōkishin to Nihonjin* (Tokyo: Kōdansha gendai shinsho, 1972), pp. 126–28.

52. Thomas C. Smith, *Political Change and Industrial Development in Japan, 1868–1880* (Palo Alto, CA: Stanford University Press, 1955), especially pp. 23, 35.

53. Ivan P. Hall, *Mori Arinori* (Cambridge, MA: Harvard University Press, 1973), p. 72.

54. *Kōbushō enkaku hōkoku*, MZKS 17: 5–6.

55. Hoshino Yoshirō, "Kōgyō gijutsu no hatten," *Keizai shutaisei kōza*, 6 *rekishi* 1, edited by Arisawa Hiromi

(Tokyo: Chūō kōronsha, 1960), pp. 80–119.

56. Umetani Noboru, *Oyatoi gaikokujin: Meiji Nihon no wakiyakutachi* (Tokyo: Nihon keizai shimbunsha, 1965), especially pp. 230–37; Ishizuki Minoru, *Kindai Nihon no kaigai ryūgakusei* (Kyoto: Minerva shobō, 1972), pp. 212–15 and 233 n25. For the overview see the Studies in the Modernization of Japan, Princeton series.

57. G. C. Allen and Audrey C. Donnithorne, *Western Enterprise in Far Eastern Economic Development: China and Japan* (London: Allen and Unwin, 1954), pp. 193–94; T. Yamanaka, "Japanese Small Industries during the Industrial Revolution," *Annals of Hitotsubashi Academy* (1951): 30ff.; Tsuchiya Takao, *Nihon keiei rinenshi* (Tokyo: Keizai shim-

bunsha, 1964).

58. Cf. Fukushima Masao, "Meiji shonen no keizai seisaku to shihon chikuseki no mondai," *Tōyō bunka* 9 (1952): 1–20; Tsuchiya Takao, *Nihon no keieisha seishin* (Tokyo: Keizai ōraisha, 1959), expecially pp. 68–91.

59. Ronald P. Dore, "Mobility, Equality, and Individuation," *Aspects of Social Change in Modern Japan*, edited by R. P. Dore (Princeton: Princeton University Press, 1971), p. 135; cf. Ishizuka Hiromichi, "Shokusan kōgyō seisaku no tenkai," *Nihon keizaishi taikei* 5, *kindai*, edited by Osanishi Mitsuhaya (Tokyo: Tokyo University Press, 1965), pp. 35–103.

60. Cf. Allen and Donnithorne, *Western Enterprise in Far Eastern Economic Development*, p. 194.

NOTES TO CHAPTER SIX

1. John R. Black, *Young Japan: Yokohama and Yedo* (London: Trubner, 1880–81), 2: 255.

2. Robert M. Spaulding Jr., "New Bureaucrats of Late Meiji Japan," paper delivered at the American Historical Association, New York, December 1968.

3. Cf. Robert M. Spaulding, Jr., *Imperial Japan's Higher Civil Service Examinations* (Princeton: Princeton University Press, 1967).

4. Family wealth is still a characteristic of Tokyo University students today. Even though tuition is low and intellectual merit a prime criterion, the competitive level of the entrance examinations requires a previous high quality of education, which means a young lifetime of additional tutorial study and study facilities which in turn, in Japan, are available only to those who can afford that luxury.

5. Ronald P. Dore, "Mobility, Equality, and Individuation," *Aspects of Social Change in Modern Japan* edited by R. P. Dore (Princeton: Princeton University Press, 1971), pp. 129, 131.

6. Maruyama Masao, *Nihon no shisō* (1936; reprint ed., Tokyo: Iwanami shoten, 1973), especially pp. 129–51.

7. See Nakane Chie, *Tate shakai no ningen kankei: tan'itsu shakai no riron* (1967; reprint ed., Tokyo: Kōdansha, 1973); cf. Albert M. Craig, introduction, *Personality in Japanese History*, edited by A. M. Craig and Donald H. Shively (Berkeley and Los Angeles: University of California Press, 1970), pp. 15–16, whose comments in this connection prompted the rereading of Maruyama.

8. Mizuta Nobutoshi, *Reimeiki no waga kaigun to Oranda* (Tokyo: Yūfūkan shobō, 1940), pp. 138–39, 157–61.

9. Ōtsuka Takematsu, "Fukkoku kōshi Reon Rosshu no seisaku kōdō ni tsuite," *Shigaku zasshi* 46: 7 (1935): 831.

10. Cf. Tsurumi Kazuko, *Kōkishin to Nihonjin* (Tokyo: Kōdansha gendai shinsho, 1972), pp. 15–24.

11. Ibid., pp. 21, 36, 54, 121–27.

12. Dr. Reona Esaki, recipient of the 1973 Nobel prize in physics, provides a practical illustration of a Japanese

view towards foreign borrowing and modernization. His work, when published in Japan, went unrecognized, and he made pointed comments about that in the public press. In summary, he suggested that in Japan there is no consistent flow of knowledge linking basic science, applied science, and practical research; that there is a tendency by Japanese scholars to pursue the latest Western fads; and that the institutional mechanism of Japan's vertical group society hampers the progress of knowledge in related disciplines because Japanese society is hostile to horizontal lines of intergroup co-operation and lateral mobility (editorial, *Asahi Evening News,* March 23, 1974).

13. Quoted in Umetani Noboru, *Oyatoi gaikokujin: Meiji Nihon no waki-yakutachi* (Tokyo: Nihon keizai shimbunsha, 1965), pp. 193–95.

14. Iizuka Kōji, *Nihon no seishinteki fūdo* (1952; reprint ed., Tokyo: Iwanami shinsho, 1972), pp. 11–24.

15. Ibid.

16. Ishizuki Minoru, *Kindai Nihon no kaigai ryūgakusei* (Kyoto: Minerva shobō, 1972), chap. 10, especially pp. 219–48.

17. Kano Masanao, *Nihon kindaika no shisō* (Tokyo: Kenkyūsha, 1972), especially pp. 50–56.

18. Tōyama Shigeki, *Sengo no rekishigaku to rekishi ishiki* (1968; reprint ed., Tokyo: Iwanami shoten 1973), pts. 1 and 3, especially pp. 43–55.

19. E. Herbert Norman, *Japan's Emergence as a Modern State* (New York: Institute of Pacific Relations, 1940), p. 102.

20. Bernard S. Silberman, "Bureaucratic Development and the Structure of Decision-Making in the Meiji Period: The Case of the Genrō," *Journal of Asian Studies* 27:1 (1967): 84–85.

21. John W. Hall, *Japan from Prehistory to Modern Times* (Tokyo: Tuttle, 1971), pp. 243, 246.

22. Ibid., p. 244.

23. Cf. ibid., especially pp. 236–37; Kano, *Nihon kindaika no shisō*, pp. 23–104. For a concise and lucid summary of the problems in modernization terminology see John W. Hall, "Changing Conceptions of the Modernization of Japan," *Changing Japanese Attitudes toward Modernization,* edited by Marius B. Jansen (Princeton: Princeton University Press, 1965), pp. 7–41.

24. Shinohara Hajime, *Nihon no seiji fūdo* (1968: reprint ed., Tokyo: Iwanami shinsho, 1973), pp. 6, 30.

25. Tsurumi, *Kōkishin to Nihonjin,* especially pp. 8–9ff.

26. Ivan P. Hall, *Mori Arinori* (Cambridge, MA: Harvard University Press, 1973), p. 72 from correspondence of Yoshida Kiyonari.

27. ŌM: C61, J. M. Batchelder to Ōkubo and Ōkuma.

28. Iizuka, *Nihon no seishinteki fūdo,* pp. 11–24.

29. "Four American Makers of Japan" in William Elliot Griffis Collection, Rutgers State University Library, New Brunswick, N. J., Box 8.

30. Cf. Irwin Scheiner, *Christian Converts and Social Protest in Meiji Japan* (Berkeley and Los Angeles: University of California Press, 1970), and Takeda Kiyoko, *Haikyōsha no keifu* (Tokyo: Iwanami shinsho, 1973).

31. George Akita, *Foundations of Constitutional Government in Modern Japan, 1868–1900* (Cambridge, MA: Harvard University Press, 1965).

32. Shinohara, *Nihon no seiji fūdo,* pp. 175–98.

33. Miyakawa Toshio, "Henna shimin undō," unpublished paper, Tokyo, 1974.

34. Cf. Kano, *Nihon kindaika no shisō,* preface, pp. 50–56.

35. GK: Gaikokujin Nihon seifu e yatoi-ire seigan ikken (French-language letter).

Selected Bibliography

MANUSCRIPT DOCUMENTS

Tokyo. Fuken shiryō [Prefectural Government Materials]. Yūshōdō Microfilm, especially Hyōgo: reel 230, Kanagawa: reels 79, 85–86, 89, Nagasaki: reels 346–47, Niigata: reels 96, 100. (府県史料)

Tokyo. Gaimushō hikitsugishorui [Papers Handed Over to the Foreign Ministry]. Tokyo University Historiographical Institute. (外務省引継書類)

Tokyo. Gaimushō kiroku [Foreign Ministry Records]. Foreign Ministry Records Bureau. (外務省記録)

Washington, D. C. Kaigunshō shiryō [Japanese Imperial Navy General Files]. Library of Congress Microfilm, especially reels 2–6 (T1–21: 1872-92, 1898). (海軍省資料)

New Brunswick, N. J. William Elliot Griffis Collection. Rutgers the State University Library.

Tokyo. Naikaku bunko [Cabinet Collection]. (内閣文庫)

Fuken oyatoi gaikokujin ichiran [Prefecture Foreign Employees], Chūgaidō, 1872. (府県御傭外国人一覧)

Mombushō gaikokujin yatoi hyō [List of Education Ministry Foreign Employees], 1880. (文部省外国人傭表)

Mombushō oyatoi gaikokujin meisaihyō [Detailed List of Education Ministry Foreign Employees], 1869-74. (文部省御傭外国人明細表)

Mombushō yatoi gaikoku kyōinroku [Education Ministry Foreign Employee Faculty Roll], 1880, 1881, 1887. (文部省傭外国教員録)

Seiin honyakukyoku oyatoi gaikokujin kankei shorui: Fu-Bu-Shi-Ga koshi ikkensho [Papers Related to Foreign Employees in the Seiin Translation Bureau: Items on the Employment of Verbeck, Black, Siebold, and Galy]. (正院反訳局御傭外国人関係書類布貝偲伽雇使一件書)

Tokyo. Naimushō dai ikkai nempō [Home Ministry First Annual Report], July 1875–June 1876, 4 fols. Waseda University Library. (内務省第一回年報)

Tokyo. Ōkuma monjo [Ōkuma Shigenobu Papers]. Waseda University Library (see catalogue titles). (大隈文書)

Washington, D.C. United States National Archives: Despatches of U.S. Ministers to Japan to the Department of State, 1862-1900.

OTHER WORKS

Abosch, David. "Katō Hiroyuki and the Introduction of German Political Thought in Modern Japan: 1868-1883." Ph.D. dissertation, Berkeley: University of California, 1964.

Akamatsu, Paul. *Meiji 1868: Revolution and Counter-Revolution.* London: Allen and Unwin, 1972.

Akita, George. *Foundations of Constitutional Government in Modern Japan, 1868-1900.* Cambridge, MA.: Harvard University Press, 1965.

Alcock, Sir Rutherford. *Capital of the Tycoon.* 2 vols. New York: Longman, Green, Longman, Roberts & Green, 1863.

Allen, George C. *A Short Economic History of Modern Japan 1867-1937.* 2d ed., rev. London: Unwin University Books, 1972.

Allen, George C. and Audrey C. Donnithorne. *Western Enterprise in Far Eastern Economic Development: China and Japan.* London: Allen and Unwin, 1954.

Anesaki Masaharu. *History of Japanese Religion.* Tokyo: Tuttle, 1963.

Anthony, David F. "The Administration of Hokkaido under Kuroda Kiyotaka, 1870-1882." Ph.D. dissertation, Yale University, 1951.

Arima Seiho, "The Western Influence on Japanese Military Science, Shipbuilding, and Navigation." *Monumenta Nipponica* 14 (1964): 352-79.

Asiatic Society of Japan. *Transactions of the Asiatic Society of Japan.* Tokyo: 1872-.

Baelz, Erwin. O. von. *Baelz no nikki* [Baelz Diary]. Translated by Suganuma Ryūtarō. 4 vols. Tokyo: Iwanami, 1964. (ベルツの日記)

Beasley, William G. *Great Britain and the Opening of Japan 1834-1858.* London: Luzac, 1951.

——. *The Meiji Restoration.* Palo Alto, CA: Stanford University Press, 1973.

——. *The Modern History of Japan.* London: Weidenfeld and Nicolson, 1963.

——. *Select Documents on Japanese Foreign Policy 1853-1868.* London: Oxford University Press, 1955.

Beauchamp, Edward R. *An American Teacher in Early Meiji Japan.* Asian Studies at Hawaii 17. Honolulu: The University Press of Hawaii, 1976.

Biographical Sketches Read at the Council of Missions, 1909. Tokyo: Meiji Gakuin University Library.

Black, John Reddie. *Young Japan: Yokohama and Yedo.* 2 vols. London: Trubner, 1880-81.

Blacker, Carmen. *The Japanese Enlightenment*. Cambridge, Eng.: Cambridge University Press, 1964.

Bousquet, Georges. *Le Japon de nos jours et les échelles de l'extrême Orient*. 2 vols. Paris: Librairie Hachette, 1877.

Bowers, John Z. *Western Pioneers in Feudal Japan*. Baltimore: Johns Hopkins University Press, 1970.

Boxer, C. R. *Jan Compagnie in Japan 1600–1850*. The Hague: Nijhoff, 1950.

Brandt, Maxim von. *Reimei no Nihon* [Dawn of Japan]. Tokyo: Kokusai bunka shinkōkai, 1942. (黎明の日本)

Brinkley's *Japanese-English Dictionary*, 2 vols. 1896 Reprint. Ann Arbor: University of Michigan Press, 1963.

Brooks, Van Wyck. *Fenollosa and His Circle*. New York: E. P. Dutton, 1962.

Buck, James H. "The Satsuma Rebellion of 1877." *Monumenta Nipponica* 28:4 (1973): 427–46.

Burks, Ardath W. and Jerome Cooperman. "The William Elliot Griffis Collection." *Journal of Asian Studies* 20:1 (November 1960): 61–69.

Capron, Horace. *Reports and Official Letters to the Kaitakushi*. Tokei: Kaitakushi, 1875.

Chamberlain, Basil Hall. *Things Japanese*. London: Kegan Paul and Trench, 1890.

Choi Kee-il, "Tokugawa Feudalism and the Emergence of the New Leaders of Early Modern Japan." *Explorations in Entrepreneurial History* 9 (1956): 72–90.

Church, Deborah C. "The Role of the American Diplomatic Advisers to the Japanese Foreign Ministry, 1872–1887." Ph.D. dissertation, University of Hawaii, 1978.

Craig, Albert M. and Donald H. Shively, eds. *Personality in Japanese History*. Berkeley and Los Angeles: University of California Press, 1970.

DaiNihon komonjo: Bakumatsu gaikoku kankei monjo, 1853–1868. [Ancient Documents of Nippon: Documents Relating to Foreign Affairs in the Last Days of the Shogunate, 1853–1868]. Tokyo University Historiographical Institute 1910–. (大日本古文書幕末外国関係文書)

Daniels, Gordon. "The British Role in the Meiji Restoration." *Modern Asian Studies* 2:4 (1968): 291–313.

———. "The Japanese Civil War (1868): A British View." *Modern Asian Studies* 1:3 (1967): 241–63.

Dore, Ronald P., ed. *Aspects of Social Change in Modern Japan*. Studies in the Modernization of Japan. Princeton: Princeton University Press, 1971.

Egashira Tsuneharu. "Takashima tankō ni okeru kyūhan makki no NichiEi kyōdō kigyō" [Anglo-Japanese Co-operative Enterprise in the Takashima Coal Mine during the

Closing of the Old Han Period]. *Keizaishi kenkyū* [Studies in Economic History] 13:2 (1935): 1–25. (江頭恒治,「高島炭坑における旧藩末期の日英共同企業」)

Fox, Grace. *Britain and Japan, 1858–1883*. London: Oxford University Press, 1968.

Fukuchi Genichirō. *Bakumatsu seijika* [Late Tokugawa Political Figures]. Tokyo: Min-yūsha, 1900. (福地源一郎, 幕末政治家)

Fukufuji Hiroji. "Teikoku kempō no yōgo: Meiji nijūninen no jōyaku kaisei o megutte" [The Phrasing of the Imperial Constitution Regarding the 1890 Treaty Revision]. *Nihon rekishi* [Japanese History] 53:10 (1952): 40–48. (服藤弘司,「帝国憲法の擁護 明治二十二年の条約改正をめぐって」)

Fukushima Masao. "Meiji shonen no keizai seisaku to shihon chikuseki no mondai" [Early Meiji Economic Policy and the Problem of Capital Accumulation]. *Tōyō bunka* [Oriental Culture] 9:6 (1952): 1–20. (福島正夫,「明治初年の経済政策と資本蓄積の問題」)

Fujita Tōichirō. "Daigaku Nankō no ichi kenkyū" [A Study of the University School Nankō]. *Meiji bunka no shinkenkyū* [New Studies of Meiji Culture]. Edited by Osatake Takeki, pp. 179–200. Tokyo: Ajia shobō, 1944. (藤田東一郎,「大学南校の一研究」)

Gaimushō: *Jōyaku kaisei kankei Nihon gaikō bunsho* [Foreign Ministry: Japanese Diplomatic Documents Related to Treaty Revision]. 7 vols. Tokyo, 1948–53. (外務省, 条約改正関係日本外交文書)

———. *Nihon gaikō bunsho* [Japan Diplomatic Documents]. Especially vols. 1, 2, 3, 8, 18. Tokyo, 1936–63. (日本外交文書)

———. *Tsūshō jōyaku kankei Nihon gaikō bunsho* [Japanese Diplomatic Documents Related to Commercial Treaties]. 3 vols. Tokyo, 1954. (通商条約関係日本外交文書)

"George Burchett Williams." *National Cyclopedia of American Biography* 11 (New York: J.T. White & Co., 1901), p. 331.

Great Britain. Foreign Office. *State Papers*. Edited and compiled by Edward Parkes, John W. Field, and Robert C. Thomson. London: Harrison and Sons, 1841–.

Griffis, William Elliot. *Mikado's Empire*. New York: Harper Brothers, 1877.

———. *Verbeck of Japan*. New York: Fleming H. Revell, 1900.

Hackett, Roger F. *Yamagata Aritomo in the Rise of Modern Japan, 1838–1922*. Cambridge, MA: Harvard University Press, 1971.

Hall, John W. *Japan from Prehistory to Modern Times*. Tokyo: Tuttle, 1971.

———. and Marius B. Jansen. *Studies in the Institutional History of Early Modern Japan*. Princeton: Princeton University Press, 1968.

Hall, Ivan P. *Mori Arinori*. Cambridge, MA: Harvard University Press, 1973.

Hanabusa Nagamichi. *Meiji gaikōshi* [Meiji Diplomatic History]. Tokyo: Shibundō, 1960. (英 修道, 明治外交史)

Harrison, John A. *Japan's Northern Frontier*. Gainesville: University of Florida Press, 1953.

Hattori Kazuma. "Kaikō to Nihon shihonshugi" [Open Ports and Japanese Capitalism]. *Nihon keizaishi taikei 5 kindai 1* [Japan Economic History Series 5 Modern 1], Edited by Osanishi Mitsuhaya, pp. 3–32. Tokyo: Tokyo University Press, 1965. (服部一馬, 「開港と日本資本主義」)

Helbig, Frances Y. "William Elliot Griffis: Entrepreneur of Ideas." M.A. thesis. University of Rochester, 1966.

Hidemura Senzō. "Meiji shonen zōheiryō ni okeru oyatoi gaikokujin no kaiko mondai" [The Early Meiji Problem of Dismissal of Foreign Employees in the Mint Bureau]. *Keizaigaku kenkyū* [Economics Studies] 31:3–4 (1965): 215–32. (秀村選三, 「明治初年造幣寮における御雇外国人の解雇問題」)

Hirschmeier, Johannes, S.V.D. *The Origins of Entrepreneurship in Meiji Japan*. Cambridge, MA: Harvard University Press, 1964.

Hōki bunrui taizen [Classified Collection of Laws]. 85 vols. Tokyo: Naikaku kirokukyoku, 1890– . (法規分類大全)

Hokkaidōshi [Hokkaido History]. 7 vols. Sapporo: Hokkaidō-chō, 1937. (北海道史)

Holtham, Edmund G. *Eight Years in Japan, 1873–1881*. London: Kegan Paul and Trench, 1883.

Honjō Eijirō, ed. *DaiNippon kaheishi* [Great Japan Coinage History]. 8 vols. Tokyo: Naikaku insatsukyoku, 1936–37. (本庄栄治郎編, 大日本貨幣史)

———. ed. *Nihon keizaishi jiten*. [Dictionary of Japanese Economic History]. 2 vols. Tokyo: Hyōronsha, 1965. (日本経済史辞典)

Hora Tomio. "Bakumatsu ishin ni okeru EiFutsu guntai no Yokohama chūton" [Late Tokugawa and Early Meiji Stationing of English-French Troops in Yokohama]. *Meiji seiken no kakuritsu katei* [Process of Establishment of Meiji Administrative Power], pp. 166–269. Tokyo: Meiji shiryō kenkyū renrakukai, 1957. (洞 富雄, 「幕末維新における英仏軍隊の横浜駐屯」)

Horie Yasuzō. "Ichibugin" [Silver One-Piece]. *Nihon keizaishi jiten* 1:50. (掘江保蔵, 「一分銀」)

Horigome Yōzō. "Hōkensei saihyōka e no shiron" [Essay on Re-evaluating the Feudal System]. *Tenbō* [Viewpoint] 87:3 (1966): 16–49. (掘米庸三, 「封建制再評価への試論」)

Hoshino Yoshirō. "Kōgyō gijutsu no hatten" [Development of Industrial Technology]. *Keizai shutaisei kōza 6 rekishi 1* [Lectures on Economic Independence 6 History 1]. Edited by Arisawa Hiromi, pp. 80–119. Tokyo: Chūō kōronsha, 1960. (星野芳郎, 「工業技術の発展」)

Iizuka Kōji. *Nihon no seishinteki fūdo* [Japan's Spiritual Climate]. 1952. Reprint. Tokyo: Iwanami shinsho, 1972. (飯塚浩二, 日本の精神的風土)

Ichijima Kenkichi, "Meiji bunka hasshō no kaiko" [Recollections of the Beginnings of Meiji Culture]. *Meiji bunka hasshō kinenshi* [Commemorative History of the Beginnings of Meiji Culture]. Bummei taikan [Civilization Series] 6: 3–19. Tokyo: DaiNihon bummei kyōkai, 1924. (市島謙吉,「明治文化発祥の回顧」)

Ike Nobutaka. *Beginnings of Political Democracy in Japan.* Baltimore: Johns Hopkins University Press, 1950.

Imai Shōji. "Denison no hansei" [Half of Denison's Life]. *Nihon rekishi* 80:1 (1955): 24–25. (今井庄次,「デニソンの半生」)

Inō Tentarō. "Meiji nananen ni okeru Mori Arinori no jōyaku shian to gaikō iken" [Mori Arinori's 1874 Treaty Proposal and Diplomatic Opinion]. *Kokugakuin zasshi* [Kokugakuin (University) Magazine] 63: 10–11 (1962): 130–39. (稲生典太郎,「明治七年における森有礼の条約試案と外交意見」)

Inoue Kaoru Kō denki hensankai [Prince Inoue Kaoru Biographical Records Editing Society]. *Segai Inoue Kō den* [Biography of Prince Inoue Kaoru]. 5 vols. Tokyo: Naigai shoseki, 1933–34. (世外井上公伝)

Irisawa Tatsukichi. "Reeoporudo Myurureru" [Leopold Müller] in *Chūō kōron* [Central Review] 48:9: 291–301. (入沢達吉,「レエオポルドミュルレル」)

Ishii Kendō. "Meiji no genkun wa kokumin shūshin no kyōiku o wasuretari" [Meiji Leaders Forgetting the People's Moral Education], *Meiji bunka no shinkenkyū* [New Studies in Meiji Culture]. Edited by Osatake Takeki, pp. 233–54. Tokyo: Ajia shobō, 1944. (石井研堂,「明治の元勲は国民修身の教育を忘れたり」)

Ishinshi [Restoration History]. 5 vols. Tokyo: Ishin shiryō hensan jimukyoku, 1939–41. (維新史)

Ishizuka Hiromichi. "Shokusan kōgyō seisaku no tenkai" [Evolution of the Policy of Encouraging Industry]. *Nihon keizaishi taikei* 5 *kindai* 1 [Japan Economic History Series 5 Modern 1]. Edited by Osanishi Mitsuhaya, pp. 35–103. Tokyo: Tokyo University Press, 1965. (石塚裕道,「殖産興業政策の展開」)

Ishizuki Minoru. *Kindai Nihon no kaigai ryūgakusei* [Modern Japan's Overseas Students]. Kyoto: Minerva shobō, 1972. (石附実, 近代日本の海外留学生)

Jansen, Marius B., ed. *Changing Japanese Attitudes toward Modernization.* Studies in the Modernization of Japan. Princeton: Princeton University Press, 1965.

Japan Directory, 1879–1914 (in Naikaku bunko).

Jones, H.J., "Bakumatsu Foreign Employees." *Monumenta Nipponica* 29:3 (1974): 305–27.

———. "The Formulation of Meiji Policy toward the Employment of Foreigners." *Monumenta Nipponica* 23:1–2 (1968): 9–30.

———. "Meiji seifu to oyatoi gaikokujin" [Meiji Government and Foreign Employees]. *Meiji bunka kenkyū* [Studies in Meiji Culture]. 3, pp. 139–55. Tokyo: Nihon Hyōron-sha, 1969. (「明治政府と御傭外国人」)

———. Review of *Shiryō oyatoi gaikokujin. Monumenta Nipponica* 30:4 (1975): 465–68.

Kagoshima kenshi [Kagoshima Prefecture History]. Tokyo: Kagoshima ken, 1926–28. (鹿児島県史)

Kaide Sumiko. "Mori Arinori *Saishōron* no rekishiteki shisōteki haikei: *Saishōron* to minpōten hensan" [Background History and Thought of Mori Arinori's Wife-Mistress Discourse: Saishōron and the Compilation of the Civil Code] in *Nihon rekishi* 302:7 (1973): 83–101. (貝出寿美子,「森有礼「妻妾論」の歴史的思想的背景「妻妾論」と民法典編纂」)

Kamata Hisaaki. "Kuruto Netto no Nihon kōzangyō shinkōsaku" [Curt Netto's Measures for Promotion of Japanese Mining]. *Keizaishi kenkyu* 29:3 (1933): 42–59. (鎌田久明,「クルトネットーの日本鉱山業振興策」)

Kanai Madoka. "Eijin Burakku to Nihon" [The Englishman Black and Japan]. *Kokusai bunka shinkōkai* [Society for International Cultural Relations] 156–62 (1967): 2–6, 8–13, 10–5, 9–13, 11–15, 7–11. (金井圓,「英人ブラックと日本」)

Kaneko Tadashi, "Gurifuisu to Nihon sono ichi" [On Griffis and Japan]. *Kyōto daigaku kyōikugakubu kiyō* [Kyoto University Education Department Bulletin]. 12 (1973): 197–214. (金子正,「グリフィスと日本その一」)

Kaninroku [Records of Officials]. Tokyo: Juntakusha, 1874–83. (官員録)

Kano Masanao. *Nihon kindaika no shisō* [Japan Modernization Thought]. 1972. Reprint. Tokyo: Kenkyūsha, 1973. (鹿野政直, 日本近代化の思想)

Katō Fusazō. *Hakushaku Hirata Tōsuke den* [Biography of Count Hirata Tōsuke]. Tokyo: Hirata Haku denki hensan jimusho, 1927. (加藤房蔵, 伯爵平田東助伝)

Katsu Kaishū. *Kaishū zenshū* [Kaishū's Collected Works]. 10 vols. Tokyo: Kaizōsha, 1927–29. (勝海舟, 海舟全集)

Kawakita Rinmei. "Bijutsu to Meiji shoki no gaijin kyōshi" [Fine Arts and Early Meiji Foreign Teachers]. *Nihon rekishi* 26:7 (1950): 16–21. (川北倫明,「美術と明治初期の外人教師」)

Kido Kōin monjo [Kido Kōin Papers]. 6 vols. Tokyo: Nihon shiseki kyōkai, 1932. (木戸孝允文書)

Kojima Chōsui, "Chishitsu gakusha Nauman to Mori Ōgai no ronsō" [Geologist Naumann and Mori Ōgai's Dispute]. *Shomotsu tembō* [Book Review] 7:9, pp. 162–69. (小島烏水,「地質学者ナウマンと森鷗外の論争」)

Kyū-Kōbu daigakkō shiryō [Documents of the Former Engineering School]. Tokyo: Kyū-Kōbu daigakkō shiryō hensankai, 1937. (旧工部大学校史料)

Le Bon, Georges. "Au Japan il y a quarante ans: Lettres de M. le Général G. Le Bon." *Bulletin de la Société Franco-Japonaise de Paris* 21 (1911): 113–18.

Lebra, Joyce. *Ōkuma Shigenobu: Statesman of Meiji Japan*. Canberra: Australia National University Press, 1973.

Lockwood, William W. *The Economic Development of Japan: Growth and Structural Change 1868–1938*. Princeton: Princeton University Press, 1954.

———, ed. *The State and Economic Enterprise in Japan*. Studies in the Modernization of Japan. Princeton: Princeton University Press, 1965.

Maclay, Arthur Collins. *A Budget of Letters from Japan: Reminiscences of Work and Travel in Japan*. New York: A. C. Armstrong, 1886.

Maruyama Masao. *Nihon no shisō* [Japanese Thought]. 1936, Reprint. Tokyo: Iwanami shoten, 1973. (丸山真男, 日本の思想)

Mayo, Marlene J. "The Iwakura Embassy and the Unequal Treaties, 1871–1873." Ph.D. dissertation, Columbia University, 1961.

———. "A Catechism of Western Diplomacy: The Japanese and Hamilton Fish, 1872." *Journal of Asian Studies* 26 (1967): 389–410.

Medzini, Meron. *French Policy in Japan during the Closing Years of the Tokugawa Regime*. Cambridge, MA: Harvard University Press, 1971.

Meiji bunka hasshō kinenshi [Commemorative History of Meiji Culture and Development]. Bummei taikan [Civilization Series], 6. Tokyo: DaiNihon bummei kyōkai, 1924. (明治文化発祥記念誌)

Meiji shiyō [Elements of Meiji History]. 2 vols. Tokyo University Historiographical Institute, 1933. (明治史要)

Meiji Taishō nenkan [Yearbook]. Tokyo: Kunaishō shoryōbu. (明治大正年鑑)

Meissner, Kurt. *Deutsche in Japan, 1639–1960*. Tokyo: Deutsche Gesellschaft für Natur und Volkerkunde Ostasiens, 1961.

———. "Die Deutsche in Yokohama." *Deutsche Gesellschaft für Natur und Volkerkunde Ostasiens*. Tokyo: Deutsche Gesellschaft, 1956.

Miyakawa Toshio. "Henna shimin undō" [The Queer Citizen Movement]. Tokyo: unpublished, 1974. (宮川利夫,「変な市民運動」)

Mizuta Nobutoshi. *Reimeiki no waga kaigun to Oranda* [Holland and the Beginnings of Our Navy]. Tokyo: Yūfūkan shobō, 1940. (水田信利, 黎明期の我が海軍と和蘭)

Motoki Seigo. *Hoppō torai* [Transmission to the North]. Tokyo: Jiji tsūshinsha, 1962. (元木省吾, 北方渡来)

Morley, James, ed. *Dilemmas of Growth in Prewar Japan*. Studies in the Modernization of Japan. Princeton: Princeton University Press, 1972.

Murakami Nobuhiko. *Meiji joseishi* [Meiji Women's History]. 4 vols. Tokyo: Rironsha, 1969–72. (村上信彦, 明治女性史)

Nagasaki igaku hyakunenshi [Hundred-Year History of Nagasaki Medical Studies]. Nagasaki: Nagasaki University Medical Department, 1961. (長崎医学百年史)

Nihon teikoku tōkei nenkan [Imperial Japan Statistical Yearbook]. 59 vols. Tokyo: Naikaku tōkeikyoku, 1882–1940. (日本帝国統計年鑑)

Naimushō chirikyoku [Home Ministry Geography Bureau], ed. *Chihō yōran* [Regional Survey]. Tokyo: Naimushō, 1881. (地方要覧)

Nakahara Kunihei. *Itō Kō jitsuroku* [Authentic Record of Prince Itō]. Tokyo: Keibunsha, 1909. (中原邦平, 伊藤公実録)

Nakamikado ke monjo [Nakamikado Family Papers]. 2 vols. Tokyo: Waseda daigaku shakai kagaku kenkyūjo, 1965. (中御門家文書)

Nakamura, James I. *Agricultural Production and the Economic Development of Japan, 1873–1922.* Princeton: Princeton University Press, 1966.

Nakamura Kōya. *Shishaku Nakamuta Kuranosuke den* [Biography of Viscount Nakamuta Kuranosuke]. Tokyo: Kyōrinsha, 1919. (中村孝也, 子爵中牟田倉之助伝)

Nakamura Magoichi. *Meiji igo hompō doboku to gaijin* [Foreigners and Japanese Public Works since Meiji]. Tokyo: Doboku gakkai, 1942. (中村孫一, 明治以後本邦土木と外人)

Nakamura Takeshi. "The Contributions of Foreigners." *Journal of World History*, 9:1 (1966): 294–319.

Nakamura Yoshimi. "Meiji shonen oyatoi gaijin no sararii" [Salaries of Early Meiji Foreign Employees]. *Nihon rekishi* 80:1 (1955): 43–45. (中村尚美,「明治初年御雇外人のサラリー」)

──── . "Wagakuni bokuyō jigyō no senkusha Jyōnzu no jiseki" [Contribution of (D. W. A.) Jones, Pioneer of Our Sheep-Raising Industry]. *Nihon rekishi* 52:9 (1952): 14–18. (「わが国牧羊事業の先駆者ジョーンズの事蹟」)

Nakane Chie. *Tate shakai no ningen kankei: Tan'itsu shakai no riron* [Human Relations in a Vertical Society: Theory of Singular Group Society]. 1967. Reprint. Tokyo: Kōdansha, 1973. (中根千枝, タテ社会の人間関係単一社会の理論)

Negishi Iwai. *Izumo ni okeru Koizumi Yakumo* [Koizumi Yakumo (Lafcadio Hearn) in Izumo]. Matsue: Yakumokai, 1931. (根岸磐井, 出雲における小泉八雲)

Ness, Gayl D. "Central Government and Local Initiative in the Industrialization of India and Japan." Ph.D. dissertation, Berkeley: University of California, 1961.

Newspapers: *Hiogo News, Japan Gazette, Japan Herald, Japan Weekly Mail, Nagasaki Express, Tokio Times.*

Nihon kagaku gijutsushi taikei [Japanese Science and Technology History Series]. Tokyo: Nihon kagakushi gakkai, 1964. (日本科学技術史大系)

Nihon kindaishi jiten [Dictionary of Japanese Modern History]. Kyoto: Kyoto University, Press, 1958. (日本近代史辞典)

Niigata shishi [Niigata City History]. 2 vols. Niigata: Niigata shiyakusho, 1934. (新潟市史)

Nishikawa Midori. "Meiji shoki ni okeru Kōbushō setchi no igi" [Significance of the Establishment of the Public Works Ministry in Early Meiji]. *Shiron* [History Essays] 10 (1962): 719–36. (西川みどり,「明治初期における工部省設置の意義」)

Norman, E. Herbert. *Japan's Emergence as a Modern State.* New York: Institute of Pacific Relations, 1940.

Numata Jirō. "Bakumatsu ni okeru Ranjin kyōshi Pompe no jiseki" [Accomplishments of the Dutch Teacher Pompe in the Bakumatsu Era]. *Shigaku zasshi* [History Studies Magazine] 56:8 (1946): 803–55. (沼田次郎,「幕末における蘭人教師ポンペの事蹟」)

―――. "Rangaku kara Eigaku e" [From Dutch Studies to English Studies]. *Nihon rekishi* 14:3–15:4 (1949): 30–35, 47–51. (「蘭学から英学へ」)

Ogata Hiroyasu. "Kindai Nihon kensetsu no chichi Furubekki hakase" [Dr. Verbeck, Founding Father of Modern Japan]. *Shakai kagaku tōkyū* [Social Science Studies] 18 (1961): 1–40. (尾形裕康,「近代日本建設の父フルベッキ博士」)

―――. "Meiji no honyaku shakai kagakusho" [Meiji Translations of Social Science Books]. *Shakai kagaku tōkyū* 3 (1960): 213–59. (「明治の翻訳社会科学書」)

―――. "Meiji seifu no bunkyō seisaku: oyatoi kyōshi o chūshin to shita kōsatsu" [Meiji Government Education Policy: A Study of (Foreign) Teacher Employees]. *Ōkuma kenkyū* [Ōkuma Studies] 4 (1954): 118–67. (「明治政府の文教政策御雇教師を中心とした考察」)

―――. "Meiji shoki no kaigai ryūgakusei seiritsu katei" [The Process of Organizing (the Programme for) Overseas Students in Early Meiji]. *Shakai kagaku tōkyū* 2:3 (1960): 1–31. (「明治初期の海外留学生成立過程」)

―――. "Ōkuma Shigenobu to Furubekki" [Ōkuma Shigenobu and Verbeck]. *Waseda daigakushi kiyō* [Waseda University History Bulletin] 1 (1965): 115–17. (「大隈重信とフルベッキ」)

―――. *Seiyō kyōiku inyū no hōto* [Ways of Importing Western Education]. Tokyo: Kōdansha, 1961. (西洋教育移入の方途)

Ōhama Tetsuya, "Ito o tsumugu onnatachi" [Women Spinners]. *Kindai no josei gunzō* [Modern Women Group Images]. Edited by Kasahara Kazuo, pp. 23–28, 131–88. Nihon joseishi [Japanese Women's History] 7. Tokyo: Hyōronsha, 1973. (大浜哲也,「糸を紡ぐ女たち」)

Ōi Narimoto. *Mekkeru shōgun no omoide* [Memories of General Meckel]. Tokyo: Gunjishi gakkai, 1939. (大井成元, メッケル将軍の思い出)

Okada Shumpei. *Meiji zenki no seika seisaku* [Early Meiji Specie Policy]. Tokyo: Tōyō keizai shimpōsha, 1958. (岡田俊平, 明治前期の正貨政策)

Ōkubo Toshimichi nikki [Diary of Ōkubo Toshimichi]. 2 vols. Tokyo: Nihon shiseki kyōkai, 1927. (大久保利通日記)

Ōkuma monjo [Ōkuma Papers]. 5 vols. Tokyo: Waseda daigaku shakai kagaku kenkyūjo, 1962. (大隈文書)

Ōkuma Shigenobu, ed. *Fifty Years of New Japan*. 2 vols. New York: E. P. Dutton, 1909.

Ōno Katsumi. "Meiji gaikō to Denison komon no kenshin" [Meiji Diplomacy and the Devotion of Adviser Denison]. *Bungei shunjū* [Literary Arts] 11 (1966): 180–88. (大野勝己,「明治外交とデニソン顧問の献身」)

Osatake Takeki. "Oyatoi gaikokujin ichiran kaidai" [Annotation for a Glance at Foreign

Employees]. *Meiji bunka zenshū* [Collected Works on Meiji Culture] 16: 20–21, 347–62. Tokyo: Hyōronsha, 1928. (尾佐竹猛,「御雇外国人一覧解題」)

Ōtsuka Takematsu. *Bakumatsu gaikōshi no kenkyū* [Studies in Late Tokugawa Diplomatic History]. Tokyo: Hōbunkan, 1952. (大塚武松, 幕末外交史の研究)

———. "Fukkoku kōshi Reon Rosshu no seisaku kōdō ni tsuite" [About the Policy Activities of French Minister Léon Roches] in *Shigaku zasshi* 46:7–8 (1935): 809–50, 982–1001. (「佛国公使レオンロッシュの政策行動について)

———. ed. *Iwakura Tomomi kankei monjo* [Papers Related to Iwakura Tomomi]. 5 vols. Tokyo: Nihon shiseki kyōkai, 1927. (岩倉具視関係文書)

Ōuchi Hyōe and Tsuchiya Takao, eds. *Meiji zenki zaisei keizai shiryō shūsei* [Collection of Early Meiji Financial and Economic Materials]. Tokyo: Kaizōsha, 1931–36. (大内兵衛土屋喬雄, 明治前期財政経済資料集成) Selected volumes:
Kaikei kensainshi [Audit Board History].
Kōbushō enkaku hōkoku [Public Works Ministry Chronicle Report].
Ōkurashō enkakushi [Finance Ministry Chronicle].
Sainyūshutsu kessan hōkokusho [Report of Income and Accounts].

Ōyama Azusa, "Ansei jōyaku to gaikokujin kyoryūchi" [Ansei Treaties and the Foreigners Residence Areas]. *Nihon gaikōshi kenkyū: Bakumatsu jidai* [Studies in Japanese Diplomatic History: Late Tokugawa Era] (1960): 111–23. (大山梓,「安政条約と外国人居留地」)

———. "Jōyaku kaisei to gaijin hōkan" [Treaty Revision and Foreign Jurists]. *Kokusaihō gaikō zasshi* [Magazine of International Law and Diplomacy] 59:4 (1960): 1–29. (「条約改正と外人法官」)

———. "Jōyaku kaisei to gaikokujin kyoryūchi" [Treaty Revision and the Foreigners Residence Areas]. *Rekishi kyōiku* [History Education] 9:1 (1961): 60–69. (「条約改正と外国人居留地」)

———. *Kaishi kaikō no kenkyū* [Studies on Open Cities and Open Ports]. Tokyo: Ōtori shobō, 1967. (開市開港の研究)

Oyatoi gaikokujin [Foreign Employees]. 17 vols. Tokyo: Kashima shobō, 1968– . (御雇外国人)

Piggott, Francis S. G. *Broken Thread: An Autobiography*. Aldershot, Eng.: Gale and Polden, 1950.

Pittau, Joseph. *Political Thought in Early Meiji Japan 1868–1889*. Cambridge, MA: Harvard University Press, 1967.

Presseisen, Ernst. *Before Aggression: Europeans Train the Japanese Army*. Tucson: University of Arizona Press, 1965.

Pyle, Kenneth B. *The New Generation in Meiji Japan: Problems of Cultural Identity 1885–1895*. Palo Alto, CA: Stanford University Press, 1969.

Raoulx, Jean. *Yokosuka kaigun kōshō no sōsetsu to Furansujin no mitaru reimeiki no Nihon* (The Foundation of Yokosuka Naval Studies and French Observations of the Beginnings of Japan). Translated by Kuranaga Shōzō. Yokosuka: Yokosuka shi kyōiku kenkyūjo, 1952. (See *Maritime Revue,* May 1939.) (横須賀海軍工廠の創設と仏蘭西人の見たる黎明期の日本)

Redesdale, Algernon Bertram Freeman-Mitford, baron. *Memories.* 5th rev. ed. 2 vols. London: Hutchinson & Co., 1915.

Refardt, Otto. "Die Deutsche in Kobe." *Deutsche Gesellschaft für Natur und Volkerkunde Ostasiens.* Tokyo: Deutsche Gesellschaft, 1956.

Reischauer, Edwin O. "The Hour of the Ox." *Horizon* 11 (1969): 12–25.

Reischauer, Robert K. *Alien Land Tenure in Japan.* Transactions of the Asiatic Society of Japan. 2d Series 13 (Tokyo, July 1936).

Rikugunshō nempō [Army Ministry Annual Report]. 3 vols. Tokyo: Rikugunshō, 1875– (in Naikaku bunko). (陸軍省年報)

Rohan, Kieran M. "Lighthouses and the Yatoi Experiences of R. H. Brunton." *Monumenta Nipponica* 20:1 (1965): 65–80.

Saigusa Hiroto. *Gijutsushi* [Technology History]. Gendai Nihon bummei shi [History of Recent Japanese Civilization] 14. Tokyo: Tōyō keizai shimpōsha, 1940. (三枝博音, 技術史)

———. *Nihon kindai seitetsu gijutsu hattatsushi* [History of the Development of Japan's Modern Iron and Steel Technology]. Tokyo: Tōyō keizai shimpōsha, 1957. (日本近代製鉄技術発達史)

———. et al. *Kindai Nihon sangyō gijutsu no seiōka* [Westernization of Modern Japan's Industrial Technology]. Tokyo: Tōyō keizai shimpōsha, 1960. (近代日本産業技術の西欧化)

Sakata Yoshio. *Meiji ishinshi* [Meiji Restoration History]. Tokyo: Miraisha, 1960. (坂田吉雄, 明治維新史)

———. ed. *Meiji ishinshi no mondaiten* [Problems in Meiji Restoration History]. Tokyo: Miraisha, 1962. (明治維新史の問題点)

———. *Meiji zenhanki no Nashonarizumu* [Early Meiji Nationalism]. Tokyo: Miraisha, 1958. (明治前半期のナショナリズム)

———. and J. W. Hall, "The Motivation of Political Leadership in the Meiji Restoration." *Journal of Asian Studies* 16:1 (1956): 31–50.

Sakurai Takeo. *Fueska Nihon chisanron* [Fesca on Japan's Agricultural Productivity]. Tokyo: Hyōronsha, 1944. (桜井武雄, フェスカ日本地産論)

Sansom, George B. *The Western World and Japan.* New York: Knopf, 1950.

Satow, Ernest. *A Diplomat in Japan.* London: Seeley Service, 1921.

Sawa Kannojō. *Kaigun nanajūnenshidan* [Navy Seventy-Year History Account]. Tokyo: Bunsei dōshisa, 1943. (沢鑑之丞, 海軍七十年史談)

Scheiner, Irwin. *Christian Converts and Social Protest in Meiji Japan*. Berkeley and Los Angeles: University of California Press, 1970.

Schmiedel, Otto. *Die Deutsche in Japan*. Leipzig: K. F. Koehler, 1920.

Schwantes, Robert S. *Japanese and Americans: A Century of Cultural Relations*. New York: Harper Bros., 1955.

Shibusawa Eiichi. *Jijoden* [Autobiography]. Tokyo: Ijin resshi den hensanjo, 1937. (渋沢栄一, 自叙伝)

Shibusawa Keizō, ed. *Japanese Life and Culture in the Meiji Era*. Translated by Charles S. Terry. Tokyo: Ōbunsha, 1958.

Shichū torishimari enkaku [History of City Regulation]. Tōkyō-to toshi kiyō [Tokyo Municipal Records]. Tokyo: Shinyōdō, 1953– . (市中取締沿革)

Shidehara Kijūrō. *Gaikō gojūnen* [Fifty Years of Diplomacy]. Tokyo: Yomiuri shimbunsha, 1951. (幣原喜重郎, 外交五十年)

Shigehisa Tokutarō. "Meiji jidai ni okeru seiyōjin no bunka jigyō" [Westerners' Cultural Activities in the Meiji Period]. *Dōshisha kōshō ronsō* [Doshisha Commerce Essays] 20 (1939): 134–48. (重久篤太郎,「明治時代における西洋人の文化事業」)

———. "Wakayama han ni okeru Doitsujin" [Germans in Wakayama Han]. *Kyōto Rangaku kenkyū hōkoku* [Kyoto Dutch Studies Research Report] 166 (1965): 1–8. (「和歌山藩におけるドイツ人」)

———. "Wakayama bunka hattatsu ni kōken seru Doitsujin" [German Contribution to Development of Wakayama Culture]. *Eiryō* 17 (1936): 1–7. (「和歌山文化発達に貢献せるドイツ人」)

———. and Amano Keitarō. "Meiji bunka kankei Ō Bei jimmeiroku" [Name List of Europeans and Americans Related to Meiji Culture]. *Toshokan kenkyū* [Library Research] 10:4 (1937): 347–72. (天野 敬太郎 共著,「明治文化関係欧米人名録」)

Shimomura Fujio. *Meiji ishin no gaikō* [Meiji Restoration Diplomacy]. Tokyo: Ōyasu, 1948. (下村富士男, 明治維新の外交)

———. *Meiji shonen jōyaku kaiseishi no kenkyū* [Studies in Early Meiji Treaty Revision History]. Tokyo: Yoshikawa kōbunkan, 1962. (明治初年条約改正史の研究)

Shinohara Hajime. *Nihon no seiji fūdo* [Japan's Political Climate]. 1968. Reprint. Tokyo: Iwanami shinsho, 1973. (篠原一, 日本の政治風土)

Shively, Donald H., ed. *Tradition and Modernization in Japanese Culture*. Studies in the Modernization of Japan. Princeton: Princeton University Press, 1971.

Siemes, Johannes. "H. Roesuraa no kempō riron ni okeru shakai hatten to rikkenshugi no kankei" [The Relation of Social Development and Constitutionalism in H. Roesler's Constitutional Theory]. *Kokka gakkai zasshi* [Journal of the Association of Political and Social Science]. Pts. 1–3. 75: 1–6 (1962): 1–41, 181–202, 307–30. (「H, ロエスラーの憲法理論における社会発展と立憲主義の関係」)

————. "Heruman Roesuraa to Nihon ni okeru Doitsukokuhō no saiyō" [Hermann Roesler and the Adoption of German Law in Japan]. *Sophia* 10:1 (1961): 1–24. (「ヘルマン ロエスラーと日本における独逸国法の採用」)

————. "Meiji seifu shunōtachi to shakaiteki rikken shisō" [Meiji Government Braintrust and Social Constitutional Thought]. *Kokka gakkai zasshi* 75:7–8 (1962): 418–24. (「明 治政府首脳達と社会的立憲思想」)

————. "Roesler und die Rezeption des deutschen Staatsrechts in Japan." *Japonica* 1 (1961): 1–7.

————. *Hermann Roesler and the Making of the Meiji State.* Tokyo: Sophia University Press and Tuttle, 1968.

Silberman, Bernard S., "The Bureaucracy and Economic Development in Japan." *Asian Survey* 5:11 (1965): 529–37.

————. "Bureaucratic Development and the Structure of Decision-Making in the Meiji Period: The Case of the Genrō." *Journal of Asian Studies* 27:1 (1967): 81–94.

————. "E. H. Norman: Structure and Function in the Meiji State: A Reappraisal." *Pacific Affairs* 41:4 (1968–69): 553–59.

————. *Ministers of Modernization.* Tucson: University of Arizona Press, 1964.

————. and H. D. Harootunian, eds. *Modern Japanese Leadership.* Tucson: University of Arizona Press, 1966.

Smith, Thomas C. *The Agrarian Origins of Modern Japan.* Palo Alto, CA: Stanford University Press, 1959.

————. *Political Change and Industrial Development in Japan, 1868–1880.* Palo Alto, CA: Stanford University Press, 1955.

Spaulding, Robert M. *Imperial Japan's Higher Civil Service Examinations.* Princeton: Princeton University Press, 1967.

————. "New Bureaucrats of Late Meiji Japan." Paper read before the American Historical Association, New York. December 1968.

Spence, Jonathan. *To Change China: Western Advisers in China, 1620–1960.* Boston: Little, Brown and Company, 1969.

Starr, Merritt, "General Horace Capron, 1804–1885." *Journal of the Illinois State Historical Society,* 18 (1925): 259–349.

Stead, Alfred, ed. *Great Japan: A Study of National Efficiency.* London: William Heineman, 1904.

Takahashi Korekiyo. *Jiden* [Autobiography]. Tokyo: Chikura shobō, 1936. (高橋是清, 自伝)

Takeda Kiyoko. *Haikyōsha no keifu* [Apostates' Lineage]. Tokyo: Iwanami shinsho, 1973. (武田清子, 背教者の系譜)

———. *Ningenkan no sōkoku* [Conflicts of the Views of Man]. Tokyo: Kōbundō, 1959. (人間観の相剋)

Tamura Eitarō. *Kawamura Sumiyoshi-Nakamuta Kuranosuke den* [Biographies of Kawamura and Nakamuta]. Tokyo: Nihon gunji tosho, 1944. (田村栄太郎, 川村純義中牟田倉之助伝)

Tanaka Tokihiko. *Meiji ishin no seikyoku to tetsudō kensetsu* [Railway Construction and the Political Situation of the Meiji Restoration]. Tokyo: Yoshikawa kōbunkan, 1963. (田中時彦, 明治維新の政局と鉄道建設)

Tetsuka Yutaka, "Meiji hōseishijō ni okeru Ju Busuke to Busuke" [Du Bousquet and Bousquet in Meiji Legal History]. *Meiji bunka* [Meiji Culture] 15:12 (1942): 1–9. (手塚豊, 「明治法制史上におけるジュブスケとブスケ」)

Tokutomi Iichirō. *Kōshaku Yamagata Aritomo den* [Biography of Prince Yamagata Aritomo]. 3 vols. Tokyo: Yamagata Aritomo Kō kinen jigyōkai, 1933. (徳富猪一郎, 公爵山県有朋伝)

Tōkyō teikoku daigaku gakujutsu taikan [General View of the Arts and Sciences in Tokyo Imperial University]. 5 vols. Tokyo: Kokusai shuppan, 1942. (東京帝国大学学術大観)

Tōkyō teikoku daigaku gojūnenshi [Tokyo Imperial University Fifty-Year History]. 2 vols. Tokyo: Chūgai, 1932. (東京帝国大学五十年史)

Tōyama Shigeki. *Meiji ishin* [Meiji Restoration]. Tokyo: Iwanami zenshū, 1951, (遠山茂樹, 明治維新)

———. *Sengo no rekishigaku to rekishi ishiki* [Postwar Historiography and History Consciousness]. Nihon rekishi sōsho [Japanese History Series]. 1968. Reprint. Tokyo: Iwanami shoten, 1973. (戦後の歴史学と歴史意識)

Toyohara Jirō, "Kōbushō to oyatoi gaikokujin ni tsuite: Meiji sangyō kindaika no issetsu" [Public Works Ministry and Foreign Employees: A Chapter in Meiji Industrial Modernization]. *Shōdai ronshū* [Commercial College Papers] (Kobe) 60:1 (1964): 35–56. (豊原治郎, 「工部省と御雇外国人について明治産業近代化の一節」)

Tsuchiya Takao, "Eijin Arekisandaa Shando no gyōseki" [Achievements of the Englishman Alexander Shand]. *Kin'yu jānaru* [Finance Journal] 4:1–12 (1963): 14–19, 55–59, 60–64, 78–82, 68–71, 54–57, 52–55, 50–54, 70–73, 32–36, 68–72, 62–69. (土屋喬雄, 「英人アレキサンダーシャンドの業蹟」)

———. *G. Wakuneru ishin sangyō kensetsu ronsaku shūsei* [Gottfried Wagner's Collected Works on the Establishment of Restoration Industry]. Tokyo: Hokuryūkan, 1944. (G. ワグネル維新産業建設論策集成)

———. "Keizai seisakuka to shite no Ōkubo Toshimichi" [Ōkubo Toshimichi as an Economic Planner]. *Chūō kōron* 50:4 (1935): 95–110. (「経済政策家としての大久保利通」)

———. *Nihon keiei rinenshi* [History of Ideas of Japanese Management]. Tokyo: Keizai shimbunsha, 1964. (日本経営理念史)

———. *Nihon no keieisha seishin* [Japanese Managerial Attitudes]. Tokyo: Keizai ōraisha, 1959. (日本の経営者精神)

――. *Nihon shihonshugishijō no shidōshatachi* [Leaders in the History of Japanese Capitalism]. Tokyo: Iwanami shinsho, 1940. (日本資本主義史上の指導者達)

――. "ŌBeijin no Nihon shihonshugi seiritsu ni hatashita yakuwari" [The Roles Europeans and Americans Performed in the Establishment of Japanese Capitalism]. *Keizai shutaisei kōza 6 rekishi* 1 [Lectures on Economic Independence 6 History 1]. Edited by Arisawa Hiromi, 265–305. Tokyo: *Chūō* kōronsha, 1960. (「欧米人の日本資本主義成立に果した役割」)

――. "Ōkubo naimukyō jidai no shokusan kōgyō seisaku" [Industrial Development in the Era of Home Minister Ōkubo]. *Keizaigaku ronshū* 4:9–10 (1934): 79–146, 30–92. (「大久保内務卿時代の殖産工業政策」)

Tsukiji kyoryūchi [Tsukiji Residence Area]. Tōkyō-to toshi kiyo. Tokyo: Shinyōdō, 1953– . (築地居留地)

Tsunoda Ryusaku, W. T. deBary, and Donald Keene. *Sources of the Japanese Tradition.* New York: Columbia University Press, 1958.

Tsurumi Kazuko. *Kōkishin to Nihonjin* [Curiosity and the Japanese]. Tokyo: Kōdansha gendai shinsho, 1972. (鶴見和子, 好奇心と日本人)

Umetani Noboru. *Meiji zenki seijishi no kenkyū* [Studies in Early Meiji Political History]. Tokyo: Miraisha, 1963. (梅渓昇, 明治前期政治史の研究)

――. "Meiji shinsei no guntai no kensetsu tōsho ni okeru Furansushugi no saiyō to Ju Busuke no kōken" [Adoption of the French Pattern in the First Establishment of the New Meiji Army System and the Contribution of Du Bousquet]. *Ōsaka daigaku bungakubu sōritsu jisshūnen kinen ronsō* [Essays Commemorating the Tenth Anniversary of the Establishment of the Faculty of Letters in Osaka University], pp. 97–120. Osaka: Osaka University Press, 1959. (「明治新制の軍隊の建設当初におけるフランス主義の採用とジュブスケの貢献」)

――. *Oyatoi gaikokujin: Meiji Nihon no wakiyakutachi* [Foreign Employees: Meiji Japan's Supporting Cast]. Tokyo: Nihon keizai shimbunsha, 1965. (お雇い外国人 明治日本の脇役たち)

――. "Shoki jōyaku kaiseishijō ni okeru Ju Busuke no kiyo [Participation of Du Bousquet in Early Treaty Revision History]. *Uozumi sensei koki kinen kokushigaku ronsō* [Essays in National History Commemorating the Seventieth Birthday of Professor Uozumi], pp. 103–18. Osaka: Kansai University Press, 1959. (「初期条約改正史上におけるジュブスケの起用」)

UNESCO Higashi Ajia bunka kenkyū sentā [UNESCO East Asia Culture Research Center]. *Shiryō oyatoi gaikokujin* [Source Materials on Foreign Employees]. Tokyo: Shōgakukan, 1975. (資料御雇外国人)

U.S. *Congressional Record,* 42d Congress, 2d Session, 1874, nos. 3629, 4876, 5210.

Ward, Robert E., ed. *Political Development in Modern Japan.* Studies in the Modernization of Japan. Princeton: Princeton University Press, 1968.

Watanabe Minoru, "Japanese Students Abroad and the Acquisition of Scientific and Technical Knowledge." *Journal of World History,* 9:1 (1966): 254–93.

———. "Meiji seifu no Ōka seisaku to gaijin kyōshi" [Meiji Government's Europeanization Policy and Foreign Teachers]. *Nihon rekishi* 38:7 and 39:8 (1951): 16–21, 22–25. (渡辺実, 「明治政府の欧化政策と外人教師」)

Watanabe Shūjirō. "Meiji nenkan rikugun kaku hōmen koyō no gaikokujin" [Meiji Era Employment of Foreigners in Each Area of the Army]. *Meiji bunka kenkyū* 4:10 (1928): 56–62. (渡辺修二郎, 「明治年間陸軍各方面雇用の外国人」)

Wilkinson, Rupert. *The Prefects: British Leadership and the Public School Tradition.* London and New York: Oxford University Press, 1964.

Williams, Harold S. *Foreigners in Mikadoland.* 1963. Reprint. Tokyo: Tuttle, 1972.

———. *Tales of the Foreign Settlements in Japan.* 1958. Reprint. Tokyo: Tuttle, 1972.

Yagisawa Zenji, "P. Mayeto no Nihon ni okeru jiseki" [P. Mayet's Achievement in Japan]. *Keizaishi kenkyū* 12: 1–3 (July–September 1934): 1–16, 27–44, 25–33. (八木沢善次, 「ペーマイエットの日本における事蹟」)

Yajima, S. "Lettres d'un ingénieur français en Japon de 1877 à 1881." *Japanese Studies in the History of Science* 10 (1971): 27–57.

Yamanaka, T. "Japanese Small Industries during the Industrial Revolution." *Annals of Hitotsubashi Academy* (October 1951).

Yasuoka Akio "Iwakura shisetsu no haken to sono seika" [Despatch of the Iwakura Mission and Its Results]. *Rekishi kyōiku* 40:1 (1966): 32–38. (安岡昭男, 「岩倉使節の派遣とその成果」)

Yokohama zeikan enkaku [Chronicles of Yokohama Customs]. 5th ed. Yokohama: Yokohama zeikan, 1902. (横浜税関沿革)

Yokosuka zōsenshi [Yokosuka Dockyards History]. Tokyo: Yokosuka chinjufu enkakushi hensan iin (Tōyōdō), 1880. (横須賀造船史)

Zōheikyoku enkakushi [Mint Bureau Chronicle]. Osaka: Zōheikyoku, 1921. (造幣局沿革史)

Index